Pleasure and Meaning in the Classical Symphony

MELANIE LOWE

Pleasure and Meaning in the Classical Symphony

INDIANA UNIVERSITY PRESS
Bloomington and Indianapolis

Publication of this book is made possible in part with the assistance of a Challenge Grant from the National Endowment for the Humanities, a federal agency that supports research, education, and public programming in the humanities. Any views, findings, conclusions, or recommendations expressed in this publication do not necessarily reflect those of the National Endowment for the Humanities.

This book is a publication of

Indiana University Press
601 North Morton Street
Bloomington, IN 47404-3797 USA

http://iupress.indiana.edu

Telephone orders   800-842-6796
Fax orders   812-855-7931
Orders by e-mail   iuporder@indiana.edu

Portions of chapter 4 appeared on Lowe, "Falling from Grace: Irony and Expressive Enrichment in Haydn's Symphonic Minuets," *Journal of Musicology* 19, no. 1 (2002): 171–221. Reprinted by kind permission of the University of California Press.

Portions of chapter 6 appeared in Lowe, "Claiming Amadeus: Classical Feedback in American Media," *American Music* 20, no. 1 (2002): 102–19. Reprinted by kind permission of the University of Illinois Press.

The paper used in this publication meets the minimum requirements of American National Standard for Information Sciences—Permanence of Paper for Printed Library Materials, ANSI Z39.48-1984.

Manufactured in the United States of America

Library of Congress Cataloging-in-Publication Data

Lowe, Melanie Diane, date
  Pleasure and meaning in the classical symphony / Melanie Lowe.
      p.   cm. — (Musical meaning and interpretation)
  Includes bibliographical references (p.) and index.
  ISBN 0-253-34827-7 (cloth : alk. paper)
  1. Symphony. I. Title.
  ML1255.L69 2007
  784.2′184—dc22

                                        2006025687

1 2 3 4 5   12 11 10 09 08 07

To Stan Link

Contents

Acknowledgments

Many people deserve my deepest gratitude. I begin with the pleasure of thanking them.

I am indebted to Robert Hatten, whose explorations of musical meaning have greatly influenced my own. His initial enthusiasm for this book made its completion possible, his later suggestions greatly improved its content, and his generous and close reading of the manuscript saved me from many errors. For their keen insights and invaluable suggestions, I owe many thanks to the two anonymous readers of the original proposal and to the anonymous reader of the manuscript. I also thank Harold Powers and Scott Burnham for their advice on earlier versions of parts of chapters 2 and 4.

At Indiana University Press, Gayle Sherwood, music editor when this book was contracted, supported my work in its earliest stages. When my daughter arrived in the middle of the second chapter, she generously adjusted my production schedule. Jane Quinet, music and humanities editor, directed the manuscript through its publication. Donna Wilson, assistant music editor, provided constant support and expertly guided me though the production process from start to finish. David Anderson carefully edited the final draft. My heartfelt thanks to all of them.

Mark Wait, dean of the Blair School of Music at Vanderbilt University, granted me research leave in the spring of 2002, supplying much needed time to think and write. My musicology and ethnomusicology colleagues at Vanderbilt—Gregory Barz, Joy Calico, Cynthia Cyrus, Jim Lovensheimer, and especially Dale Cockrell—provided a supportive, collegial, and enriching academic environment. I am grateful for their generosity of spirit and collective intellectual energies.

For countless hours of patient listening, I owe Gayle Shay, Director of the Vanderbilt Opera Theater and true friend, many cups of coffee. I also owe her my sincere thanks for encouraging me not to shy away from some of the riskier moves in this book.

Finally, it is my greatest pleasure to thank my wonderful family for their love and enduring patience. My parents, Donald and Diane Lowe, are always a source of strength. My daughter, Wednesday Link, lifts my spirits and unknowingly provides me endless encouragement. I can only hope to offer her the same. To my husband, Stan Link, for his love, generosity, and abiding confidence, I owe more than any words of gratitude can express. I dedicate this book to him.

Pleasure and Meaning in the Classical Symphony

Introduction

On 18 June 1778 the Parisian audience at the *concert spirituel* was supremely entertained by Mozart's music. So too were the Viennese who attended Mozart's many "academies" in the 1780s. And London audiences could hardly have been more pleased by Haydn symphonies, the featured works of Salomon's concert series in the early 1790s. Accounts of thundering applause, spontaneous encores, and packed theaters and halls attest to the enjoyment of those present and their patent approval of both the music and its performance.[1]

Depending on the year, the city, and the venue, aristocrats and members of the bourgeoisie, journalists and travelers, men and women, musically literate and illiterate alike were in attendance at public concerts in the late eighteenth century. As the many references to a "fashionable attendance" and "the best and most brilliant company" reveal, the majority of listeners in late-eighteenth-century public concert audiences were undeniably leisured and wealthy.[2] But during the last two decades of the century, especially in London and Paris, members of Europe's growing middle classes began to participate in concert life in steadily increasing numbers. From musical societies dedicated to "the Mercantile Interest," as *The Oracle* named the moneyed, middle-class subscribers, to garden concerts catering to the "melange" [*sic*] of citizens described by *The Morning Chronicle*,[3] opportunities for London's citizenry to enjoy concert music abounded. While some concert societies in Paris were more hospitable to the members of the Third Estate than others (the *concert spirituel* and the Concert des Amateurs catered primarily to elites), after Thermidor the social mix of concert audiences reflected the political pluralism of contemporary French society. Ex-nobles, ex-revolutionaries, and "royal thieves," as one police agent colorfully labeled the *nouveaux riches* in 1795, were among the listeners.[4]

The democratization of Europe's concert halls in the late eighteenth century reached across the Atlantic, bringing the masterpieces of the German symphonic repertoire to the general American public. "Come One Come All," the Germania Musical Society's advertisement for a "Grand Concert of Music" in Baltimore in 1849 announced,[5] capturing the ethos of public concert life in nineteenth-century America. But during the first half of the twentieth century, concert music in the Western world's "great democracy" returned, ironically, to its earlier "courtly" status as the cultural property of the elite class. Whether one locates the "sacralization" of musical culture during the Gilded Age or during the decades between the First and Second World Wars,[6] by the middle of the century those who attended public concerts of classical music in the United States were members of the genteel class, educated professionals, and the newly rich.

And so it remains in America today. The symphonies of Haydn and Mozart, along with Beethoven, of course, constitute the heart of symphony orchestra repertoires and classical radio play lists, sustaining concert subscriptions and bolstering membership to public radio. But these perennial favorites are just as unavoidable in Hollywood film soundtracks, waiting rooms, television commercials, fine restaurants, hotel lobbies, and cartoons. We are even occasionally treated to classical music—always instrumental—when put on hold on the telephone. Late-eighteenth-century music, particularly the public instrumental music, is heard as part of the soundscape of our everyday, twenty-first-century lives. People from nearly all walks of life still encounter this music and, presumably, find it somehow entertaining—if somewhat less rousing than did Haydn's and Mozart's first listeners.

Given the centrality of music in the construction of social and cultural identity, why would individuals among the diversity of groups and social strata in this music's first audience, late-eighteenth-century Europe's concert-going public, have found the same music so appealing? How has the public instrumental music of late-eighteenth-century Europe remained accessible, entertaining, and distinctly pleasurable to such a variety of people for over two hundred years? In what ways is it intelligible to audiences from different times, cultures, and social situations? Through what channels does it communicate with its listeners so that monarch and merchant, philanthropist and pianist, psychiatrist and soccer mom are all somehow able to understand it? What might it mean to such different individuals?

This book explores the potential meanings listeners—primarily historical listeners but also contemporary ones—may have heard in the public instrumental music of the late eighteenth century and the pleasures they may have experienced while constructing these meanings. Premised on the aesthetics of the Enlightenment, the politics of entertainment in the late eighteenth century, and postmodern inquiries into the constitution of pleasure, the theoretical core of this book posits that "pleasure" results from the listener's interpretive control over, rather than mere apprehension of, musical meaning.

As we shall embrace it in the context of this book, musical meaning resides entirely within the individual listener during a musical experience. It is subjective, ephemeral, and contingent upon a multiplicity of factors and conditions of that listening experience, many of which are wholly unknowable. The frustrating lack of documentation of individual listeners' personal responses to public concert music in the late eighteenth century effectively prohibits definitive answers to many questions of musical meaning in this repertory. My musical interpretations and the conclusions I draw from them are therefore necessarily more speculative than those that result from traditional composer- and score-oriented approaches to this music. Moreover, because I am particularly interested in how eighteenth-century listeners who were not all that musically informed may have understood and interpreted Classical symphonies, my analytical observations are by and large limited to those features a lay listener would have been able to hear in the "real time" of a first and likely *only* hearing of a given work. For these reasons, this book will not appeal to everyone. But to my way of thinking, the reality that questions of what precise meanings listeners heard in late-eighteenth-century public instrumental music are ultimately unanswerable should not prevent us from asking them anyway as a way to understand the possible scope and variety of those meanings.

A Qualification of Public Music

My qualification of late-eighteenth-century symphonic music as "public" music rests not only on the often noted distinctions between public and private musical styles,[7] but also on the social makeup of its original audience and its position within the capitalist marketplace of late-eighteenth-century consumer culture. Delimited most influentially by Jürgen Habermas as the "bourgeois public sphere" ([1962] 1989), the enlightened public was the new cultural and political arbiter. It was comprised of private individuals who engaged in rational discourse on matters of the state, public policy, morality, and taste. Although some women did participate in the discourse, the individuals of the enlightened pubic were primarily men who were sufficiently propertied and educated to support Europe's burgeoning print culture of novels, newspapers, periodicals, and literary criticism. I am primarily concerned with the potential meanings these historical listeners plausibly could have constructed during their concert experiences.

Although Habermas implies an emancipatory role for the public sphere, one that challenged the individuals and institutions of the *ancièn regime,* it is important that we not exaggerate a politically subversive agenda—especially one that would stem from historical hindsight. To do so fails to acknowledge not just the significant noble leadership within the public sphere of the eighteenth century but also the prescience, adaptability, and resilience of the society, institutions, and traditional power structures of the *ancièn regime.* "Public opinion" mattered to the ruling powers as much as to their opposition. Moreover, the cultural and leisure activities enjoyed by the enlightened public invited—encouraged, even—social interaction between members of the nobility and the propertied middle classes. Education and taste became the new social determinants, culturally uniting the nobility and the bourgeoisie to form a new elite class (see Melton 2001, 11–12).

Driving this ostensible reordering of social class was the commodification and democratization of culture. Anyone with the means to pay could partake of entertainments and diversions previously enjoyed exclusively by the aristocracy. To accommodate the marked increase in sociability, places for the enlightened public to socialize, from coffeehouses to concert halls, spread rapidly throughout Europe. That concert music had become a highly profitable commodity in this new public marketplace of culture is demonstrated by comparing the compensation Haydn received for a single benefit concert in the Hanover Square Rooms on 16 May 1791 with the honorarium he received for his twenty-six appearances for the Prince of Wales at Carlton House during his first visit to London: £350 versus 100 guineas, respectively (Geiringer 1968, 114–16), over three times as much for one public performance as for twenty-six private ones.

"Public" music, then, in the context of this book, is defined socially and economically as much as stylistically. It comprises music composed within the late eighteenth century's commercial culture, performed in its public spaces, consumed by the enlightened public, and aimed at pleasing the bourgeois public sphere's diversity of private individuals.

The Accessibility of Musical Meanings

In contemplating the meanings "everyday" eighteenth-century listeners may have constructed for this "public" music, I am engaging in overtly political business. From our contact with new cultural theories, poststructuralist and postmodern critical theories, and reception theory, musical thinkers of all types now generally acknowledge that the interpretation of a musical work is a political activity. Those remaining who would still insist that art and its interpretation are not inherently political are, of course, also asserting a political statement. As George Orwell put it, "the opinion that art should have nothing to do with politics is itself a political attitude" (1953, 313). When we interpret anything—a piece of music, events in history, or even interpretations themselves—we engage in activities of analysis, criticism, value judgment, signification, and the construction of meaning. Such actions, by asserting the authority, dominance, and power of one discourse over another, ultimately empower certain people over others (Goehr 1993, 178–79). For example, given the sustained ridicule of eighteenth-century conceptions of musical imitation during the nineteenth century, embarrassment over Wackenroder's *Schwärmerei* in the twentieth (Sparshott 1980; see also Bonds 1997, 388), the formalist conviction that emotional intimations contaminate music (Burnham 1999, 196), and a widespread discomfort with the frequently gushing sentimentality of Romantic criticism, it is not surprising that the modernist values underlying the institutionalization of musical understanding assuaged anxiety by asserting music as an objective art and musical thought as an empirical and scientific enterprise. The "subjectivities of the past" (Epstein 1987, 202) were deemed counterproductive and misguided, if not downright foolish. But with objectivity came exclusivity, and musical meaning, once accessible to the many, became inaccessible to all but the few.

The philosophical construct of absolute music, a cornerstone of twentieth-century musical aesthetics, effectively excised all but purely musical meanings from the instrumental music of the late eighteenth century, anachronistically rendering this music among the most objectified repertories in the history of Western music. Whether intended or not, the critical process of philosophically removing from Classical instrumental music not just the capacity but the obligation of meaning beyond the purely musical ultimately excluded all but the initiated from interpretive engagement. While imitations, depictions, topical references, and other types of musical associations could be heard, presumably, by most listeners in the late eighteenth century, metaphysical interpretation became the professional domain of philosophers, critics, writers, and other learned minds in the early nineteenth century. Similarly, theoretical explication, the dominant discourse of twentieth-century musical thought, is the exclusive province of music scholars, inaccessible even to other learned communities, not to mention the lay listener.

During the past two centuries there has been a decided increase in what is required not just to understand and interpret but merely to appreciate the instrumental music of the Classical era. As this music became more autonomous in musical thought and musical meaning came to reside more in structural abstractions, meaning itself became inaccessible to those who lacked the musical education and knowledge to perceive such structures. Even among music scholars, only committed specialists may claim to be comfortably conversant in the complex tonal theories of the later twentieth and early twenty-first centuries. We seem to have forgotten that in its original eighteenth-century context, public instrumental music had direct and immediate expressive capabilities for its diversity of listeners. Its meaning was hardly consigned to the depths of the purely musical. Indeed, the whole notion of internal or self-sufficient musical meaning is ideologically incompatible with eighteenth-century musical thought.

The immediate task of chapter 1, then, is to fashion a working definition of musical meaning for the purposes of this book. My point of departure is that the prevailing binary opposition of musical and extra-musical meaning is deeply flawed, particularly when applied to Classical instrumental music, the very music that might seem to illustrate most compellingly the oppositionality of the two categories.[8] After presenting various logical, aesthetic, historical, and musical problems that question the applicability of both categories to late-eighteenth-century music, I jettison this seemingly neat but all too comfortable binary opposition in favor of a rather messy but more useful interdependence of music, reference, structure, expression, contingency, and an ever-present listening subjectivity.

In a first step toward asserting the historical accessibility of meaning in late-eighteenth-century public instrumental music, chapter 2 argues that an interdependency of expressive and formal meanings rendered this music structurally intelligible to its original listeners in the real time of a first hearing. At issue here is not just expressive significance but expressive *consequence*. The identification of topics, literary themes, and other stylistic references may reveal much about this music's potential for expressive meaning, but it tells us frustratingly little about things like a movement's expressive syntax or a symphony's cyclic organization. By exploring interrelationships between the expressive surface of Classical symphonies and the broader eighteenth-century entertainment culture, I explore how conventionalized signs associatively communicate such basic rhetorical functions as opening, continuing, and closing within a single movement. At the discursive level of the symphony's multi-movement cycle, I identify a broad expressive descent from exalted to terrestrial passions and suggest within it resonances of human mortality, secular humanism, and enlightened social thought.

Entertainment, Pleasure, and the Listening Subject

The theoretical orientation of this book clearly embraces a postmodern critical agenda. But rather than simply drop a late-twentieth-century critical apparatus onto a two-hundred-year-old musical repertory, my otherwise anachronistic application rests on the presence of two tenets of postmodern critical theory—

intertextuality and subjectivity—in the aesthetics of the Enlightenment. Their manifestation in critiques of imitation and in constructions of the enlightened subject are my primary concern in chapter 3. To side with the Enlightenment's own distrust in the authority of facts, to endorse heartily the legitimacy of the fictive in historical narrative, and to demonstrate the reciprocity of the aesthetic object and the bourgeois subject, this chapter concludes with an unabashedly fanciful experiment in music-historical writing. I create three historically informed but otherwise fictional listening subjects—a count in Joseph II's Vienna, one of the *nouveaux riches* in post-Thermidorian Paris, and a merchant-banker from the City of London—and imagine their interpretations of Haydn's Symphony in G Major, No. 88, during the "real time" of their "first hearings" of this music.

To address the specific pleasures historical listeners may have experienced while hearing public concert music, in chapter 4 I abandon the notion of "mere entertainment" and the prejudice implied by such an assessment of music—any music. Indeed, that which provides its audience with amusement and diversion may also be a formidable wellspring of ideas. Drawing from such varied sources as the discourse of taste in the late eighteenth century, Bourdieu's social theory of cultural capital, Kant's aesthetic philosophy, French critical theory, Freud's pleasure principle, feminist film theory, and John Fiske's pioneering study of television culture, I argue that the pleasure experienced by a listener, whether historical or contemporary, is a direct result of his or her control over the ideas music communicates—its meaning. The relationship between entertainment and pleasure, then, is less interdependent than dialectical. An inherently political phenomenon, the entertainment of the public can thus supply the homogenizing pleasures of the imagination while at the same time sustaining an underlying social heterogeneity. Because the minuet is arguably the most socially readable movement type in the Classical symphony, I consider how meanings historical listeners may have constructed for Haydn's and Mozart's symphonic minuets could operate as both centripetal and centrifugal political forces in Enlightenment Europe.

My interpretive engagement with late-eighteenth-century public instrumental music in its historical context culminates in chapter 5's exploration of the social and political meanings Haydn's original English listeners may have constructed while hearing his Symphony in D Major, No. 93. Inviting such sociopolitical meanings in this symphony are its unusually frequent and salient juxtapositions of stylistic registers, communal and individual voices, and patrician and common expressions. The underlying sophistication of Haydn's legendary accessibility is a principal source of the distinct pleasure this symphony afforded its diversity of listeners. While its expressive echoes of the immediate cultural surroundings are largely unambiguous, they may easily be interpreted to support more than one social agenda or political orientation. *Kenner* and *Liebhaber*, commoner and king alike are thereby empowered to construct meanings aligned with the needs of their own social, political, and personal situations.

Both a conclusion and an epilogue, chapter 6 explores striking similarities between the position of late-eighteenth-century public instrumental music within its original historical context and its position within the capitalist marketplace of contemporary American consumer culture. As in the late eighteenth century, the instrumental music of the Classical style currently sounds as part of an intensely commercial culture. While many may bemoan the present economic reality and blame the commodification of culture for contributing to (or sustaining) the demise of classical concert life in America, classical music is actually thriving in less traditional venues—especially visually mediated contexts. Ironically, in today's more public entertainment contexts of film and television this music may now more easily accomplish what it only occasionally could in the public venues of eighteenth-century entertainment: encourage its audience to construct politically subversive meanings. But the possible overdetermination of the meanings of classical music in contemporary American culture has also led to a stagnation in signification, the effect of which is a near forfeiture of listening pleasure in the concert hall. To recover the pleasure of listening to the Classical symphony in more traditional listening situations, I suggest we wholeheartedly embrace the many points of crosstalk between our experiences of this music in live or recorded performances and its use in visually mediated contexts. As we negotiate through the resulting web of intertextual meanings, we may also, surprisingly, regain something of this music's historical ways of meaning.

1 On Meanings of Musical Meaning

That music might, could, or should mean something is the perennial concern of Western musical thought. Since Antiquity investigations into the existence and nature of musical meaning have been tethered to questions of musical mimesis—whether insisting that imitation of natural phenomena is an essential requirement, as was the dominant aesthetic position from Antiquity through the Enlightenment, or categorically denying music's capacity to imitate, represent, or express anything, a tenet of late-nineteenth-century aesthetics and twentieth-century formalism and modernism. The historical insistence on music's reference to something outside of itself, combined with the later denial of its capacity for any such reference, gave rise to the now commonplace dichotomy of musical and extra-musical meaning, a division that has been entangled with various notions of absoluteness in music since the turn of the nineteenth century. Because the instrumental music of the late eighteenth century is so often anachronistically championed as "absolute music," it is with this slippery philosophical construct that we must begin.

The Construct of Absolute Music

For the last century and a half, historians, theorists, philosophers, and critics have interpreted the instrumental music of the Classical style as absolute music—an ideal of musical purity fashioned by the Romantics that, following decades of increasing abstraction, became a cornerstone of twentieth-century music theory and aesthetics. As it is commonly understood today, a piece of absolute music is completely autonomous, understandable only in terms of objectifiable, abstract features. The near monopoly of strategies in our analytical toolbox that scrutinize an actual or presumed manifestation of this abstraction, from formal to motivic to structural-tonal voice-leading analysis, bears witness to the extent to which music has been rendered an absolute text awaiting the revelation of its structural secrets. To be sure, we remain indebted to these sorts of analytical strategies, for they reveal fascinating aspects of construction, but too often they leave unengaged questions of signification and meaning. By design, they concern themselves with only the realm of the "purely" musical, thereby tacitly sustaining a theoretical and philosophical separation between that which is musical and that which is extra-musical.

But in the musical thought of the early Romantics, those critics with whom the notion of absoluteness in music originated, a ready division between musical and extra-musical meaning was not nearly so secure. For Wackenroder, Tieck, Hoffmann, and other early Romantic critics, the very writers who found the music of Haydn, Mozart, and (early) Beethoven a "new" and "romantic" art, the aesthetics of late-eighteenth-century instrumental music was nothing short of metaphysics. Embracing German idealism, they celebrated the symphony in particular as the art best suitable for expressing the spiritual, the ideal, the infinite, and the absolute. Toward the middle of the nineteenth century, however, when Wagner's term "absolute music" ironically became associated with Eduard Hanslick's argument against that composer's *Gesamtkunstwerk,* the notion of ideal purity removed from instrumental music all external reference, representation, and generation, even of such an abstract concept as infinity.[1] Through a philosophical slight of hand, the expression of the spiritual and the ideal, hitherto an extra-musical obligation, became a purely musical matter, an essence capturable only in the "abstract interiority of pure sound."[2] As Lydia Goehr explains, "the distinction between the musical and the extra-musical was allowed to function on a worldly but not on a transcendent level . . . [enabling] one to accept a double-sided view of musical meaning, that it be transcendent, embodied spirituality and purely musical at the same time. . . . The new romantic aesthetic allowed music to mean its purely musical self at the same time that it meant everything else" (1992, 156–57). Within the Romantic struggle to reconcile an idealist aesthetic with formalist tendencies, "meaning" itself, then, embraced at least two different meanings—one representational, the other (self)referential—just at the point instrumental music was allowed to be "meaningful" at all.

But the impetus behind the metaphysical readings in early Romantic music criticism came from a change in contemporary philosophy, not a paradigm shift in contemporary music (Bonds 1997, 389). Because their interpretations seem to fit the music of Beethoven's late style far better than the music contemporary to their writings, it is commonly asserted that Wackenroder, Tieck, Hoffmann, et al. were prophetic, describing a music yet to be written.[3] But despite our sense of incongruity between the music of the Classical style and early Romantic criticism, as well as the common (mis)attribution of the notion of musical autonomy to early Romantic thought, the instrumental music of the late eighteenth century was compelling to the early Romantics precisely because of its affinity with the extra-musical. Indeed, we must not overlook the link the early Romantics maintained to the aesthetics of mimesis.[4] The idealist underpinnings of their aesthetics may have altered the notion somewhat—what was represented was not the real but the ideal, not physicality but spirit. But the expectation that music should mean something beyond itself remained central. Extra-musical meaning was essential to the early Romantic notion of the absolute in music, a concept constructed while the instrumental music of Haydn and Mozart enjoyed immense popularity.

Although the early Romantics introduced absoluteness to musical discourse, the construct of absolute music itself—essentially the wholesale excision of extra-musical meaning from instrumental music—began to emerge only with the mid-nineteenth-century polarization of musical thought and the consequent dichotomy of program music and nonnarrative instrumental music. But even with such a seemingly obvious statement of formalism as Hanslick's (in)famous line—"sounding forms in motion are the only and exclusive content and object of music"—we must be careful not to jump to an immediate establishment and defense of absolute music as absolutely and exclusively musical. Despite Hanslick's uncompromising arguments for music as a nonrepresentational art, the many echoes of the Hegelian notion of art as the materialization of the idea in the first volume of *Vom Musikalisch-Schönen* suggest,[5] at least in his early thought, an idealist conception of musical form: form is spirit; spirit is form.[6] In other words, since at this point we cannot limit Hanslick's sense of the word "form" *(Formen)* to mere musical structure, the "purely" musical cannot be the "only and exclusive content and object of music," at least not until well into the second half of the nineteenth century and the publication of the later editions of Hanslick's treatise, which are "purged . . . of all overt references to idealism" (Bonds 1997, 419). But perhaps it is ultimately not until such later metalinguistic theories of musical content as Schenker's *Ursatz*, Schoenberg's developing variation, and Réti's thematicism that instrumental music was construed as "pure"—a wholly objective and self-contained art.

The construct of absolute music seems firmly in place only when conceived in terms of what the music lacks.[7] Absolute music contains no object, reference, representation, content, expression, or idea external to music itself. At this point (in an admittedly simplified historical narrative) hermeneutic interpretation becomes divorced from theoretical explication in the dominant discourses of musical thought. Even such listener-oriented landmarks in postwar tonal theory as Leonard Meyer's expectation-based theories (1956, 1973), developed further by Eugene Narmour as the implication-realization model (1977), and Fred Lerdahl and Ray Jackendoff's linguistics-based generative theory (1983) search for rules of musical structure, not mechanisms of meaning—musical or otherwise. What began around the turn of the nineteenth century as an expressive ideal of musical purity—an ideal that celebrated the imprecision, not the absence, of meaning in instrumental music—now embraces nearly the opposite: autonomous music liberated from any and all expressive expectation, representational capacity, and subjective content. Freed of extra-musical baggage, the "absolute music" of the Classical style in particular can be assured objectivity by its structural clarity. Its meaning resides only in its lack of meaning beyond the musical.

To be sure, several musicologists have recently revisited the philosophical construct of absolute music, often dispelling this anachronistic concept from the music of the late eighteenth century. Carl Dahlhaus's seminal essay *The Idea of Absolute Music* ([1978] 1989) sets the conception of the autonomous artwork in opposition to eighteenth-century bourgeois thought and moral philosophy. Bonds distinguishes between idealism as an aesthetic principle as it emerged in the writings of the early Romantics around the turn of the nineteenth century and later concepts of absolute music (1997, 420). Daniel Chua's quixotic contextualization of absolute music within an astounding range of intellectual discourses begins with the claim that absolute music was "a discovery unveiled by the German Romantics, as if [it] had always been there, eternal and absolute" (1993, 3). James Webster reveals that much of Haydn's instrumental music incorporates extra-musical associations and explains that Haydn "never intended to compose 'absolute music' in the nineteenth-century sense" (1991a, 335). Roger Scruton, noting that the absolute ideal existed long before "the jargon of its name," asserts that paradoxically "the rise of instrumental music and the development of Classical forms saw the temporary disappearance of the absolute ideal" (1980, 1: 27). And Leo Treitler keeps us honest, reminding readers that the construct of absolute music does not necessarily lead to formalism and nothing else (1989, 212–13).

But despite our acknowledgment of the "absolute problem" (among others), a concerted recent effort to avoid the pitfalls of positivism, and a compelling argument that for much nineteenth-century German music "the absoluteness of absolute music . . . is the very condition of its meaning" (Hoeckner 2002, 4), we have yet to formulate—whether as musicologists, philosophers, or theorists—a conditional notion of meaning in eighteenth-century instrumental music that reconciles the purely musical ideal of nearly two centuries of reception with the extra-musical reality of this music's inception. V. Kofi Agawu's *Playing with Signs* (1991), a semiotic interpretation of Classic music, makes a fine attempt at delineating a theory that encompasses both expressive meaning and structural coherence. But in the end, his imaginative synthesis notwithstanding, the specificity of his "extroversive semiosis" and the generality of his "introversive semiosis" remain quite far apart.[8] Robert Hatten's *Musical Meaning in Beethoven* (1994) perhaps comes the closest to integrating the two, but, while he makes good on his promise of a semiotic model that embraces both expressive and formal meanings, I would argue that we need to explore still further the range of mechanisms for their interaction. In general, our endeavors to exorcise from this music its absolute possession too often admit extra-musical associations only to revert to the more comfortable "absolute" discourse of abstract musical analysis, or remain within the realm of philosophy and criticism, never fully engaging the sounding experience. Questions of musical meaning endure.

The Constructs of Musical and Extra-Musical Meaning

Perhaps, though, the greatest obstacle to new considerations of musical meaning in Classical instrumental music is our easy acceptance of the long-established but deeply flawed musical/extra-musical opposition itself. The obstacle lies not so much in the rigidity of our distinction between the categories of the binary structure, which Lawrence Kramer, for one, questions by "show[ing] 'internal' and 'external' meanings intertwining closely and widely" (1995, 67). Rather, the problem resides largely within the delineations of the categories themselves. Goehr has suggested a tacit distinction between the extra-musical and the non-musical in Romantic musical discourse, a distinction provided by the ambiguity of the term *ausser* in *das Aussermusikalische*. In the nineteenth century, this ambiguity accommodated the budding formalist need for music to "engage with and within the world purely musically" but still retain its "broader human and expressive significance" (1998, 6–18). But for the instrumental repertory of the Viennese Classical tradition and the aesthetics of music in the eighteenth century, the initial category of the musical/extra-musical dichotomy is the more problematic one.

Implicit in the category of the musical is the absolutist notion of the "purely musical," the objectivist stance of high modernism captured perfectly in Stravinsky's polemic about his Octet: "My *Octuor . . .* is a musical composition based on objective elements which are sufficient in themselves" (White [1924] 1966, 575). Any meaning intended or ascribed to the work would be the purely musical meaning of the music itself. Resonance with the later philosophical construct and theoretical assumptions of absolute music could hardly be louder. But the construction of the category of the musical, particularly when set in opposition to the extra-musical, implies the notion of the *intra*-musical: the purely musical meaning of the musical elements—"sufficient in themselves"—*within* an individual work. As Stravinsky puts it, "the play of the musical elements is the thing" (577). The construction of the intra-musical is thus dependent on a conception of the musical work as an independent and objectified entity.

This construction of the "work-concept," however, is itself dependent on what Goehr has termed the "separability principle": the belief, fashionable at the end of the eighteenth century, that works of art are separated completely from the everyday world, are self-sufficient, and "bear no external resemblance to anything else" (1992, 171). But, the historical currency of such aesthetic constructs notwithstanding, a musical work does not exist in isolation. Its very nature (or definition) as music presupposes an affinity with other musical works. We cannot recognize a musical element as such without some a priori understanding of what a musical element is, an understanding that comes only from our individual musical experiences. In other words, the listening subject is the essential ingredient in the delineation of the musical element. A "purely" intra-musical meaning for a given work, even one whose "objective elements are sufficient in themselves," is inescapably formed in relation to musical elements outside of that work, a reality that relegates the intra-musical to a philosophical abstraction quite divorced from the nature and reality of our musical experiences.

Musical meanings, then, even when construed as "purely" musical and designed to exist only within a specific work, are nevertheless in a continuous dialogue with the meanings of other musical entities, whether the composer or analyst wants them to be or not.[9] The inevitable intertextuality of music and its meanings, particularly when used to refer to the *meaningful* content in and of an individual composition, effectively nullifies the category of the musical.[10] As a result, the category of the extra-musical vanishes as well, for its definition is wholly dependent on the boundaries of the musical. No set of "purely" musical meanings remain for which extra-musical meanings can constitute a complementary set.

In addition to such logical problems with the musical/extra-musical binary construct in general, the appropriateness of these oppositional categories runs into aesthetic, historical, and musical trouble when applied to the music of the Classical style—the very music that might, because of an enduring appreciation of its structural architecture, seem to demonstrate most clearly their oppositionality. Grounded in the writings of Plato and Aristotle, the aesthetics of mimesis dominated musical thought in the eighteenth century. Imitation of natural phenomena, especially the human affections, was considered the primary, if not the only, mechanism of musical meaning. *Affektenlehre,* for example, combined the classical concept of mimesis with the Cartesian objectification of human passions to rationalize a theory of emotional representation in music. Such representations are today readily conceptualized as extra-musical meanings. But if the category of the extra-musical requires for its delineation the category of the purely musical, an ideological incompatibility emerges, for eighteenth-century theorists were hardly inclined to afford music any internal or self-sufficient meaning. Representations of human affections in eighteenth-century music, then, should not be considered extra-musical meanings, for just as musical meaning at the time could not be "pure," neither could it be "extra."

The opposition of the musical and the extra-musical is historically inappropriate for the music of the Classical style, for it depends on a philosophical separation of music from its earthly context, a quintessentially Romantic development. For all but the last few years of the eighteenth century the mimetic principle—the imperative that art imitate nature—was firmly in place. According to this aesthetic doctrine, the significance and meaning of music originate only in relationships with objects in the natural world—from imitation of audible sounds of nature to representation of human affections. Despite occasional flirtations with the notion of music as abstract expression,[11] the artistic expectations of the age are encapsulated in Charles Batteux's rhetorical question: "What would we think of a painter who was content to throw on the canvas bold shapes and masses of the liveliest color without reference to any known object? The same argument can be applied to music" ([1746] 1981, 49). To remove from eighteenth-century instrumental music its tangible relations to the known objects of the contemporary world is to ignore the aesthetic conditions under which this music was composed. Like the construct of absolute music, the application of the "separability principle" (Goehr 1992, 157–59) to the music of the Classical style is anachronistic.

Moreover, the notion that eighteenth-century music could be separated from the world of the ordinary goes against its primary means of musical expression—references to the music and sounds of everyday life, or "topics," as Leonard Ratner first theorized them twenty-five years ago. Topics are musical commonplaces. Some are conventionalized musical types—fully worked-out pieces—like the minuet, funeral march, and operatic aria; others are characteristic styles—rhythms, textures, melodies, accompanimental patterns, etc.—that imitate, evoke, or are otherwise associated with the music, sounds, and objects an ordinary listener was likely to encounter.[12] Translated into a more explicit semiotic vocabulary, "a topic is a semiotic code that associates a conventional label with a constellation of musical signs" (Klein 2005, 56). While the referents might be extra-musical, the initial mechanism of topical signification is usually an evocation of the *sounds* of everyday objects, and these sounds themselves, for characteristic styles as well as conventionalized types, are quite often musical: a hunting call, a peasant dance, a ceremonial fanfare, a popular song, a military procession. For the sounds that are not innately musical, topical signification typically involves a mediating agent that is musical. Opera and theater are obvious sources for these mediators, for the words and dramatic situations effectively assign the reference: for example, the summoning of the supernatural with the fantasia style,[13] or the evocation of storms or stormy passions with tremolos, driving rhythms, sudden turns to the minor mode, dissonances, and chromaticism—that is, the topic we now conventionally label *Sturm und Drang*. While topics in instrumental music might inspire the listener to construct affective, social, political, or even personal meanings, their first and most immediate "extra-musical" reference is usually to something "musical," an oxymoronic situation that in and of itself questions the boundaries of both categories on purely musical grounds.

We shall therefore leave behind the tired and flawed "musical/extra-musical" binary construction. To theorize just how and what late-eighteenth-century public instrumental music might mean, we shall explore in its place the interdependence of music and reference, expression and structure, and an ever-present listening subjectivity.

Some Meanings of Musical Meaning

I have so far been tossing around the word "meaning" somewhat casually, as if *its* meaning is both singular and self-evident to any and all readers. In common English usage, we treat many words as synonymous with "to mean": to express, represent, signify, refer to, denote, connote, imply, indicate, etc. But in philosophical and critical considerations of musical meaning, we cannot be so casual (even though many are), for to say that a piece of music "means" something is not necessarily the same thing as to say that it "expresses" something, "represents" something, or "signifies" something. When we consider the nouns corresponding to the verbs above—meaning, expression, representation, signification, reference, denotation, connotation, implication, indication, etc.—it becomes increasingly clear that, philosophically speaking, we are dealing with several related but quite different concepts and categories.

Music philosophers, in recent considerations of the nature of musical meaning, generally proceed by identifying and examining categories of meaning, taking great care to analyze each and to differentiate among them. Nelson Goodman (1968, esp. 85–95), Vernon Howard (1972), Peter Kivy (1984, 124–42), Stephen Davies (1994, 79–121), and Roger Scruton (1997, 118–70), for example, all stress the importance of a conceptual distinction between expression and representation in music.[14] But there are, of course, as many conceptions of these terms as there are writers who theorize about them. Representation and expression are much more closely related in Goodman's aesthetic theory than in Scruton's, to offer but two writers' divergent ideas among the many analyses of these particular aesthetic concepts. For Scruton, "reference is the *route* to representation in literature just as resemblance . . . is the *route* to representation in painting" (122–23). But music, he argues, is not a representational art at all; rather, it is an expressive art.[15] Goodman, on the other hand, in an aesthetic theory that does not separate music from the arts in general, posits that expression and representation simply operate through opposite directionalities of denotation.[16] It is unnecessary for our present purpose to encapsulate other philosophers' delineations of these and other categories of musical meaning. Suffice it to say that the aesthetic discourse is rich, diverse, complex, generally abstract, and not a little contentious.

In semiotic aesthetics, those theories of musical meaning that regard music as a sign system, expression is joined analytically to signification. Susanne Langer's seminal works from the 1940s and 1950s, for instance, posit musical meaning as dependent on iconicity, and music itself as symbolic of mental states or emotions (1942, 204–45; 1953, 24–41). More recently, several musicologists and music theorists have embraced semiotics (though not always explicitly acknowledged as such) in the analysis and interpretation of music. More than the philosophical investigations, these studies, particularly those that explore topics as conventionalized signs of a musical surface, offer detailed analyses of musical works in a direct engagement of musical meaning.

In her trailblazing analyses of *Le nozze di Figaro* and *Don Giovanni*, Wye Jamison Allanbrook demonstrates how Mozart communicates topically the "virtues and vices" of his characters (1983, 70). In Figaro's cavatina "Se vuol ballare," for example, Mozart reveals Figaro's wit and control by "cloaking his insolence in the noble *politesse* of the minuet"—a dance topic that, because of its noble class associations, is the Count's proper music, not Figaro's. In the following B section, in which Figaro announces his plans to take revenge on the Count, Mozart switches to a contredanse, the "danceless dance" for middle-class amateurs, a dance whose "democracy of meters is a sign of its democracy of spirit": Figaro "has lured his victim onto his own turf" (61, 80–81). In Allanbrook's interpretation of Mozart's operas, the meanings of the expressive signs of the musical surface are primarily character definition and social commentary.

In her analyses of instrumental music, however, topical meaning is restricted to the purely musical realm. As Allanbrook herself acknowledges, her primary concern is "the interaction . . . of process and expression" (1992, 128). The meaning of the minuet in the second group of Mozart's Piano Sonata in F Major K. 332/I, for example, would seem to carry none of the class associations it does in Mozart's operas. Rather, Allanbrook finds that its "undeniable formedness . . . is a means of firmly fixing the position of the new key in the harmonic argument" (137). Her analyses of certain Mozart string quartet movements likewise confine the meaning of topics to structural implication and reinforcement. We learn of a fugal exposition decomposed into a contredanse in the finale of K. 387 and a Ländler cast too early and in the "wrong" key for a second-theme appearance in the first movement of K. 464 (1996, 135–37, 145). Social, political, or interpersonal meanings, such as those expressed topically in Mozart's operas, Allanbrook finds instrumental music incapable of communicating. Moments of interpretation beyond formal process— for instance, our awareness "at once of authority and its repression" (1996, 153) in the opening of K. 428/I—are rare. (And, as acknowledged, that particular observation comes from Janet Levy's analysis of textural meaning in the movement.) Elsewhere she states unequivocally that she is "uncomfortable with reading musical structures symbolically as political or philosophical positions" (1994, 176). The expressive surface of instrumental music, then, for Allanbrook, lacks the ability to inspire the rich and revealing interpretations of matters human she finds so compelling in opera's topical discourse.

Topical signs mingle with rhetorical figures in both theory and practice in Elaine

Sisman's rich and rewarding analyses of Mozart's "Prague" and "Jupiter" symphonies. By separating structural meaning from expressive meaning, she allows for observation of their interaction and cooperation in a work's formal processes. Building on Ratner's identification of the *ombra* topic and the rhetorical figure *apostrophe* at measure 16 of the slow introduction of the "Prague" Symphony, for example, she relates the *ombra*'s echoing of opera's supernatural to the *apostrophe*'s address to a personified thing (1997, 41). But beyond noting these kinds of topical and rhetorical associations, their interaction reveals primarily formal motivations, effectively assigning, like Allanbrook, only structural meanings to the topics and figures of the expressive surface in a given instrumental musical context. That the meanings of topics are ultimately formal is perhaps clearest in Sisman's exploration of the relations between gestures and topics. Drawing on the basic gestures of actors and orators as described in eighteenth-century manuals, she relates, for instance, "commencing gestures" such as grand hand-waving flourishes to the "Prague's" opening *coup d'archet*, concluding that "in the theatre and in oratory, the eloquent gesture accompanies or stands in for words; in instrumental music, the gesture is an essential conveyor of meaning" (65).[17] Like her categories of "formal" topics of interior reference (e.g., the false recapitulation) and "generic" topics that point to other musical genres (e.g., symphonic ritornello), the meaning of topics in general is essentially musical. The meaning of the "controlling" pastoral topic of the "Prague" Andante, for instance, while idyllic in expression, is ultimately the mediation "between the complex and multiple nature of the first movement and the much simpler single-topic *buffa* finale" (79). For Sisman, the "sources of *inventio* for composers" become "sources of shared"—and here I insert a word—structural "understanding by audiences" (50).

The "categories of meaning delimited by a work" are Hatten's concern in his exploration of expressive musical meaning in Beethoven's music (1994, 10). Like Allanbrook and Sisman, he is interested in relations between the formal (or "strategic") and the expressive (or "stylistic") dimensions of music. Central to Hatten's theory is the concept of an "expressive genre," a category of musical works defined by particular articulations of "conventionally encoded expressive states and processes," for example, tragic, triumphant, transcendent, spiritual, pastoral, and resignational. But it is not merely the musical delineation of expressive states but rather the formal or strategic process of their unfolding that defines an expressive genre—for example, a "change-of-state schema" (e.g., tragic-to-transcendent) or an "overarching topical field" (e.g., pastoral). Once identified, just as unusual structural details imply deeper expressive significance, expressive genres allow striking structural events to yield rich hermeneutic possibilities. In the end, Hatten's musical meaning relies on a reciprocal relationship between structure and expression. His interpretation of the third movement of Beethoven's *Hammerklavier* sonata as "acceptance through resignation" and ultimately "transcendence through a positively resigned acceptance—or spiritual abnegation," for instance, requires first the identification of the tragic-to-transcendent expressive genre and then a reading of significant strategic and surface features within that generic context as a troping of meaning.[18]

We might even say, as Hatten himself does later, that his theory and interpretations blur the distinctions between expressive and structural meanings.

But Hatten nevertheless maintains that "expressive meanings are as purely musical as the forms and structures that serve to distinguish them" (1994, 2). Assuming that "acceptance through resignation" is an example of an interpreted expressive meaning, his notion of *musical* meaning would seem to be much broader than Allanbrook's or Sisman's. The nature of the relationship between expression and structure, more than a philosophical delineation of meaning itself, supports Hatten's conception of such a seemingly extra-musical meaning as purely musical.[19] As he writes in conclusion, "in music, as in art, that which is structural *is* so because of its expressive significance, and that which is expressive in turn depends on a structuring which enables us to infer its expressive meaning" (278). Although Hatten's argument is grounded in his belief that "expressive meanings, and the stylistic competency they presuppose, were a part of Beethoven's compositional process (whether consciously or tacitly)" (2), not in a philosophical analysis of the categories themselves, his work clearly implies a rejection of the musical/extra-musical dichotomy.

In *Playing with Signs*, Agawu likewise examines how meaning and significance are communicated via music's structural and expressive features. His interpretation of the first movement of Mozart's String Quintet in C Major K. 515, for example, offers three analytical accounts: (1) a reading of the movement's topical content as "a tussle between high- and low-born characters"; (2) a hearing of the movement through a "sonata-form grid"; and (3) a capturing of its rhetoric of harmony through a "beginning-middle-ending paradigm." Each account is fragmentary, and the meaning of the movement therefore "resides in a large number of inter- and intradimensional connections"—the "play" that "serves to mediate between these accounts" (1991, 98–99). Just what that meaning might be, however, Agawu stops short of suggesting. While he notes that certain contradictions in topical situation "serve to enrich [the movement's] musical meaning," Agawu's profound discomfort with the notion of "plot" in instrumental music—he finds it "a result of sheer indulgence" (34)—prevents him from further speculation. The analysis of Mozart's tonal-harmonic strategy that follows thus feels like a retreat into the more comfortable and objective realm of traditional analysis, a realm in which musical meaning is again purely—and safely—musical. Agawu ultimately sidesteps the question of *what* a piece of music means for *how* a piece means, thereby avoiding direct engagement with the notion of musical meaning itself.[20]

Occasionally in musical scholarship, particularly in studies of musical semiology, we do find direct engagement with meanings of musical meaning, and the definitions posited, while tailored for use within the immediate context of a singular study, often seem applicable to a wider field of inquiry. Jean-Jacques Nattiez, for one, embraces Peircean semiotics to theorize that meaning, both musical and otherwise, is constructed in an endless web of interpretants. Meaning is therefore in a constant state of flux.[21] Hatten, likewise a Peircean semiotician but also a sometime critic of Nattiez (see Hatten 1980), contends (as noted above) that music's expressive meaning is purely musical. Raymond Monelle focuses on music's "inherent signification," which "implies a listening subject [but] is not dependent on individual listeners." His conception of musical meaning is thus independent of words, different from linguistic meaning, and comprehensible only through references to cultural units and history (2000, 11).

While methodologies, repertories, theoretical goals, and analytical strategies vary widely, many musicologists, music theorists, and semioticians take great care to assert the subjective nature of meaning itself. But then, perhaps surprisingly, most proceed to approach musical meaning *inter*subjectively. Nattiez's theory allows for a "constellation of possible meanings," and he explicitly acknowledges that "there is no guarantee that the webs of interpretants will be the same for each and every person involved in the process" (1990, 11). But the limitation of his musical analyses to only the "neutral level"—in essence, the score—jettisons in application the subjective aspects of his theory to embrace only its structuralist origins.[22] Hatten, in his exploration of musical meaning in Beethoven, likewise notes that interpretation is infinitely subjective but reconstructs, through his analyses, only "plausible *intersubjective* (shared, or sharable) interpretations" (1994, 5, emphasis in original). Agawu, too, acknowledges the "multiplicity of potential meanings of any single work," but in his own work hopes to "reduce away the fanciful meanings that are likely to crop up in an unbridled discussion of the phenomenon, and to approach the preferred meanings dictated by both historical and theoretical limitations" (1991, 5). The negative spin Agawu puts on the word "fanciful" and the stamp of authority granted those "preferred" historical and theoretical meanings seem, in the end, to remove individual subjectivity from the equation. By contrast, subjectivity is a central concern throughout Monelle's exploration of the "sense" of music. When engaging the issue of subjectivity directly, however, his argument that what is heard during a musical performance is the implied subjectivity of the text ultimately exposes his conception of subjectivity as structural (2000, esp. 147–69). If the work of these four writers is at all representative, an intersubjective approach locates musical meaning within music's own semantic and syntactic structures—that is, within an autonomous musical text, despite its undeniable (and, to be fair, usually acknowledged) dependence on history, culture, and myriad other things contextual.

In interpretations of music that privilege the contingencies of culture and context over an autonomy of the music itself (or at least consider the two more equally), musical meaning resides not so much in the musical text but in the intertextual spaces between musical experiences, historical, social, political, and intellectual contexts, and various other cultural phenomena. Kramer, for example, in an exploration of the nature of musical representation and meaning in his musical, textual, political, and cultural analysis of Haydn's "Representation of Chaos" in *The Creation,* theorizes an open-ended dialogic exchange between text and context (1995, 67–97). In a similar combination of musical and cultural analysis, Susan McClary interprets Mozart's "Prague" Symphony in light of bourgeois subjectivity, oppressive authority, and regression into nostalgia (1994). Rose Rosengard Subotnik, on the other hand, explores tangible connections between aspects of musical structure and Enlightenment rationality to read Mozart's last three symphonies as reflecting a shift toward a modern and critical worldview (1991, 98–111). Such ideological approaches, however, have been repeatedly disparaged for their apparent self-indulgence and presumed evanescence, as well as the salience of the personal—and often political—agenda of the interpreter. In other words, because the illumination of enduring aspects of the musical object is usually not its intention, this type of criticism is judged (and sometimes condemned) for its unabashed subjectivity.[23]

While it seems that much of the discomfort with an open-ended, intertextual, and even personal approach to musical meaning is due to our widely differing relationships to self-reference, Naomi Cumming gets it right, I think, when she suggests that academic writers of all types—even many self-defined New Musicologists—typically avoid reports of their own listening experiences out of a preference for certainty, or perhaps even "a less obvious fear of uncertainty" (2000, 46). And yet we, as a discipline, have recently acknowledged that the interpretation of any musical work—whether grounded in score analysis or cultural criticism—is at best a subjective and speculative activity. In the ongoing debate between various musicologies, theories, and criticisms, this is one point on which we all seem to agree. Indeed, Hatten, a music theorist and semiotician deeply invested in exploring musical meaning, who (as noted above) maintains that expressive meaning is purely musical, and whose work is chock full of rich and rewarding score analysis, nevertheless defines hermeneutic work as the "historical and *speculative* pursuit of *potential* meanings" (1994, 5, my emphasis). We can hear the same chord of contingency within a similar dedication to historical situation in the words of music and cultural critic Lawrence Kramer, whose sociopolitical readings have blazed the trails of New Musicology: "The intent is to say something consistent with what *could* have been said, whether or not it actually was, and in so doing to *suggest* how the work may have operated in, with, on, and against, the life of its culture" (1995, 20, my emphasis). When two scholars—both of whom engage problems of musical meaning but ask wildly different questions and employ widely varying interpretive strategies—concur on the speculative nature of the enterprise, it would seem that we have at least jettisoned our modernist desire for analytical and interpretive certainty. Why, then, do we still remain uncomfortable admitting personal and subjective listening experience not as merely an inevitable part, but in fact a *desirable* part, of musical scholarship?

My Meaning of Musical Meaning

As an interpretation of the public instrumental music of late-eighteenth-century Europe, this book is about suggesting musical meanings. But despite the cursory discussion above of some of the many historical, philosophical, and musicological conceptions of musical meaning, I have yet either to embrace or delineate a notion of musical meaning that can serve as a working definition for my present purpose. To be sure, the question of what it means to "mean" is, as Anthony Pople puts it, "a semiological Pandora's Box of differences, deflections, and deferrals" (1994, xi). But by posing a few intentionally simple questions and offering a deliberately uncomplicated sketch of what I mean by musical meaning in the immediate context of this book, I hope to suggest some provisional boundaries to contain my hermeneutic venture, despite the various ambiguities and contradictions that will arise when this definition is put to work.

What constitutes musical meaning? Musical meaning, for our purpose here, is simply those ideas, constructed in the mind of the listener, or those emotions, generated in the body (and mind) of the listener, upon experiencing a musical entity and performing the mental and physical activity of interpreting that experience. There are as many interpretations as experiences, as many experiences as listeners, and as many meanings constructed as listening subjects capable of performing even the simplest interpretive acts.

Does a piece of music have meaning? If "have" implies some sort of possession, then no. We shall maintain that a piece of music in and of itself does not have meaning. Meaning is constructed by human subjects and therefore resides within us, within human beings, not within inanimate objects, artistic or otherwise. A piece of music may be the most immediate stimulus or the conduit for meaning communicated between human subjects, but the construction of meaning takes place within the mind and body of an individual, animate person.

To be sure, more than one person may arrive at the same, or at least very similar, set of meanings for a particular musical composition, an actuality that suggests the presence within a musical work of certain features we can recognize as a style or code. Listeners who enjoy a certain "stylistic competency," to borrow Hatten's term (1994), may thus construct meanings that would seem to be intersubjective. But since for many readers a conceptualization of meaning as intersubjective may imply at least some residence of meaning within the work itself, to underscore my listener-centered approach I shall theorize here that such shared musical meanings are the product of the same "interpretive community," Stanley Fish's name for those who "share interpretive strategies not for reading (in the conventional sense) but for writing texts, for constituting their properties and assigning their intentions." As Fish explains, "these strategies exist prior to the act of reading and therefore determine the shape of what is read rather than, as is usually assumed, the other way around" (1980, 171). Listeners who are able to and choose to hear meanings that are sensitive to the musical, aesthetic, and historical circumstances of a musical work's composition, and perhaps even aligned with the presumed intentions of its composer, belong to the same interpretive community. But (Fish's later elimination of the subject-object dichotomy from the critical debate notwithstanding) the meanings these listeners hear, however shared or conditioned by the values and beliefs of a particular interpretive community they may be, remain nonetheless the constructions of *individual* members of that interpretive community. Even seemingly reconstructable meanings are therefore individual, subjective meanings ascribed to the musical work by its present interpreter. They are not reconstructions of meanings that exist within the piece itself.

Who determines musical meaning? The listener, when he actively interprets the music he hears. While a composer may determine specific meanings, maintain these meanings during the activity of composition, believe she is composing these meanings into a piece, and expect a piece of music to transmit her meanings, such intended meanings may or may not be perceived or re-created in the mind and body of a listener. He may interpret that musical work differently.[24] By the same logic, once the compositional activity is completed, the composer herself becomes another listener. Interpretation—the process of constructing meaning—is in this sense no different for a piece's composer than for its listener. The composer simply enjoys a unique listening subjectivity: she knows what was intended and may (or may not) interpret her own work accordingly.

We listeners, however, cannot know what the composer intended. Despite whatever documentary or textual evidence may be out there to discover, a composer's intended meanings are ultimately unknowable to anyone but the composer herself, and therefore irrelevant for our present purpose. But lest this assertion sound like yet another call to avoid the trap of the "intentional fallacy," I would argue that limiting the study of a work of art to its intrinsic nature (as argued by Wimsatt and Beardsley in their hugely influential 1954 essay) ironically prohibits all but individual and subjective meanings, no matter how objective such meanings are intended to be. To speculate constructively about the meanings listeners, whether historical or contemporary, hear in a composition, we must consider not only the work's intrinsic musical aspects but also its musical, historical, cultural, aesthetic, social, and political situations, for a listening subject cannot divorce a text from its various contexts. The "separability principle" (Goehr 1992, 171) does not apply to the listening experience. It is rather an aesthetic *belief*—part of the philosophical context conditioning the interpretive activity of particular listening subjects at certain points in history.

Are some meanings more "meaningful" than others? This question hinges first on whether one type of interpretive activity is more tangible than another. There are, of course, many degrees of interpretation, as well as many degrees of being conscious of performing interpretive acts. As I write this book, for instance, I am necessarily intensely self-conscious in my interpretive engagement; when I am at a concert, I am less so. But are the interpretations actualized at my computer upon hearing in my head an idealized performance of a given work better, more significant, or more valid than the ones actualized for the same piece performed on, say, a student recital? I would maintain that they are simply different. The same listener hearing the same piece under the same set of circumstances but at two different times will not necessarily arrive at the same interpretations because the *experience* is different. The musical text is crucial, of course, but I shall maintain that listening context and listener subjectivity control and ultimately determine musical meaning.[25]

Are some meanings more "correct" than others? If they are the product of the interpretive activity of an individual listener, no matter who, where, or when she is, then no. Interpretations of musical experiences are subjective; they cannot be incorrect. Some interpretations may seem to carry more weight than others because of the authority of the listening subject who performed them—a "professional interpreter," for instance, whose job it is to produce criticism that persuades others of a particular meaning for a particular text (see Fish 1980, 356–71). Within the context of this book, the interpretations of someone with, say, considerable musical training or vast historical knowledge are not more correct, in and of themselves, than those of someone who professes to be "tone deaf" or has not dedicated his career to studying musical-historical cultures. Such listeners are simply members of different interpreting communities.

Moreover, whether an interpreter has authority remains the judgment—also the result of interpretation—of another human subject. Authority, like meaning, is something we construct within our own minds. The authority I respect in certain teachers, like the authority I grant the *Oxford English Dictionary*, resides not in that person or object but in myself. When speculating about the potential meanings listeners construct during musical experiences, judgment as to the authority of the listening subject remains the responsibility of the one doing the speculating. And traditional understandings of what constitutes authority—education, experience, profession, reputation, historical situation, etc.—may not always apply. In an exploration of meanings the contemporary American public maintains for Mozart's music, for instance, I may find the interpretations of someone *not* trained in music more valuable and representative—and hence more meaningful within the context of my inquiry—than those of someone who has spent decades in a practice room. In other words, one interpretation becomes more authoritative than another only when we decide for ourselves what constitutes authority in a given situation, and then choose to privilege that quality while interpreting the interpretations. (Of course, as Fish points out, such "anti-professionalism is a form of professional behavior engaged in for the purpose of furthering some professional project" [1989, 207]. My "behavior" in this case reveals my own commitment to a particular academic practice and therefore also my membership in a particular interpretive community.)

What, then, might "meaning" mean? While musical meaning may be simply those ideas and emotions constructed by a listening subject during the activity of interpreting a musical experience, the meaning of those constructed meanings is the result of a subsequent interpretation. If to engage the meaning of meaning, then, is like Zeno's paradox—we spend forever approaching but never arrive—it behooves us to remember Pople's words: "meaning is a journey rather than a destination" (1994, xi).

2 The Immediacy of Structural Understanding

An exasperated reviewer of Beethoven's 22 December 1808 concert at the Theater an der Wien, on which was programmed both the Fifth and Sixth Symphonies, a piano concerto, three vocal works, and two keyboard fantasies, throws up his hands, overwhelmed by the task of saying anything meaningful about this music having heard it but once: "To judge all of these pieces after one and only one hearing, especially considering the language of Beethoven's works, in that so many were performed one after the other, and that most of them are so grand and long, is downright impossible" (*AMZ*, 23 January 1809, col. 268).[1] Who could not sympathize? But in the decades around 1800 the number and variety of pieces on this concert was not at all unusual. Each half of a public concert program typically opened with a symphony, followed by an aria or two, a concerto, perhaps some chamber music and keyboard improvisations. Another symphony, or at the very least the finale of one, usually closed the concert. Surely this reviewer possessed the endurance to enjoy several hours of musical entertainment in a day, as such was the norm. Perhaps it was the music itself he found challenging. Indeed, just six months earlier the same music journal articulated what had become conventional wisdom: "As is well known, one can rarely form a definite opinion about a Beethoven composition upon first hearing" (*AMZ*, 23 June 1808, cols. 623–24; quoted and trans. in Morrow 1989, 220). The reviewer then explains that further comment about the piece under consideration, Beethoven's "Triple Concerto" in C Major for piano, violin, cello, and orchestra, Op. 56, will be withheld until it can be heard several times.

Reviewers a decade earlier, however, seemed perfectly capable of finding something meaningful to say about the music of Haydn, Mozart, and their contemporaries after only one hearing.[2] For example, the journalist reviewing Salomon's 17 February 1792 concert in Hanover Square for *The Times* writes the following about Haydn's Symphony in D Major, No. 93, which was premiered that evening: "Such a combination of excellence was contained in every movement, as inspired all the performers as well as the audience with enthusiastic ardour. Novelty of idea, agreeable caprice, and whim combined with all *Haydn's* sublime and wonten grandeur, gave additional consequence to the *soul* and feelings of every individual present" (Landon 1976, 134). To be sure, such comments may seem little more than the usual conventional appellations ascribed to the works of an undisputed compositional genius. But what is significant here is not so much *what* was said, but that something *was* said; in fact, until Beethoven's heroic period and the dawning of

Romantic criticism, something was *always* said. Listeners found public instrumental music accessible and intelligible, as was not only expected but prescribed in the theoretical and aesthetic writings of the day.[3] Kirnberger, for one, instructs that "in works destined for public use . . . everything must be simple and cantabile, so that everyone understands it" (Sulzer [1792–97] 1967–70, 1:441; quoted and trans. in Zaslaw 1989, 516). While we may question the general applicability of "simple and cantabile" to the instrumental music of the late eighteenth century, the public of the time, even after only one hearing, certainly seemed to understand it.

But what is *understanding*, and how shall we regard it in this musical context? As a concept increasingly theorized in many disciplines, there is of course no singular understanding of understanding. In the present work, however, we shall define "understanding music" simply but narrowly—as the listener's self-reflexive physical and cognitive ability to translate musical elements into terms more familiar and tangible to her. While the particular musical elements and the terms into which they are translated vary with both listener and listening modality (the terms are not necessarily nonmusical, for instance), the activity of understanding music requires a certain consciousness about the relationships between the musical object and the experiences of the listening subject that mediate that translation. To understand music, then, theorized here for the eighteenth century as well as today, requires the listener to be able to hear and be conscious of relationships between the music and her experiences, musical or otherwise, of everyday life. Text and context are thus entangled in this process.

Ultimately forming the foundation for musical expressivity, these connections between text and context, grounded in intertextual echoes, are interdependent with musical structure.[4] Without the ability to process immediately and on one hearing the structural unfolding of a movement in time, a listener is unable to experience the meeting or foiling of expectation, instances of musical surprise, the appearance of expected material in an unexpected location, and other similar types of expressive play dependent on structural situation—stylistic devices common enough in late-eighteenth-century music to be a cornerstone of its expressive discourse. Indeed, late-eighteenth-century instrumental music was immediately intelligible to its original listeners largely because they could hear expression structurally and structure expressively. A structural understanding grounded in surface expression is not dependent on the usual assortment of strategies in our analytical toolbox, many of which, when applied to eighteenth-century music, anachronistically embrace teleology, unity, complexity, or hidden structure as institutional musical values—values that came into being only in the nineteenth century with the redefinition of instrumental music as an autonomous artistic entity.

In this chapter, by hearing the symphony within an inclusive echo chamber of late-eighteenth-century entertainment culture, we shall explore how the expressive surface of public instrumental music interacts with musical structure in such a way that the music's formal process became immediately intelligible to its listeners—listeners who, we must remember, did not have the benefit of subsequent hearings, miniature scores, deep-structural analysis, or even quiet concert halls.

Topical Questions

In musicological literature, references in eighteenth-century music to the music of everyday life have been theorized as "topics"—"subjects for musical discourse" in Ratner's original definition (1980). In recent years, topical analysis has become a fresh and insightful tool to rival the firm hold of tonal and formal analysis as the primary means for understanding the music of the Classical style. For example, this engagement with the expressive surface is an integral component in Allanbrook's sociopolitical reading of Mozart's operas (1983) and her examination of expressive and formal features in certain instrumental works (1992; 1996), Sisman's topical and rhetorical analysis of Mozart's "Jupiter" and "Prague" Symphonies (1993b; 1997), Agawu's semiotic interpretation of various chamber works by Haydn, Mozart, and Beethoven (1991), and Hatten's delineation of expressive genres in Beethoven's music (1994). These studies are diverse in methodologies but joined by the conviction that both "composers and audiences invested these commonplaces with meaning" (Sisman 1993b, 46).

But despite the great enthusiasm for considering the musical surface along with hidden and not-so-hidden musical structures, not to mention some brilliant demonstrations of just how revealing topical analysis can be, several challenges face those who look to relationships with contextual soundscapes in pursuit of musical meaning. The most significant concerns the identification of a topic. Sisman puts her finger precisely on this most crucial aspect of topical analysis. She asks: "What is a topic and what is not? Is every tremolo passage in a minor key a 'reference' to *Sturm und Drang* or every imitative passage 'learned style'?" (1993b, 46). Questioning the signified of the former, she notes that the literary category of the *Sturm und Drang* "was not even associated with a musical style of this period until the twentieth century, so how could it have been a topic of shared understanding?" (1997, 64). And her own studies of the "Prague" and "Jupiter" Symphonies suggest that imitative but nonlearned (or, in Charles Rosen's parlance, "classical" [1997, 117]) counterpoint, an "ordinary resource of style," is not a topic but may nevertheless, in certain contexts, operate as a rhetorical figure.[5]

The details, evidence, and persuasiveness of Sisman's argument notwithstanding, our ears alone may be able to determine easily and immediately whether or not a particular musical texture or style supplies a topical reference. For example, in the context of a late-eighteenth-century symphony, learned counterpoint (i.e., fugue, fugato, *alla breve,* and *style legato*) is exceptional (or marked, stylistically)—it stands out—and thus provides opportunity for stylistic signification that the more ordinary (for the style) "classical counterpoint" cannot. Learned counterpoint, by echoing music both archaic and sacred, communicates authority;[6] classical counterpoint, a musical texture of the "here and now," lacks conspicuity and therefore also such potential signification.

A similar argument can be made for the use of the *Sturm und Drang* at structural points requiring modulation. As Allanbrook notes about the frequent use of these kinds of stylistic devices in transitions from the first theme group to the second in sonata-form movements, the *Sturm und Drang* is "typical 'travelling music.' It provides the agitation necessary to alert the listener to the undermining of the tonic and the struggle upwards to the dominant, and it provides the harmonic and motivic freedom to ensure that the modulation will be dramatic" (1992, 136–37). But while Allanbrook might consider every instance of turbulent melodies and chromatic harmonies topical references (she labels all such moments in K. 332/I *Sturm und Drang*, for example), in some instances any meaning beyond the musical indication that we are traveling is questionable. So too, therefore, is the topical designation of a passage, something that indicates an expressive means by reference to music external to that of the immediate presentation. The usual interpretation of the *Sturm und Drang* as an "expression of subjective and intense personal feelings" (Ratner 1980, 21) or "supernatural intrusions upon human beings" (Sisman, 1997, 42) would thus seem inappropriate or forced in many cases, particularly when the appearance of the *Sturm und Drang* is not surprising or unexpected.[7]

Agawu points to another challenge facing the topical analyst. He writes:

> Perhaps the most fundamental limitation of any topical analysis is its lack of consequence. . . . While topics can provide clues to what is being "discussed" in a piece of music—thus making them authentic semiotic objects—they do not seem able to sustain an independent and self-regulating account of a piece; they point to the expressive domain, but they have no syntax. Nothing in Ratner's scheme tells us *why* the singing style [in the first movement of Mozart's Prague Symphony] should come after the outbursts of sensibility, or why fanfare is used toward the conclusion of the [first] period. (1991, 20)

Agawu's solution for this shortcoming is to embrace rhetoric and harmonic process as a means to provide the syntactic logic apparently lacking in the expressive surface. He then looks for "play" between a movement's referential surface topics and its nonreferential, that is, purely musical, underlying harmonic structures as revealed by Schenkerian structural-tonal voice-leading reduction. But still, despite several engaging discussions of this "play," the topical foreground and harmonic background remain separate entities. Agawu does relate a few surface topics to the musical functions of his beginning-middle-ending paradigm, implying that certain topics make rhetorical sense in a given location. Horn calls, for instance, signify beginning and sometimes ending (1991, 59). And, like Allanbrook,[8] he finds some syntactic logic for topical expression within an individual piece—Mozart's syntactic control in the first movement of the String Quintet in C Major K. 515, derives from the "grouping of similarly functioning topics" (1991, 90). But in the end his semiotic theory does not really suggest *why* a given topic makes sense (or is intelligible) at a particular point in the musical processes of Classic music in general.

While they do not necessarily explain the intricacies of syntactic logic for the expressive surface of a specific piece, the distinctly audible features of many topics do reveal just why certain topics make good musical sense for certain formal processes within the Classical style. The *Sturm und Drang* style, for one, is, as Allanbrook suggests, tailor-made for transitional passages. Similarly, the predictability of dance topics and songlike melodies (not to be confused with the singing style, which is more of a texture than a melodic type), with their presentational qualities of regular periodicity, homophonic textures, and overall tunefulness,[9] promote coherence and a sense of fixedness at points requiring structural stability.[10] To be sure, we may still not always be able to articulate the sequential sense of topics at the local level—within a theme group, say, as in Ratner's topical analysis of the opening of Mozart's "Prague" Symphony. But we can understand something of "regional" topical situation, since topics are frequently key elements in the articulation of broad expressive states within large formal structures and multimovement compositions.

It is Sisman again, however, who asks arguably the most important and daunting question about the limits of topical analysis: "Does the composer intend the audience simply to recognize topics, or to understand more subtle meanings?" (1993b, 46). There is certainly much evidence in compositional and theoretical treatises to suggest that topical references were the product of conscious compositional decisions. Although frustrating in their lack of any systematic explication, there are ample descriptions of various dances, styles, textures, and stylistic registers in encyclopedias like Sulzer's *Allgemeine Theorie der schönen Künste* (1771–74) and Koch's *Musikalisches Lexikon* (1802), theoretical tracts like Türk's *Klavierschule* (1789) and Daube's *Anleitung zur Erfindung der Melodie* (1797–98), and journalistic publications like Scheibe's *Critischer Musikus* (1745), all of which bear witness to the currency and presence of topics in the minds of the writers of these publications and, presumably, the composers and musicians who read them. But a positive answer to Sisman's question, at least as it is posed, is not possible. For our purpose here, however, the question is also irrelevant. It concerns composer intention, something ultimately unknowable.

The question itself becomes more productive (and provocative) if we shift the emphasis from composer intention to listener perception. There is also much evidence to suggest that listeners in the eighteenth century heard topical references, made associations, and at least formed opinions about the appropriateness of their use in a given context. For example, reviewers in the increasingly popular music magazines, publications often disparaged by more learned music theoreticians and writers, occasionally reveal the topics they hear in instrumental music. In a review of *Six Simphonies* by Friedrich Schwindl for Johann Adam Hiller's *Wöchentliche Nachrichten*, the anonymous author acknowledges his recognition (and dislike) of a chorale in the second movement (1766–70, 3:33, 160).[11] Listeners also heard topics in vocal music, particularly references to various dances. Thomas Busby, for example, notes Handel's poor use of a minuet in *Alexander's Feast* (1819, 2:386).[12] At the very least, then, we can surmise that attentive listeners heard echoes of music from other contexts—here the chorale of the Lutheran church and the minuet of the ballroom—and, moreover, that such references were integral to a listener's sense of his own musical understanding. Indeed, by his own admission, Hiller's reviewer "did not know what to make of [Schwindl's second movement]" until he recognized the chorale.

But once a topic was recognized, did listeners engage in interpretive activity beyond merely identifying the source to which it refers? Unfortunately Busby and Hiller's anonymous reviewer tell us only that they found a particular topic inappropriate, indicating identification and disapproval, but not much in the way of further interpretation. And what about those topical references of which they did approve? Reviewers tend to be even less specific when praising a composition or performance. They reach into the same bag of lofty but frustratingly general accolades applauding a composer's "inexhaustible genius," "invention in ideas," and "creative spirit."[13] Cramer himself, in his *Magazin der Musik,* even acknowledges this problem at the beginning of a review of some of C. P. E. Bach's published sonatas. He writes, "It is always difficult to say something definite about an instrumental piece without simply breaking out in general exclamations or going into detail with barren lists of harmonic beauties, modulations, etc." (7 December 1783, 1275–76; quoted and trans. in Morrow 1997, 126). But must we take this lack of specificity in reviews as evidence that eighteenth-century listeners heard only a composer's "genius" and stopped their interpretive activity there? The fact that composers returned again and again to similar devices and references suggests not only the listener's recognition but, more crucially, his understanding.

Perhaps more constructive questions than whether a composer intends an audience to understand subtle topical meanings are (1) how might a listener construct meaning through her interpretation of topical references? and (2) what might such meanings be? We are still faced with problems of identification, interpretation, and consequence, not to mention the speculative nature of the entire enterprise, but by shifting emphasis away from composer intention and toward listener interpretation, we not only avoid the trap of the intentional fallacy but ironically end up embracing more comfortably the notion that composers planned the effects that their audiences were able to appreciate. In other words, by demonstrating how listeners were able to interpret expressive features and relate them to the musical argument, it becomes a less troubled leap of logic that composers worked such effects into the structure of a composition (as assumed by Sisman), especially when a composer, particularly one known for studying his audience, returns to the same expressive and structural devices again and again. While grounded in a listener orientation, our approach may thus be composer-oriented as well.[14]

Conventionalized Signs

In her seminal article on texture as a sign in music, Janet Levy distinguishes between two different types of textural signs. Contextual signs arise from associations or relationships among textures *within* a given piece. "What seems involved in such signifying," she writes, "is a simple mode of association (notably by identity) over a musical distance, or recognition of deviation from a characteristic presentation of thematic material." Conventionalized signs, the second type, arise from associations or relationships among textures *outside* a given piece, specifically those textures one encounters with enough regularity to be considered conventional within a broad but immediate musical context. Levy's distinction between contextual and conventionalized signs is a useful one, for while our delineation of potential carriers of musical meaning will not be limited to musical textures, we shall be concerned primarily with relationships between the expressive features of a given piece and its everyday musical contexts. In the end we shall embrace potential musical meanings beyond the syntactical, but since any broader meaning may be dependent upon the situation of expressive elements within a composition's formal argument, we must first consider how a work's expressive surface provides "instantaneous conduits to syntax" (Levy 1982, 530).

In the following exploration of relationships between expression and formal process in Classical instrumental music, there will undoubtedly be many similarities to the work of other writers in both the approach to the question and our conclusions.[15] But there will be one crucial difference: we shall consider, for the most part, only conventionalized signs, for the interpretation of contextual signs often requires "retroactive hearing"—the reinterpretation of earlier events based on the experience of later ones. I am not suggesting that listeners, whether of the eighteenth century or today, are incapable of remembering and reflecting upon previous musical happenings during or after hearing subsequent ones. But neither would I maintain that consciously recalling earlier structural detail is a normal mode of listening in an *entertainment* context, either now or especially then. Considering the noise and distractions of eighteenth-century theaters and public concert halls, it is unlikely that any but the most attentive listeners of the time would notice the more subtle reworkings of previously presented musical material, no matter how crafty or, from an analytical perspective, wholly significant to the musical argument they may be. Instead, listeners were there as much to socialize as to hear the concert, and thus were likely taking in little more than the "broad strokes" of a composition. And yet, if the accounts of thundering applause and spontaneous demands for encores are any indication, audiences enjoyed concerts immensely and found the compositions that made up a typical morning, afternoon, or evening's entertainment somehow readily intelligible.

The following discussion considers several expressive means for communicating the most basic rhetorical functions of a movement's structural unfolding—opening, continuing, and ending.[16] Simply put, openings establish strategic and expressive stability; continuations generate strategic and expressive instability; and endings regain strategic and expressive stability. While attentive and musically educated listeners may have heard more subtle rhetorical figures or varying degrees of strategic stability and instability, the ability to perceive these three fundamental functions at various levels of the discourse is all that was required for the lay listener to comprehend a movement's principal formal argument. Moreover, the perception of these basic rhetorical functions does not necessarily require the listener's ability to hear, or inclination to notice, the music's motivic, harmonic, or tonal means of establishing a particular rhetorical function.[17] As we shall see, salient references to the musical soundscape of the eighteenth-century world, particularly echoes of other types of entertainment music, did not merely reinforce but in fact could establish states of stability and instability. The expressive domain alone could thereby provide ready "roadmaps" for contemporary listeners to follow during their one and usually only journey through an instrumental composition.

To explore from the listener's perspective the interdependency of structural process and conventionalized surface topics, textural signs, and other types of references to the contemporary musical soundscape, I have chosen four works representative of various stages of the late-eighteenth-century symphonic art by its two greatest practitioners: Haydn's Symphony in B-flat Major, No. 68 (c. 1775?), and Symphony in D Major, No. 104, "London" (1795), and Mozart's Symphony in D Major, "Haffner," K. 385 (1782), and Symphony in D Major, "Prague," K. 504 (1786). Two were composed for public concerts—the "Prague" likely for a series of Mozart's academies and the "London" for Salomon's concert series in London—and two for private occasions—the "Haffner" for the ennoblement of Mozart's childhood friend Sigmund Haffner the younger[18] and Haydn's No. 68 for functional use at the Esterházy court. But all four ultimately enjoyed performances in Europe's public theaters and concert halls—the "Haffner" in Vienna's Burgtheater, for example, and Haydn's No. 68, published by Hummel (Berlin-Amsterdam, 1779), presumably in various venues throughout the continent and Britain. Audiences for these works, then, were quite varied and included bourgeois and noble listeners, *Kenner, Liebhaber,* and lay listeners alike, all of whom we can surmise were able to follow something of the musical arguments put forth.

Surface Topics and Rhetorical Process

Expressive Signs of Stability: Opening

Virtually all performances of the late eighteenth century, theatrical as well as musical, opened with the invigorating first movement of a symphony or an overture, and it was the responsibility, or function, of the opening moments of that symphony to grab hold of the audience's attention. As Mary Sue Morrow notes in her study of concert life in late-eighteenth-century Vienna, "audiences did not have the two cues that alert us to a concert's beginning: the dimming of the lights (how do you dim candles?) and the dramatic entrance of a baton-carrying conductor. The music itself had to provide the signal" (1989, 142). A loud, sudden blast of sound is a most effective way to attract the attention of a large group of chatty people, and indeed, a high percentage of Classical symphonies starts with such "noise-killer effects."[19] The "Haffner," the "Prague," and Haydn's Symphony No. 104, for example, all open with grand gestures that are clearly recognizable as signs of commencement (Example 2.1). But while such gestures may be sufficient to alert listeners that a concert is starting, especially in situations in which they would expect music to begin, the establishment of expressive stability, accomplished largely by echoing other musical openings, encourages the listener's comprehension of the rhetorical function of opening at the beginning of symphonic first movements.

The heavy march tempo and dotted- and double-dotted rhythms that mark the opening measures of Haydn's Symphony No. 104 immediately call up the pomp and stateliness of the French overture, a style of festive, ceremonial entrance music heard in courts and theaters throughout seventeenth- and eighteenth-century Europe. In its various guises as a movement type—from the processional *entrée* in

Example 2.1.
a. Mozart, Symphony in D Major K. 385, "Haffner," I, opening
b. Mozart, Symphony in D Major K. 504, "Prague," I, opening
c. Haydn, Symphony in D Major No. 104, "London," I, opening

French stage performances to the introductory first movement in instrumental suites—the French overture invariably has an opening function. Indeed, it is often suggested as a likely model for the slow introductions of Classical symphonies.[20] More than any other feature, the French overture's trademark dotted rhythms express stability by means of their association with the court, as the constancy of the sovereign was the most stabilizing force for the European citizenry of the time. The opening of the "Haffner," while too fast for a French overture, secures expressive stability by recalling, with its double-dotted and drum-call rhythms, duple meter, and noble character, the regality of ceremonial marches. In addition to projecting a similar regal magnificence, the forceful ascending flourishes at the beginning of the "Prague" Symphony echo the grand orchestral openings heard in many Italian opera overtures. Mozart, for example, used the very same ascending flourishes to open the overtures to *Idomeneo* and *La clemenza di Tito;* he returns to them once more, of course, to open the "Jupiter" Symphony.[21]

The unison texture with which these three symphonies begin also establishes expressive stability. As Levy argues, "probably the single most pervasive quality of a unison passage is its aura of authoritative control. For unanimity—as in the crowd singing together in unison—is basically contrary to our sense of the individuality of human beings. It does not appear to occur in nature, to happen naturally. It must, in some sense, be organized, preordained—imposed" (1982, 507). Undeniably, the commencement of a public concert in the late eighteenth century was an organized imposition upon the noisy socializing of the audience. But it was also a command—"Listen!"—for, as Levy notes, our association of certain types of unison textures, particularly those martial in character, with the "bold call to attention for political, social, or military events seems so basic as to be emblematic" (1982, 509). In these three symphonic openings, then, the combination of the forte "noise-killer," the reference to ceremonial entrance music, and the authority of the unison texture immediately communicates to the listener expressions of both commencement and stability.

One could certainly argue that the mere placement of such musical material at the beginning of a work is enough to establish something of an opening rhetorical function. A listener would never misunderstand the first notes of the first movement of a symphony likely placed first on a concert program as something other than an expression of opening and, by strategic association, stability. But just as formal function suggests expressive meaning, so does expressive meaning suggest formal function. For instance, it is perhaps most essential in sonata-form movements to establish a sense of stability at the opening of the second group, for not only are we in a new key (whether that is perceived by the lay listener or not), but the preceding modulatory bridge passage is likely to have been exciting, volatile, driven, and anything but strategically and expressively stable. Not infrequently is stability established strategically by means of recalling thematic material from the opening of the first group, as in the exposition of the first movement of Haydn's "London" Symphony where the restatement of the now-familiar contredanse tune (at m. 65) secures the arrival in the dominant after the rousing bridge passage. But when the musical material that opens the second group is new, the most common (and therefore presumably successful) means of affecting stability is a tuneful, singable, and predictable melody—characteristics shared by both popular tunes and dances, the most accessible, familiar, comfortable, and common music of every-day eighteenth-century life.[22]

The singing-style, eight-measure melody at the start of the "Prague" first movement's second group is a clear example (Example 2.2a). After the intensity of the cadential passage at the end of the bridge, the slowing of the harmonic rhythm, change to legato articulation, reduced scoring to stings alone, built-in repetitions, and unmistakable homophony of this material allow the listener to shift listening modalities and simply take in the easy presentation of a new and unchallenging tune (at m. 97). Likewise, the melody at the beginning of the "Prague" finale's second group (Example 2.2b), with its reduced scoring, lack of syncopation, built-in repetitions, simple three-note stepwise descents, and plain block and broken-chordal accompaniments, ensures a brief moment of expressive stability in this otherwise action-packed movement. But it is the remarkably clear periodicy of both of these second-group themes, particularly the strings' clear 4+4 phrase structure reinforced by the winds' four-measure "answer" (mm. 74–78) in the "Prague" finale, that defines both passages as unequivocally stable. As Allanbrook has observed, "strong periodicity is a means of firmly fixing the position of the new key in the harmonic argument" (1992, 137). But *why?* For the lay listener especially, it is the echoing of the phrase structure, uncomplicated harmonic and melodic procedures, and overall accessibility of popular tunes and dances that allow the listener who does not or cannot follow a movement's tonal process to be aware nonetheless of where he is in its structural design: the evocation of popular song or dance lets him know that the music will rest for the moment right where it is.

Conventional accompanimental patterns can likewise secure expressive stability. As Levy notes, they indicate "that we will hear a presentational passage—probably a full statement, such as a stable phrase-group or period." Arguing for a "kind of double psychic economy," she suggests first that when we recognize Alberti and other familiar patterns, "because there is no question of what the passage *is*, we can relax and simply experience its unfolding." Then, because the "palpable motor action" measures time regularly for us, we expend less effort in the perception of meter (1982, 489–92). In addition to throwing the melody into relief, ensuring its status as such, and suggesting a certain singing quality, all expressive aspects of the musical texture that evoke a sense of tuneful familiarity by echoing the textures of popular songs, these regular accompanimental patterns encourage a less vigilant listening modality by articulating a steady pulse and predictable harmonic rhythm. The place we are most likely to encounter such regularly measured, broken-chordal figures in sonata-form movements is, of course, the second group.[23] But they are also commonly found in slow movements, particularly at the beginning. The two locations are thereby aligned as points of repose in many late-eighteenth-century symphonies. The second group of the first movement and nearly all of the slow movement of Haydn's Symphony No. 68, the opening of the second movement and the parallel period of the second theme of the finale of Mozart's "Haffner" Symphony, and the winds' "answers" in the second group of the third movement of

Example 2.2.
a. Mozart, Symphony in D Major K. 504, "Prague," I, second group
b. Mozart, Symphony in D Major K. 504, "Prague," III, second group

Mozart's "Prague" Symphony all offer clear examples of the use of conventional accompanimental patterns to encourage the listener's sense of structural stability (Example 2.3).

Expressive Anticipation of Stability

The listener's perception of strategic stability is often intensified when the anticipation of that stability is heightened expressively. Surface expressions of expectancy, motion, and authority, for example, can promote the listener's awareness of structural situation regardless of her knowledge of musical form or her ability to hear tonal relations.

Generating expectancy, fanfares typically announce the arrival of a structurally important point or a particularly stable event in the musical discourse, a clear echo of the fanfare's traditional social function of announcing the arrival of a sovereign or dignitary at the beginning of public events or ceremonies. In the first movement of the "Haffner" Symphony, a descending fanfare at the end of the bridge (mm. 33–

Example 2.3.

a. Haydn, Symphony in B-flat Major, No. 68, I, second group

b. Haydn, Symphony in B-flat Major, No. 68, II, opening

c. Mozart, Symphony in D Major K. 385, "Haffner," II, opening

d. Mozart, Symphony in D Major K. 385, "Haffner," III, parallel period of the second theme

e. Mozart, Symphony in D Major K. 504, "Prague," III, winds' "answers" in the second group

Example 2.4.
Mozart, Symphony in D Major K. 385, "Haffner," I, end of the bridge

34) signals the modulation to the dominant key and the beginning of the second group (Example 2.4). But a nervous bass line (mm. 35–40) renders uncertain the statement in A major of the movement's opening gesture. Ironically, it is not until ascending violin fanfares announce the move "back" to D major—that is, to IV/V—for a now confident restatement of the opening gesture (mm. 41–42) that the second group enjoys any stability, however fleeting, before the closing theme at m. 59. At the parallel points in the recapitulation, the bridge is shortened and the first fanfare is omitted. This makes good musical sense, for there is no arrival in a new key to announce. The second fanfare remains (mm. 147–48), however, to mark the following brief moment of stability.

The first movement of the "Prague" Symphony provides another example of the annunciatory function of the fanfare. Following the extraordinarily tense and lengthy introduction, the exposition does not commence with a bang—or even a root-position tonic chord—to give the listener some sense of tonal stability and musical grounding (Example 2.5). In place of the more usual presentational material are syncopated Ds, which Sisman has perfectly described as giving "a strong impression of 'vamp until ready.'" The slower-moving but still syncopated lower line suggests a harmonic holding pattern, underscoring the impression that this exposition is not quite ready to begin. But a mere six measures after this tentative opening (during which a short repeated-note rhythmic figure is introduced, to be discussed presently), a wind and brass fanfare announces that we are indeed commencing (mm. 43–45). As Sisman observes, the "message is clear: 'strike up the band!'" (1997, 58). But no sooner than we have begun, the "vamping" Ds re-

Example 2.5.
Mozart, Symphony in D Major K. 504, "Prague," I, opening of the Allegro
Continued on the next page

Example 2.5.
Mozart, Symphony in D Major K. 504, "Prague," I, opening of the Allegro

turn. It is the following brilliant-style tutti section (mm. 55–71), culminating in an extended cadential fanfare, that finally affirms that this exposition is actually underway.

Related to the fanfare in both association and connotation is the drum call, a short, incisive rhythmic figure that emphasizes the downbeat by preceding it with crisp upbeat. Essential to foot regiments, drum calls not only communicate military instructions but, when repeated, form the cadences required for marching. In the eighteenth century, drum calls also fulfilled various civic duties, such as replacing the town crier's hand bell (Blades 1980, 5:647). In Classical instrumental music, drum calls, when salient in the musical texture, are as recognizable as fanfares, and likewise impart important information about structural situation and function. But while fanfares typically announce strategically important and generally stable events in the musical argument by echoing their civic function and thereby creating a sense of expectancy, drum calls imply preparation, generate energy, and heighten our sense of impending arrival by suggesting the march's inexorable forward motion. In the first movement of Haydn's "London" Symphony, for example, a tutti outburst (at m. 32) follows right on the heels of the second period of the contredanse theme and, punctuated by drum-call rhythms in the brass and timpani, gains the momentum required for this bridge passage to modulate to the dominant (Example 2.6a). Similarly, following the "Haffner's" opening call to attention, the drum call that marks the end of that antecedent phrase (mm. 4–5; see Example 2.1a) is picked up in the consequent phrase (mm. 6–13, Example 2.6b). At first simply providing continuation, the drum call ultimately propels the music forward through the bridge and modulation to the second group (mm. 14–34).

The drum calls in the second movement Andante of Haydn's Symphony No. 104 take on even greater structural significance, as they provide the listener with signposts marking some of the most important events in the movement's formal articulation. The brass and timpani, who have hardly sounded during this ternary variation movement, dramatically punch through the texture (mm. 67–70, Example 2.6c) to announce the varied return of the A section four measures later. A subsequent pianissimo drumroll quietly alerts the listener to another return within the reprise, this one somewhat unexpected. After a surprising harmonic digression (mm. 105–113) interrupts the variation of the second half of the rounded binary A section, a reflective "reaction-shot" wind cadenza (mm. 114–117) and further contemplation in the strings and bassoon (mm. 118–122) follow (Example 2.6d). Then, instead of continuing from the point of departure and completing the variation of the period, Haydn returns (or "fast-forwards") to the beginning of the opening period (at m. 122) to close the movement according to form, the timpani roll (m. 121) having subtly prepared us for this leap to the final statement.

The wonderfully quixotic slow movement of Haydn's Symphony No. 68, oddly sentimental and comic, provides an unusual example of a drum call used more to anticipate motion than to supply that motion itself. As Webster describes it, the overall effect of the first group is "non-goal-directed rumination" (1998, 236). But in the second group, the only passage devoid of the movement's incessant accompanimental "ticking" motif, rhythmic activity increases to sextuplet thirty-second notes that break off suddenly into triplet drum-call rhythms (mm. 31–32, Example 2.6e). Startled as we are by the surprising surge of energy, the sudden stop seems less abrupt because, despite their fading volume, the drum calls not only continue something of the passage's forward motion but also create a sense of anticipation. After such an unexpected swell, we know something important is sure to happen. But our expectations are foiled as the ruminating melody and ticking motif return

Example 2.6.
a. Haydn, Symphony in D Major, No. 104, "London," I, bridge
b. Mozart, Symphony in D Major K. 385, "Haffner," I, end of the first group through the bridge
Continued on the next page

Example 2.6.

c. Haydn, Symphony in D Major, No. 104, "London," II, "announcement" of the return of the A section

d. Haydn, Symphony in D Major, No. 104, "London," II, in the varied return of the A section

Continued on the next page

Example 2.6.
e. Haydn, Symphony in B-flat Major, No. 68, II, in the second group
f. Haydn, Symphony in B-flat Major, No. 68, II, end of the retransition

(at m. 34) and remain through the closing group. At the end of the retransition (Example 2.6f) Haydn again plays with our expectations by recalling the drum call (mm. 81–82), this time sustaining the forte dynamic to intensify its message of preparation and heighten the listener's anticipation of something grand. But alas (and as attentive listeners with knowledge of formal process would have suspected), in the next measure (m. 83) the pondering melody and persistent accompaniment are back. The nearly exact reprise of the exposition's drum call in the recapitulation (mm. 108–109)—and the likelihood that we are no longer tricked into anticipation—serves only to amplify the ultimate futility of the gesture.

Solo textures supply another type of preparatory expression. Like drum calls, they almost always imply the beginning of an important and structurally stable section in a movement's formal process. Levy argues that solo textures echo the individual statement that initiates group action, as seen in such varied contexts as Jewish and Christian responsorial chanting, cheerleading, political rallies, and the choruses of ancient Greek tragedy. Reflecting this particular mode of human communication, "the solo may rather literally serve to 'conduct' the action to the beginning of a major segment in a formal structure" (1982, 498). Such an extended-upbeat function is easily heard in the two-measure solo violin section's lead-in to the second group (mm. 30–32) in the first movement of Haydn's Symphony No. 68 (Example 2.7a) and in the one-measure first violin lead-in (m. 17) at the identical spot in the second movement of Mozart's "Haffner" Symphony (Example 2.7b). As Levy observes in comparable moments, "the sudden reduction of texture—particularly the absence of bass—heightens the instability" (498–99). The first violin line (mm. 48–49) that leads into the recapitulation of the "Haffner's" slow movement (Example 2.7c), however, feels less like a preparatory upbeat than a quasi-improvisatory vocal cadenza, not only because, as Levy has observed, "we tend to identify a solo line with an individual human voice" (498), but also because of other textural features that strongly suggest the imitation of an aria—the movement's conventional accompanimental pattern and "cadenza" at the end of the exposition (mm. 28–29), for example. But its strategic function as preparation for stability remains the same. Similarly, the brief fugato passages in the "Haffner" finale (e.g., mm. 53–56, Example 2.7d) are not heard as extended upbeats, for they are, in fact, rather assertive downbeats that kick off the closing group (mm. 57–70). But, as in other imitative contrapuntal textures, the solo texture's role in this context as leader of a group and initiator of response is nevertheless unmistakable.

Reining in the listener's concentration at the end of a movement can require a gesture just as authoritative as one employed at the beginning of a symphony to gain the attention of a chatty and distracted audience. Quite frequently the unison texture's authoritative stance also intensifies anticipatory passages, particularly those driving toward formal closure. The natural and human association of the unison with authority noted above is supported, if not amplified, by its most conventional expressive use in the theater. Count Almaviva's many demands in Mozart's *Le nozze di Figaro* are among the countless examples in late-eighteenth-century opera of the communication of power and authority by means of a unison texture.

Example 2.7.
a. Haydn, Symphony in B-flat Major, No. 68, I, second group
b. Mozart, Symphony in D Major K. 385, "Haffner," II, second group
c. Mozart, Symphony in D Major K. 385, "Haffner," II, preparation for the recapitulation
d. Mozart, Symphony in D Major K. 385, "Haffner," IV, closing group

The very first line of the Count's first full musical number, the Act I trio, is a question followed by a command. "What do I hear? Go at once and send the seducer packing." This command—the first line that we hear the Count sing (as opposed to recite)—Mozart sets nearly in unison, musically asserting his power (Example 2.8a). For the first part of the phrase the strings back the Count's line exactly, adding little anticipatory gestures to each note of his scalar climb (mm. 4–11). Only at the end of the phrase does the full band join him to provide the period's punctuation (mm. 12–15). Throughout the trio, as the Count's anger builds, he reiterates not the entire scalar motive, but *only* its unison opening. Another example can be heard in the Count's unisons at the beginning of the Act II finale (mm. 55–56, 58–59, Example 2.8b), the point in the opera at which is he most menacing: he believes his wife's lover is hiding in her closet, and demands the key. Most compelling, however, are the Count's unisons at the end of the Act II finale, when he acts as judge in Marcellina's case against Figaro. His gavel is his voice: "Olà silenzio," backed by unison strings for all but the cadence, cuts through the dramatic and musical chaos, focusing all attention—the audience's as well as the characters'—on the Count's action and authority. The third of these unison demands for silence (mm. 769–81, Example 2.8c) leads directly to the finale's last section, a Più Allegro constructed almost entirely of rushing scales, dotted rhythms, fanfares, and drum tattoos—the stock cadential material that so often marks large-scale strategic closure in late-eighteenth-century music.

Echoing such dramatic, attention-focusing moments in opera, the authority of a unison passage rouses the audience and unites its energy in the drive to formal closure in the first movements of the "Haffner" and "London" Symphonies. In the exposition of 104/I, all forward momentum converges and intensifies in two measures of unison (mm. 90–91, Example 2.9a) during the tutti outburst in the second group, compelling listeners to anticipate the satisfying arrival that is surely seconds away. The new melody that immediately follows the cadence at m. 101 thus sounds all the more surprising, for the whole band was just united for an eight-measure cadential drive that could have convincingly closed the exposition. Because the parallel cadential passage in the recapitulation lacks the "acceleration effect" of the two-measure unison lead-in, it does not gain the momentum of its prior iteration—which, after all, makes good musical sense, for the new melody would not be as unexpected and the cadential "fake-out" less effective. Near the end of the second group of the "Haffner's" first movement (in both the exposition and recapitulation), a sudden shift to the minor mode, a drop to piano dynamic, and string tremolos evoke the *ombra* at m. 66, interrupting a cadential passage on its way to formal closure (Example 2.9b). A forceful tutti unison at m. 74, however, cuts off the excursion into the realm of the otherworldly just before it can cadence there, and then—with considerable effort—tows the music back to the cadential business at hand. The sheer force and startling authority of this extended unison passage (mm. 74–80), echoing the remarkable power of individuals united in a common purpose, serve to alert the listener to both the digression and subsequent correction of the movement's structural course.

Example 2.8.
a. Mozart, *Le nozze di Figaro,* Act I Trio, the Count's rising anger
b. Mozart, *Le nozze di Figaro,* Act II Finale, the Count demands the key
c. Mozart, *Le nozze di Figaro,* Act II Finale, the Count calls for silence

Example 2.9.

a. Haydn, Symphony in D Major, No. 104, "London," I, tutti outburst in the second group

Continued on the next page

Example 2.9.
b. Mozart, Symphony in D Major K. 385, "Haffner," I, in the second group

Expressive Signs of Stability: Ending

As required by the tonal argument, closural passages, particularly closing groups of sonata-form movements and finales, confirm the tonic (or temporary tonic) key as "home" by reiterating short, formulaic harmonic progressions. It is the rare listener who does not hear the resolution of such insistent authentic cadences, even if she lacks the training or vocabulary to describe the harmonic mechanisms at work. But the comfort and immediate recognition of the stock cadential gestures that typically articulate such harmonic progressions, combined with a lack of presentation of new musical ideas, contribute just as much to the listener's sense that we are at a final point of stability, stasis, or conclusion in the formal process.

Indeed, cadential passages are easily the most conventional in the public instrumental music of the late eighteenth century, and one could hardly hear a symphony without encountering at moments of structural closure generic scales, arpeggios, tattoos, fanfares, and tutti chords articulated in short, symmetrical, and entirely predictable phrase structures marked by heavy downbeats.[24] Examples abound: the closing groups and brief codetta passages of both first movements and finales of all four of our example symphonies are comprised of such conventional closing material arranged in symmetrical, two-measure phrase structures. As much as echoing music from other activities and contexts of everyday life, closing groups echo each other. The stability of endings in late-eighteenth-century public music is ultimately generated by means of a self-defining and self-reinforcing convention.

Expressive Signs of Instability: Continuing

In between moments of structural stability lie unstable passages that communicate to the listener the necessity of continuation. On the small scale are transition and bridge passages, points in the strategic argument that involve modulation or substantial change in expressive stance. On the large scale are development sections and slow introductions, structural points that demand broad formal resolution. While the anticipatory topics and textures discussed above contribute to the sense of instability we hear at such points, the *need* for musical continuation we often perceive in transition and development sections goes beyond a sense of mere anticipation. In addition to the modulations and shifting, unresolved harmonies required by the tonal argument, evocations of music associated with tension, excitement, agitation, insecurity, unrest, or anxiety encourage the listener to associate such connective passages and larger formal sections with dramatic change. Theater music, especially *mélodrame* and obbligato recitative, provides the most readily identifiable musical signs of instability. Not surprisingly, the references heard most frequently at points of large-scale structural instability are to the textures, topics, and rhetorical gestures of musical theater that are explicitly tied by text and plot to volatile emotions, dramatic conflict, and irresolution—expressive states in which neither story nor music can rest.

In the public instrumental music of the late eighteenth century, we can recognize two broad categories of unstable passages. In the first, the musical material itself expresses the instability. The nervous energy of string tremolos, for example, is easily heard as a sign of unrest whether situated in a transitional passage, a development section, or even as an interruption in an otherwise stable passage. Listeners in the eighteenth century would have encountered this simple string-textural device, defined in the seventeenth century by Monteverdi as *stile concitato,* primarily in the theater. String tremolos frequency accompany moments of dramatic tension, conflict, agitation, or impending change in nearly every musical-theatrical genre. Among countless examples are Ariadne's fears of death in Georg Benda's widely popular melodrama *Arianna a Naxos* (Example 2.10a); Ilia's acknowledgement of conflicting emotions of love and hate in the opening obbligato recitative of Mozart's opera *Idomeneo* (Example 2.10b); and the treachery of the general Pheron in fourth entr'acte of Mozart's music for Thobias Philipp Freiherr von Gebler's *Thamos, König in Ägypten* (Example 2.10c).

Echoing such dramatic moments of change, the violin tremolos in the bridges to the second groups of the first movement of Haydn's Symphony No. 68 (mm. 23–30, Example 2.11a), the first movement of the "Haffner" Symphony (mm. 13–18, see Example 2.6b), and the finale of the "Prague" Symphony (mm. 47–59, Example 2.11b) generate a sense of motion and unrest, two qualities necessary not only for the modulation to the dominant to be dramatic but also for its strategic purpose

Example 2.10.
a. Georg Benda, *Arianna a Naxos*, Arianna's fears of death
b. Mozart, *Idomeneo*, opening obbligato recitative
c. Mozart, *Thamos, König in Ägypten*, fourth entr'acte

Example 2.11.
a. Haydn, Symphony in B-flat Major, No. 68, I, bridge
b. Mozart, Symphony in D Major K. 504, "Prague," III, bridge
c. Haydn, Symphony in B-flat Major, No. 68, I, in the development section

Example 2.12.
Mozart, Symphony in D Major K. 504, "Prague," I, minor-mode statement of the second theme

to be audible to those listeners not following the tonal argument.[25] Similarly, the sudden, forte violin tremolos at mm. 68, 72, and 82 in the short development section of No. 68/I (Example 2.11c) interrupt the soft, staccato, tip-toeing scales three times with a startling "boo"; the final tremolo is then sustained to intensify the drive to the cadence on V/VI (at m. 87). The violin tremolos at the beginning of the minor-mode interruption of the closing group in the "Haffner" first movement (mm. 66–67, see Example 2.9b) are likewise unexpected and, as a defining element in the musical evocation of the *ombra*, immediately generate a sense of unease. By hearing in instrumental music clear echoes of volatile musico-dramatic moments, listeners can immediately align these kinds of passages with unstable affective states and dramatic situations that require resolution. By means of association, then, certain aspects of surface expression enable listeners to perceive directly— and without a musician's understanding of tonal or formal process—the most immediate strategic function of unstable passages: to ensure continuation.

In the second category of unstable passages, the expression of instability depends on location within the formal argument at least as much as on the nature of the musical material. Momentary shifts to the minor mode, for example, require expressive as well as tonal resolution, even when the music itself has all the hallmarks of musical stability, for in the late eighteenth century the minor mode was expressively marked, reserved for the expression of unusual emotions, threatening circumstances, and tragedy. While the parallel, minor-mode statement of the eight-measure singing-style theme (mm. 104–111, Example 2.12) in the second group of the "Prague's" first movement may seem to sustain stability by affirming the dominant as the new tonic while offering familiar material and modal contrast, it in fact undermines the dominant's harmonic achievement both tonally and expressively. On the tonal front, as Charles Rosen points out, "the change from V to v . . . attacks [v's] character as a dominant as well as its stability, for the minor mode cannot be used as a dominant—at that time, it was inherently less stable than the major" (1980, 154). Underscoring the minor dominant's tonal instability are the expressive associations of the minor mode itself. Without resolution of both tonal and affective issues, the music cannot proceed strategically to cadential material—it cannot close. To regain the temporary loss of stability engendered by the modal shift, Mozart returns momentarily to the major at m. 112 to restate the opening of the theme, this time with a countermelody to ensure interest and variety (the ternary structure of this second theme also suggests variation), before moving on to the closing group at m. 121. Listeners thus briefly return to both the calmer affect and the more relaxed listening modality encouraged at the opening of the second group, just in time to be excited by the rousing closing material.

The strongest communication of instability in late-eighteenth-century public instrumental music, however, is generated when the strategies of both categories are used in tandem: musical material associated with instability situated in an unexpected location. Arguably the most immediately recognizable musical expression of unrest is the so-called *Sturm und Drang* style, particularly when it is used in dramatic works to evoke the *ombra*—supernatural phenomena such as ghosts, the anger of the gods, and storms so violent they seem otherworldly in origin. Examples abound, but among the most well known today are the final Allegro (No. 25) of Gluck's pantomime ballet *Don Juan,* the Furies' chorus in Gluck's *Orfeo ed Euridice,* the storm scenes and terror of the sea monster in Mozart's *Idomeneo,* and of course the Statue's music, foreshadowed in the overture, in Mozart's *Don Giovanni.* References to the *Sturm und Drang* in instrumental music, by echoing the music of such fearsome dramatic moments, would certainly promote a sense of unease in the listener, if not quite the feelings of awe and terror experienced in the theater.[26]

As is often noted, the abrupt shift to D minor at m. 16 in the slow introduction of the "Prague" Symphony (Example 2.13) bears a striking resemblance to the music Mozart would compose one year later for the slow introduction to the *Don Giovanni* overture, itself an anticipation of the music for the Statue's arrival for

Example 2.13.
Mozart, Symphony in D Major K. 504, "Prague," I, shift to minor mode in the slow introduction

dinner. Clearly Mozart intended this style of music to stir the minds and souls of his audience. What is so striking about its appearance in the "Prague" Symphony, however, is not only the sudden intensity of the *Sturm und Drang* topic but its situation in a slow introduction that expressively, if not strategically, is just at that moment prepared to give way to the following Allegro. Only those listeners who hear the tonal preparation for a cadence in the tonic rather than on the dominant would expect the introduction to continue. But even attentive and harmonically astute listeners would likely not expect such a dramatic shift of affect in a symphonic slow introduction. Indeed, the "Prague" introduction is among the longest and most expansive in the late-eighteenth-century symphonic repertory. In Haydn's and Mozart's symphonies, only the introduction to Haydn's Symphony in E-flat Major, No. 103, "Drum Roll," is longer. But unlike the "Prague" introduction, it maintains a single affect throughout its thirty-nine $\frac{3}{4}$ measures. Perhaps, as Sisman has suggested, Mozart's model was the introduction to Haydn's Symphony in D Major, No. 75, which with its dramatic shift to D minor "manifests, in miniature, the principal elements that Mozart expanded in the 'Prague'" (1997, 45).[27] But whether preceded by Haydn or not, and granting that certain harmonic and structural techniques noted by Sisman are also essential to the overall effect, there is no denying that the intensity and unexpectedness of the *Sturm und Drang* is largely responsible for the unusual weight of the "Prague" introduction.

Similar surprising moments of *Sturm und Drang* can be heard interrupting the closing groups of the "Prague" finale (mm. 110–20, Example 2.14a), the "Haffner" first movement (mm. 66–71, Example 2.9b), and the finale of Haydn's Symphony No. 104 (mm. 287–93, Example 2.14b). In the last two cases, extraordinary means are required to force the music back from its momentary lapse into subjective emotion or temporary excursion into the realm of the otherworldly. As in the "Haffner" first movement (discussed above), a forceful unison passage at m. 293, strikingly similar in contour and expression to the unison in the "Haffner," returns the Haydn finale to the stability of ending. To compensate for the last-minute digression, the following material is all the more assertive in its cadential obligation. In contrast, the lack of a redirecting passage in the "Prague" finale—the outburst of *Sturm und Drang* simply cadences into the cheerful energy of buffa triplets—fits well with the quick changes demanded by this finale's comic pacing.

Expressive Kinship and Cyclic Organization

Openings: Overtures and First Movements

On a considerably broader scale, entire movements of symphonies may be heard to echo various other types of musical entertainment, and, like topics and textures within a movement, these surface echoes contribute to the syntactic logic of multimovement works. As mentioned above, virtually all public performances in the late eighteenth century, theatrical as well as musical, opened with the invigorating first movement of a symphony or overture,[28] and it was this movement's responsibility—its immediate function—to focus the attention of the noisy audi-

Example 2.14.
a. Mozart, Symphony in D Major K. 504, "Prague," III, in the closing group
b. Haydn, Symphony in D Major, No. 104, "London," IV, in the closing group

ence. The topics and gestures of commencement that open Mozart's "Haffner" and "Prague" Symphonies and Haydn's Symphony No. 104 would certainly alert the listener to the concert's beginning. But if the only requirement of the first piece was that it start with the customary call to attention, why were symphonies and overtures always the choice? Why not concertos, many of which also begin with the required effect in full orchestration? Or a sufficiently energetic aria that opens with a grand, dramatic gesture? For those concerts featuring both orchestral and soloistic music, Sisman has suggested that "the programs metaphorically traversed a rhetorical pattern: from 'general' introduction to 'specific' arguments to 'general' summing up" (1993b, 6–7). The reflection of this rhetorical sequence neatly accounts for the framing aspect of orchestral music, for another symphony (or at least the finale of the opening one) usually closed as well as opened concerts. But surely the first movements of symphonies must have provided an immediate sense of opening, and finales an immediate sense of conclusion, beyond that suggested by analogy of ensemble combination and oratorical structure.

One way that the first movements of symphonies as a whole communicate opening at the rhetorical level of a concert program is by echoing both style and situation of theater overtures. The striking correspondence of expressive content and strategic process in symphonic first movements and theater overtures is, of course, neither surprising nor hidden, for the Neapolitan opera overture is widely understood as the immediate ancestor of the concert symphony.[29] Moreover, throughout the first half of the eighteenth century the terms "symphony" and "overture" were used interchangeably. Even in the later decades, when the genres were more clearly established, we still occasionally encounter a symphony listed as an overture on concert programs, as well as an opera overture referred to as a symphony.[30] Stephen Fisher has pointed out that Haydn himself never "adopt[ed] a terminology that discriminated between them" (1985, 5). Even as late as the turn of the nineteenth century, overtures and symphonies were not always considered distinct musical genres. The 1799 catalog of Johann Traeg's copying house, for example, lists all of Haydn's opera overtures among his symphonies.[31] Further, the writings of contemporary theorists reveal overlapping usage of the terms "symphony" and "overture" throughout the century. In *Der vollkommene Capellmeister,* Mattheson writes that "symphonies serve to open the most important musical plays, just as the intrades for the smaller" ([1739] 1981, 657). In *Critischer Musikus,* Scheibe states unambiguously that "since opera reached its perfection in Italy, one observes a genre of instrumental pieces performed before the stage's curtain is raised, which prepares the audience in a suitable and clever manner for the entire opera. These pieces are called symphonies" (1745, 596).[32] And Schulz begins his "Symphonie" article for Sulzer's *Allgemeine Theorie der schönen Künste* by asserting that a symphony is "a piece of instrumental music for many voices that is used in place of the now obsolete overture" (trans. in Churgin 1980, 10). Once the three-movement Neapolitan overture design of the 1740s was all but replaced by the one-movement design by the 1770s, the formal and expressive affinity between symphonic first movements and overtures would have been immediately apparent to any who frequented the theater and concert hall.

Among our four symphonies, the first movement of the "Prague" perhaps best demonstrates this generic kinship. As a sonata form with a slow introduction, the main formal differences between the "Prague" first movement and the one-movement theater overture of the late eighteenth century are the repeat of the exposition (theater overtures rarely repeat either half of the binary form)[33] and the closure of the ending (opera overtures often change expressive course and modulate just before the end of the closing group to segue into the first scene). Affectively and structurally, the "Prague's" slow introduction resembles that of the *Don Giovanni* overture: both open with an arresting, tutti "noise-killer" followed by dotted rhythms (flourishes in the symphony [mm. 1–3], plodding chords in the overture [mm. 5–11]), continue with a more lyrical passage (mm. 4–15 in the symphony; mm. 11–15 in the overture), and conclude—after an initial jolt—with an extended, suspenseful *Sturm und Drang* sequence (mm. 16–28 in the symphony; mm. 23–31 in the overture) that, at the end, brings back the dotted rhythms (at m. 13 in the symphony; at mm. 18 and 20 in the overture). To be sure, the proportions vary and the turn to the *Sturm und Drang* is certainly more shocking in the symphony than in the overture—the symphony changes abruptly from major to minor mode (at m. 16) while the overture hints at the impending unrest with syncopations and "stirring" figures a few bars earlier (at m. 13). But the order of topics and affective states presented in both introductions suggest remarkable formal and expressive affinity.

The similarities between the corresponding first groups of the following Allegros are likewise striking. Both offset the weighty introduction with reduced scoring to strings, a piano dynamic, and a certain lightness of touch; pulsing eighth notes are balanced with slow-moving, syncopated (counter)melodies in nearly identical rhythms; and fanfares in the winds, brass, and timpani close both opening periods (mm. 43–44 in the symphony; mm. 38–39 in the overture). Further, in both movements a partial repetition of the first period leads to a brilliant-style tutti (at m. 55 in the symphony; at m. 48 in the overture) for the ensuing bridge and modulation to the second group. The same order of expressive events (up to the *Sturm und Drang* outburst) as in the "Prague" introduction is also heard in the overture to *Die Zauberflöte*—tutti "noise-killer" (mm. 1–3), dotted rhythms (mm. 4–13), and singing-style melody (mm. 4–16). And the buffa-style repeated-note motive with which this overture's following Allegro commences bears a striking resemblance to the repeated-note motive that develops out of the "vamping" syncopated Ds at the beginning of the "Prague's" Allegro.

There are, of course, countless examples that demonstrate the formal and expressive kinship of late-eighteenth-century symphonic first movements and theater overtures, but surely these examples from Mozart, combined with the extant literature on Haydn's and Mozart's overtures and symphonies (not to mention our own ears),[34] suffice to suggest that listeners in the eighteenth century would have easily heard in symphonic first movements the formal logic and expressive content of theater overtures. As the overlapping terminology suggests, it is possible that, since both genres served the same function of commencement within the contexts of both a musical work and an entertainment event, listeners themselves may have hardly distinguished between them. They may simply have heard symphonic first movements and theater overtures alike as the vehicle that supplied the expected grand instrumental beginning to the day's entertainment.

Endings: Comic Opera, Popular and Comic Dances, and Finales

Symphonic finales, on the other hand, served to conclude not just a multi-movement composition but entire concerts as well. Sometimes the finale of the opening symphony was reprised at the end; other times it was withheld until the end, with the rest of the concert "inserted," as it were, between the opening symphony's third and fourth movements; or sometimes a different symphony and its finale closed the concert.[35] To understand the closing function of symphonic finales in the late eighteenth century, we must first jettison such musical values as inter-movement coherence and the related concept of the work as an integrated whole—values twentieth- and twenty-first-century listeners inherited from the nineteenth century and so often anachronistically apply to the Classical symphonic repertory. Then we must look to more general features of finales, in particular those expressive elements not dependent on tonal or motivic relationships with prior movements (which is not to deny the possibility of their existence, however),[36] to consider how presumably *any* finale could serve as a fitting conclusion for a concert lasting several hours.

A glance at the finales of our four symphonies reveals some salient expressive correspondences: the "Haffner" and "Prague" finales immediately summon up the comic liveliness and fast-paced action of the buffa stage, while the two Haydn finales exude the boisterous energy of the dance hall (Examples 2.15a–d). The comic pacing of the two Mozart finales is often commented upon, and both Sisman and Georg Knepler note obvious echoes of opera buffa. Proposing that instrumental music is "semanticized" by vocal music, Knepler finds the "Prague" finale to be "about the boldness of action" (1994, 237; quoted in Sisman 1997, 80n136). Sisman agrees that "action is everything" in this movement; she notes the closeness in affect and theme type between the "Prague" and "Haffner" finales and suggests the "Haffner" finale may be heard as an "operatic echo" of Osmin's aria "O! wie will ich triumphiren" from *Die Entführung aus dem Serail* (1997, 80–83). The finales of Haydn's Symphonies Nos. 68 and 104, on the other hand, clearly echo popular dances. The drone under the opening strain of the finale of No. 104 suggests the lively rusticity and countrified spirit of a peasant dance. Rhythmically and structurally the finale of No. 68 is a contredanse. In fact, the great majority of Haydn's symphonic finales composed after the early 1770s are contredanses. So, too, is the finale of Mozart's Symphony in E-flat K. 543. And while the "Haffner" and "Prague" finales certainly do stand out as the most action-packed, or "manic" to use Sisman's word, finales in Mozart's symphonies, they are by no means unique in their fast-paced comic energy. The finale of Mozart's "Linz" Symphony K. 425, for example, as well as those of K. 319 and K. 338 are bustling movements in the terrestrial meters of $\frac{2}{4}$ and $\frac{6}{8}$, replete with accessible tunes and comic spirit. Their expressive kinship with the arias and ensembles of opera buffa is unmistakable.

Buffa and contredanse topics are clearly the most common expressive choices for symphonic finales in the late eighteenth century. But how and why do they communicate a sense of closure to the listener? For contredanse finales we might look to a symphony's previous movement—by this point, almost always a minuet and trio—for one possible answer. The sequence of minuet followed by contredanse echoes the usual order of events of the dance hall: the aristocratic and staid minuets were danced first, a preservation of tradition and authority; the more lively, spirited, and "democratic" contredanses followed "as soon as decently possible," as Allanbrook puts it (1983, 61). For buffa finales we might look to the conventions of the comic stage, in particular the action-packed ensemble finale and the *lieto fine* in which all loose ends are tied, tensions resolved (or dissolved), and order restored. Further, by echoing one sound of comic opera, the buffa aria, another may

Example 2.15.
a. Mozart, Symphony in D Major K. 385, "Haffner," IV, opening
b. Mozart, Symphony in D Major K. 504, "Prague," IV, opening
Continued on the next page

Example 2.15.
c. Haydn, Symphony in B-flat Major, No. 68, IV, opening
d. Haydn, Symphony in D Major, No. 104, "London," IV, opening

be summoned by association—the conventional closing chorus which is, though necessarily less manic, customarily just as energetic.

While these reflections of the order of musical events in other types of musical entertainment may supply, by means of expressive kinship, some degree of closure within the context of both a multimovement instrumental work and a public concert, it may be ultimately the uniquely *human* comic expressive stance itself, heard in both the contredanse and the buffa finale, that communicates to the listener the strongest sense of conclusion. But before exploring how the humanity of the comic style may communicate closure, we must first consider the expression of continuation suggested by slow movements in an interior, usually second, position.

Continuations: The Middle Style of Internal Slow Movements

In his "Symphonie" entry for Sulzer's *Allgemeine Theorie der schönen Künste*, Schulz notes that the "andante or largo between the first and the last allegro has indeed not nearly so fixed a character, but is often of pleasant, pathetic, or sad expression" (trans. in Churgin 1980, 13). A glance at the slow movements of our four sample symphonies reveals something of the structural and expressive diversity widespread in the symphonic repertory of the late eighteenth century. The sentimental yet comic third movement Adagio cantabile of Haydn's Symphony No. 68, the easy, trouble-free Andante of the "Haffner," and the pastoral Andante of the "Prague" are sonata forms; the second movement Andante of Haydn's Symphony No. 104 is a ternary form whose uncomplicated, A-section gavotte gives way to a stormy developmental B section. But the variety of surface expressions and formal articulations notwithstanding, these four internal slow movements communicate a sense of large-scale continuation to the listener by echoing—often in a vocal style—the modesty, humility, sentimentality, and pastoral mode of middle characters from the musical stage.

Of course, the mere suggestion of an aria in second position, immediately following a movement that resembles an overture, is an obvious expressive echo of the order of events in opera and other forms of musical-theatrical entertainment in the late eighteenth century. Some sense of the continuation supplied by second movements may simply be a result of this obvious "overture-aria" reflection. Much of the texture in the slow movements of Mozart's "Haffner" Symphony and Haydn's "London" Symphony, for instance, suggests a vocal style, while many of their strategic devices are typical of operatic arias. Throughout nearly the entire movement, the "Haffner" Andante maintains a singing-style melody supported primarily by conventional accompanimental patterns that function both to ensure the dominance of the tune and to establish a broad expression of stability (see Example 2.3c). A vocal evocation is also suggested by the cadenza-like passage (at m. 28) just before the final cadence in both the exposition and recapitulation (Example 2.16a). In addition to the songlike melody and symmetrical phrase structure of the A section of the second movement of the "London" Symphony, the dramatic pause at m. 25 in the middle of the reprise of the first strain of the rounded binary form suggests a vocal evocation (Example 2.16b)—one can easily imagine a short cadenza in place of the melody's long notes and fermata (and perhaps Haydn even intended one here). With its shift to the minor mode and touches of *Sturm und Drang*, the contrasting B section, though decidedly less vocal in style, resembles the conventional internal contrast of the da capo aria, while the varied reprise of the A section, with its more elaborate melody, reflects the singer's improvised decorations of an aria's da capo. The Adagio cantabile of Haydn's Symphony No. 68, with its "ruminating," singing-style melody and conventional broken-chordal accompanimental pattern, likewise suggests the texture of song (see Example 2.3b). But unlike the slow movements of the "Haffner" or the "London," this vocal evocation is the symphony's third movement—it follows a minuet and trio rather than an overture-like first movement. The Andante of the "Prague," on the other hand, is not nearly as vocal in style, but follows arguably the most overture-like first movement of the four (see Example 2.18).

What all of these four slow movements share, beyond their slow tempo, is a middle-style expressive stance. While particular musical features and general character were, for eighteenth-century critics, central in establishing affect, the affec-

Example 2.16.
a. Mozart, Symphony in D Major K. 385, "Haffner," II, just before the end of the exposition
b. Haydn, Symphony in D Major, No. 104, "London," II, in the reprise of the first strain

tive foundation rested on the more general degree of dignity—the stylistic divisions of "lofty," "mean," and "humble" delineated in classical rhetorical theory and echoed in seventeenth-century French aesthetics. Scheibe, for one, wrote lengthy descriptions of the "high," "middle," and "low" styles in the 20 August 1737 issue (no. 13) of his *Critischer Musikus*. The middle style, he explains, "must above all be clever, pleasant, and flowing. It must delight and please the listeners rather than bring them to passionate stirrings or leave them in all too profound reflection" (1745, 128).[37] Ernst Gerber, writing over fifty years later, agrees: "[the middle style] included softer and milder feelings, such as love, calmness, satisfaction, cheerfulness, and joy" (*AMZ*, 1799, cols. 295–96; quoted and trans. in Ratner 1980, 364). Beyond general notions of character, however, Scheibe's descriptions in fact prescribe certain textural means for composing in the middle style: "the beautiful and the natural exist in [the middle] style particularly when the melody is extremely clear, lively, flowing, and sharply defined, when it without restraint makes use in various ways of improvised ornaments, when it is free, unaffected, and always new. The harmony must make the melody only clearer and more distinct; it must in no way stand out, since that is for the melody alone to do" (1745, 128).[38] Scheibe would seem to find the texture of accompanied vocal music, providing it has a pleasant character, to be the ideal means to a middle-style expression. Three of our four slow movements fit nicely with the textural details of Scheibe's middle-style prescription, those in Mozart's "Haffner" Symphony and Haydn's Symphonies Nos. 68 and 104.

The middle style of the second movement of Haydn's Symphony No. 104 is further established by Haydn's use of the gavotte style, an evocation of the dance *di mezzo carattere* (Example 2.17a). The weak second beat of the second bar of each two-bar unit generates a hypermetric pairing of weak and strong bars to articulate the gavotte's characteristic manipulation of duple meter. As Allanbrook's metrical spectrum reveals, the duple patterns of the gavotte and bourrée lie closest to those of the minuet and other stately triple dances, but their "compromise nature—they are altered marches or dances made up out of strides—prevents them from approaching the dignity of either the exalted march or the minuet" (1983, 68). The gavotte's "compromise" pattern thus places it in Sulzer's third category of theatrical dances, the dances of *halbe Charaktere*. As he describes them, "their content is an everyday action in the character of the comic stage—a love affair, or any intrigue in which people from a not completely ordinary kind of life are involved. The dances require elegance, pleasant manners, and fine taste" (1771–74, s.v. "Tanz"; quoted and trans. in Allanbrook 1983, 68–69). The class of characters portrayed is, in Allanbrook's words, "the elegant-ordinary"; the tone required is the "refined bucolic." The gavotte's long association with the pastoral argues further for its middle-style status, for the literary pastoral, though placed lower in earlier periods, was situated firmly in the middle style by Nicolas Boileau-Despréaux, the leading French literary critic of the late seventeenth and early eighteenth centuries (Sisman 1997, 74n115). The drones that close the A sections of this movement (mm. 33–36, mm. 141–45), especially when accompanied by the nostalgic, parting horn calls at the end of the movement (mm. 149–51), easily bring to mind the pastoral's rustic grace (Example 2.17b).

Without obvious vocal evocations or a clearly articulated dance topic, it is the pastoral expression alone of the "Prague's" Andante that establishes its middle-style status. Replete with such pastoral markers as drones and parallel harmonies, the idealized first and second themes likewise call up the "refined bucolic" (Example 2.18). To be sure, there are several moments in this movement that may seem to sound decidedly unpastoral—for example, the unison figure in mm. 8–9, its subsequent canonic treatment in mm. 10–14, and the sudden minor-mode, forte eruptions in the bridge in mm. 19–20, among others. But as Sisman's brilliant analysis of this movement demonstrates, the pastoral is the movement's "controlling topic"—"a mode of reference that governs all the gestures of the movement"—and as such does not preclude the expression of other topics, styles, and gestures. Moreover, Sisman suggests that the presence of such contrasting, even oppositional styles may also reflect the problematic status of the literary pastoral in the eigh-

Example 2.17.
a. Haydn, Symphony in D Major, No. 104, "London," II, rhythmic scansion of the opening strain
b. Haydn, Symphony in D Major, No. 104, "London," II, end

teenth century, as well as revealing that composers of the time were aware that the pastoral always involves "the recognition of a contrast, implicit or expressed, between pastoral life and some more complex type of civilization" (Greg 1906; quoted in Loughrey 1984, 20 and Sisman 1997, 78).

That composers would have been not only aware of such theoretical debates in literature but also inclined to reflect such topical issues in their music fits well with Neal Zaslaw's notion that the "symphony may be considered a stylized conspectus of the eighteenth century's favourite artistic subject matter." Of the movement types in Mozart's symphonies he observes that the martial and lyrical ideas in first movements represent the heroic and the amorous respectively; the andantes are pastoral; the minuets represent courtly life, the trios an antic; and the finales are based on rustic or popular dances. "Taken together," he argues, "the heroic, the

Example 2.18.
Mozart, Symphony in D Major K. 504, "Prague," II, first theme and bridge

amorous, the pastoral, the courtly, the antic, and the rustic or popular, represent the themes most often found in eighteenth-century prose, poetry, plays, and paintings" (1989, 417)—an intriguing idea that accords well with the notion that symphonies would echo other forms of *musical* art and entertainment. Recognizing the reflection of such literary themes and musical echoes, however, does not tell us *why* the heroic should be followed by the amorous within a movement or by the pastoral within a symphony, or *why* the rustic dance should follow the courtly dance. In other words, the identification of themes and topics in symphonies tells us much about expressive meaning but little or nothing about expressive syntax or cyclic organization.

Tonal and rhetorical strategy is generally considered the driving force behind structural organization and procedure within single movements of late-eighteenth-century music, and we have already explored how surface topics and stylistic references can communicate structural process immediately to listeners not following the tonal argument. Contrast between successive movements is generally considered the main organizational principle in multimovement compositions, and eighteenth-century listeners would certainly have been able to perceive changes of tempo, instrumentation, and affect. But might there also be, as in single movements, some interaction between a symphony's cyclic organization and the broad expressive stances, themes, and musical echoes of its contemporary entertainment culture that lends intelligibility to the succession of movement types?

Expressive Descents

In its reflection of the themes and sounds of contemporary art and entertainment, the late-eighteenth-century symphony generally charts an expressive course through decreasing degrees of dignity: from the high style of overture-type first movements, through the middle style of slow movements, and finally to the low style of either buffa or popular/comic-dance finales.[39] In many symphonies this affective fall occurs in one broad stroke. Mozart's "Prague" Symphony, with only three movements, is an obvious example: a grand and "difficult" first movement,[40] followed by a pastoral Andante, and a buffa Presto finale. Haydn's Symphonies No. 68 and No. 104 likewise articulate a single fall. In the former, the slow movement in third position (rather than the more conventional second position) allows for the high style of the first movement to be sustained through the second movement's noble minuet. Even the trio in this symphony maintains its courtly composure, as opposed to a more traditional countrified presentation. The minuet proper of Haydn's "London" Symphony (Example 2.19a), on the other hand, with its Allegro tempo, sforzandos on beat 3, and hemiolas, echoes the boisterous spirit of the "foot-thumping" *Deutscher Tanz,* the clumsiest of which Allanbrook notes "would support a choreography of the grotesque" (1983, 69), placing it in Sulzer's lowest class of dances. The trio's rustic but more reserved *Ländler* (Example 2.19b) would belong to Sulzer's class of comic dances, those dances that portray the customs of common people. In both cases, the degree of dignity has fallen below that of the middle-style gavotte of the second movement Andante. The only one of our four example symphonies not to traverse this affective descent in one broad stroke is the "Haffner," and in this case we can observe a double fall. Following the high-to-middle descent of the grand and brilliant Allegro con spirito and the aria-like Andante, the stately third movement minuet (Example 2.19c) returns to a high expressive stance, the tiny affective slip of the faintly countrified trio (Example 2.19d) all but neutralized by the da capo return to the noble dance. This high-style stance

Example 2.19.
a. Haydn, Symphony in D Major, No. 104, "London," III, first strain of the minuet
b. Haydn, Symphony in D Major, No. 104, "London," III, first strain of the trio
c. Mozart, Symphony in D Major K. 385, "Haffner," III, first strain of the minuet
d. Mozart, Symphony in D Major K. 385, "Haffner," III, first strain of the trio

is followed by an immediate drop to the comedy of the fast-paced buffa finale, completing the second fall of the symphony's high-to-middle, high-to-low expressive trajectory.

Of course, not all symphonies in the late eighteenth century chart such clear courses of expressive descent. The learned counterpoint and fugal coda of the finale of Mozart's "Jupiter" Symphony are elevated in style and, despite the galant style of much of the movement, raise the overall degree of dignity above what would otherwise be generally comic or nontragic.[41] Indeed, Sisman has argued that the "Jupiter" finale, despite Mozart's "finding the mean yet again between accessibility and difficulty," in the end "reveals vistas of contrapuntal infinity," "creates a cognitive exhaustion born of sheer magnitude," and "makes vivid the mathematical sublime"—hardly words to describe a common or terrestrial affect (1993b, 79). As such, the "Jupiter's" return to the high style foreshadows what becomes the transcendent/triumphant expressive trajectory of the Romantic symphony: an initial fall followed by the ultimate regaining of even higher stylistic and aesthetic ground. Haydn's Symphony in D Major, No. 101, "The Clock," on the other hand, is an inversion of the "Jupiter's" expressive course. With its martial dotted rhythms tempered by the singing style of a tuneful melody and "ticking" accompaniment, the second movement Andante's middle style achieves the symphony's highest degree of dignity; the first movement and finale are contredanses, while the minuet's brisk tempo and staccato articulations compromise the dance's traditionally noble affect. The resulting expressive trajectory is a rise from the low to the middle style followed by a return to the symphony's opening comic and common stance.

These exceptions and certainly many others notwithstanding, the expressive descent observed in our four sample symphonies is by far the one most frequently encountered in the late-eighteenth-century symphonic repertory. I would even suggest it as a general expressive paradigm for multimovement compositions throughout much of the eighteenth century, one that may have roots in the Italian sonata-style instrumental music of the seventeenth century. As Gregory Barnett postulates, a typical affective scheme found in instrumental sonatas of the late seventeenth century traverses a series of affects from "pathos to contemplation to exuberant release." Barnett concludes that "the rich drama of topoi from the Classical Era . . . owes a debt to the Italian sonata of a century earlier" (2002, 10). But the debt is likely even greater than he suspects. In addition to the use of expressive topics to impress upon the listener a discourse of affects, the particular progression of affects Barnett identifies clearly resonates in public instrumental genres of the late eighteenth century. In both degree of dignity and affective foundation, the late-seventeenth-century sonata and the late-eighteenth-century symphony travel the same general expressive course: from the exalted to the terrestrial, the noble to the common, the grand to the humble, or the serious to the comic, all of which pause in an intermediating affective state to bridge the expressive gap between high and low.

While we may eventually be able to trace the musical evolution of this particular expressive paradigm, to consider from philosophical, aesthetic, and expressive perspectives why it developed and what it may mean remains at this point speculation. But to engage in such speculation seems the only way to approach expressive meaning beyond simply noting the imitation, evocation, reflection, and echoing of musical events and sonic artifacts from the soundscape of the listener's contemporary world and everyday life. Questions such as why the high style is suitable for musical openings, why the middle style rarely opens or closes but customarily continues, and why the comic and low styles suggest closure cannot be definitively answered, of course, but they are vital nonetheless to any investigation of the interaction of form and expression as a conduit to musical meaning in late-eighteenth-century music. The reflections that follow are neither conclusive nor complete. They are intended merely to set up interpretations we shall entertain presently, as well as to encourage more dialogue about the expressive motivations, meanings, and possible interpretations of late-eighteenth-century multimovement processes.

Expressive Echoes and Possible Meanings

In the descent from exalted to terrestrial passions we may hear various expressive echoes of Western notions of human mortality, particularly those presented in Christian culture and mythology. Many stories from both the Old and New Testaments traverse a parallel expressive course from the divine to the earthly. Two among many examples are the termination of the Edenic Covenant and the incarnation of Christ, both of which involve the physical change and ultimate death of human beings. While the Enlightenment's advance of rationalism and knowledge left the Christian myth less credible and therefore also less compelling, the reality of human earthly existence remains nonetheless. In a more general sense, then, the descending expressive paradigm may reflect the natural cycles of a master narrative, Christian or otherwise, inspired by our own mortality: from the miracle of birth, through life, to the certainty of death.

Similarly, in light of the secular humanism, science of freedom, and social reforms of the day, we may hear the descent from noble to common passions, or a grand to a humble expression, as inviting enlightened political and social interpretation—as an assertion and celebration of a shared human reality. The "exuberant release" (Barnett 2002) of a closing peasant dance or the democratic spirit of a concluding contredanse may suggest a final equality among humans, just as Beaumarchais's Figaro proclaims that the Count, despite his nobility, fortune, rank, and position, "took the trouble to be born, nothing more" ([1784] 1961, 193). To be sure, as Peter Gay acknowledges, enlightened thought "was in the main reserved to the well-born, the articulate, and the lucky: the rural and the urban masses had little share in the new dispensation." But while deference, neglect, exploitation, famine, thievery, passivity, and pessimism survived, "those placed favorably enough to profit from the currents of the age were buoyed up by pleasing and unprecedented prospects" (1969, 4–5). The concert-goer of the late eighteenth century, whether noble or common, was among those favorably placed, and it is certainly within the realm of possibility that, just as composers may have intended to express enlightened values musically,[42] listeners constructed enlightened social and political meanings during their musical experiences.

3 Enlightening the Listening Subject

From investigations of Masonic and literary influences to explorations of the composer-audience relationship, several recent and compelling studies suggest that Haydn's and Mozart's music of the 1780s and '90s reflects the ideals of the Enlightenment.[1] It should not be surprising, then, that this music continues to speak to the imagination of listeners over two hundred years after its composition, for the Enlightenment's commitment to education, individual freedom, social justice, and human betterment are the sources of the same values many in the Western world maintain today. Butwhile such enlightened values endure, the Enlightenment can also be seen as a source of distasteful repressive institutions like absolutism, colonialism, racism, androcentrism, and myriad other markedly modern ideologies.[2] Would not the seeds of these less desirable values likewise be heard in late-eighteenth-century music?

Rather than dwelling on the undeniable affirmative answer to this rhetorical question, it is more productive for our present purpose to acknowledge that reductions of the Enlightenment to a handful of intellectual stances or cultural values, whether positive or negative, trade in clichés. As arguably the most significant intellectual moment in the emergence of the modern world, the Enlightenment is on the one hand idealized as the resistance to various authorities, from the supernatural to the politically ordained. On the other, it is easily criticized for glorifying such nonhuman authorities as Truth, Reason, Nature, and Progress. Supporting this ready opposition is the alignment of the Enlightenment's philosophy of instrumental reason with the tenets of modernity and the questioning of its absolutes with a postmodern critical agenda. Indeed, as postmodern thought requires the construction of a monolithic modern ideal against which to revolt, the Enlightenment conveniently provides a philosophically modern wellspring.

But the relationship between these two mighty intellectual traditions is, of course, more complicated, and their histories are intriguingly intertwined. In this chapter we shall explore surprising but tangible suggestions of two cornerstones of postmodern theory and criticism—intertextuality and subjectivity—in various eighteenth-century aesthetic writings, in particular, critiques of imitation and constructions of the enlightened listening subject. As we shall see, the Enlightenment ironically emerges as the launch pad for some of postmodernism's most significant critical insights.[3] Then, following a consideration of some anxieties that surface in the application of these tenets of postmodern critical theory in reading eighteenth-century music, we shall embark on an unabashedly fanciful journey. To embrace more heartily (and polemically) not just the inevitability but the *desirability* of the fictive in productions of historical meaning, a postmodern idea in its

own right that finds its roots in the Enlightenment, we shall construct three historically informed but otherwise fictional listening subjects and imagine their interpretations of Haydn's Symphony in G Major, No. 88, during the "real time" of
their "first hearings" of this music.

Contingencies of Meaning in Eighteenth-Century Critiques of Musical Imitation

During the Enlightenment, throughout France, England, and German-
speaking lands, it was unquestioned by composers and philosophers alike that art
should imitate nature. Grounded in the writings of Plato and Aristotle, aligned
with the classical art of rhetoric, and embracing the Cartesian objectification of
the passions, the theory of mimesis dominated musical thought. Affections were
to be imitated in music to arouse the passions of the listener. Imitation, the usual
term for this artistic obligation, rarely appears in seventeenth-century philosophical
and theoretical treatises, but it resurfaces in 1719 in Jean-Baptiste Du Bos's *Réflexions critiques sur la poësie et sur la peinture*, a work frequently touted as the beginning of modern aesthetics. For Du Bos the purpose of art is to generate feeling—in
his word, *sentiment*—and to generate feeling in music there must be imitation of
"all those sounds that nature herself uses to express the feelings and passions"
([1719], trans. in Le Huray and Day 1981, 18). The imitative imperative for music
could hardly be clearer. After this influential work, nearly all aesthetic writings
through the end of the eighteenth century devote considerable ink to music's imitative obligations, abilities, and shortcomings.

While asserting imitation as the aesthetic duty of music, Du Bos's *Réflexions critiques* bears witness to the centrality of the *perception* of the listener in eighteenth-
century philosophical constructions of music's imitative processes. On instrumental music within the context of opera, for example, he writes: "Do not we ourselves
feel that these airs make such impressions on us as the musician desires? Do we not
perceive that these symphonies enflame us, calm us, soften us, and in short, operate
upon us?" ([1719], trans. in Le Huray and Day 1981, 18). In a clear echo of John
Locke's postulate that ideas spring not just from sensation but from the perception
of sensation ([1706] 1961, 77), Du Bos suggests that as music affects the passions
of the body, the listener's mind actively discerns its effect. A successful musical
imitation for Du Bos, then, requires mental as well as physical responses from the
listener.

By the middle of the eighteenth century writers unsure of music's imitative capabilities gradually came to prefer the term "expression" when contemplating music's aesthetic condition. In Du Bos's treatise we can observe a hierarchical relationship between imitation and expression: nature herself expresses passions, but music
can only imitate nature's expression. Imitation is indirect, expression direct.[4] But
many aestheticians in the eighteenth century conceived of expression as the objective representation of affect, rendering expression and imitation nearly synony-

mous.[5] For others, however, expression retained its mimetic essence but was granted a broader and more abstract meaning as an idealized or imperfect representation of affect, usually coupled with the arousal of the listener's passions. Charles Batteux, for example, a philosopher greatly influenced by Du Bos's ideas, defines imitation not as arousal but as representation of the passions in his own widely read (and readily criticized) treatise *Les beaux-arts réduit à un même principe* ([1746] 1989). And where Du Bos expects an exactness of imitation, Batteux finds imitation to be a process of idealization.

Most remarkable in Batteux's treatise, for our purpose, is his anticipation of a key binary construction of many twentieth-century critical theories. In the third chapter of the third section of the third part of *Les beaux-arts*, titled "All music and dance must have a meaning, a sense," he writes "expressions,[6] in general, are in themselves neither natural nor artificial; they are but signs" ([1746] 1989, 239).[7] To be sure, Batteux does not follow this striking claim with a dissertation on semiotics, but the implications of his remark are profound nonetheless. Music, for Batteux, stands in an iconic relationship with something else, and the listener must recognize *in his mind* what entity is being represented in order for music to have meaning.[8] Batteux's observation that "melodic lines and dance movements are only imitations, artificial structures of tones and poetic gestures that are merely realistic" ([1746], trans. in Le Huray and Day 1981, 18) even suggests the structuralist theoretical distinction between signifier and signified.

The notion that musical expression involves not just the arousal of the passions in the body but the stimulation of ideas in the mind as well is arguably the most consequential aesthetic move to come out of the widespread critique of musical imitation during the second half of the eighteenth century. Indeed, Batteux's remark that "the passions are here as imaginary as are actions in poetry" ([1746] 1989, trans. in Le Huray and Day 1981, 48) firmly locates the construction of meaning not in the musical text but in the mind of the listener. Several writers a generation later, while conflicted as to whether the engagement of the mind enhances or detracts from the aesthetic experience, accept unequivocally the centrality of the listener's ever-present and active mind during a musical performance. Michel-Paul-Guy de Chabanon, for one, argues that music is sensual and the pleasures we take in it are solely physical, but nonetheless acknowledges the mind's ever-present activity. Bashing imitation, he writes:

Music acts immediately on our senses. But the human mind, that quick, active, curious, reflective intelligence, interferes with the pleasure of the senses: it cannot be an idle and indifferent spectator. What part can it take in sounds, which because they have in themselves no determinate meaning never offer clear and distinct ideas? It searches for relationships there, for analogies with various objects and with various natural effects. And what happens? . . . Music imitates to the extent that it can, and at the express command of the intellect, which, enticing the act further than its end directs, proposes imitation to it as a secondary goal. But the intellect, which for its own part appreciates the weakness of the means that music uses in order to succeed in imitation, makes few difficulties on this point. The slightest analogies, the most flimsy relationships suffice for it. ([1785], trans. in Allanbrook 1998, 239)

Wishing that listeners would simply shut off their brains and take pleasure in the sheer physical sensations music arouses, Chabanon must yield the point that most people either cannot or do not do this. Much to his disappointment, the mind simply "cannot be an idle and indifferent spectator."

Philosophe Denis Diderot, on the other hand, reconciles the physical requirements of mimesis with his own (perhaps untamable) urge to engage the brain. In his *Lettre sur le traité du mélodrame* he writes: "Beautiful chords . . . please my ear; [they are] abstractions made from all sentiments in my soul, all ideas in my mind. However, to tell the truth, I would not listen long to a music which had only this merit. I never listened to a good symphony, above all to an adagio or andante, that I did not interpret—at times so happily that I hit exactly upon the painting proposed by the musician" ([1771] 1875–77, 8:508, trans. in Neubauer 1986, 119). For Diderot, the sensual pleasure music affords is in itself not sufficient. He clearly expects a musical experience to be intellectually as well as physically stimulating. More to the point, however, is the implicit contingency of the ideas generated. Diderot is undoubtedly conditioned by his mimetic orientation to imagine the particular object or phenomenon to which the music refers. As John Neubauer puts it, "he interprets listening, in part, as an intellectual guesswork aimed at the composer's intention" (119). In fact, Diderot would argue that intention itself is representational. But at all times he actively maintains control over the ideas he imagines. At no point does he suggest that another interpretation, one not aligned with the composer's intended imitation, would be any less valid. For Diderot, music stimulates as much as represents ideas, and the listener is empowered to construct his own personal meaning (119).

In a claim that goes much further than Diderot in asserting the primacy of the mental over the physical in the listener's response to music, Immanuel Kant asserts in the *Kritik der Urteilskraft* that "no sensation [is the] matter of aesthetic judgment" ([1790], trans. in Le Huray and Day 1981, 220). The aesthetic idea, the central conception in Kant's Third Critique, constitutes the *Geist* of a work of fine (or beautiful) art. It is created by a genius and inspires "much that is indefinable in words," "the feeling of which quickens the cognitive faculties" of the observer's mind ([1790] 1952, 530). Defined as "that representation of the imagination, annexed to a given concept, with which, in the free employment of imagination, such a multiplicity of partial representations are bound up, that no expression indicating a definite concept can be found for it" (530), an aesthetic idea engenders thought— the creation of *new* ideas—in the mind of the beholder. None of these ideas, however, approach the creativity of the original aesthetic idea itself. For Kant, then, to receive art is undeniably cognitive activity. But his question, unlike any raised by Chabanon or Diderot, is not whether the mind of the listener is engaged during a musical experience—it clearly is—but whether music is a fine art or merely a pleasant art, for representations, regarded as mere sensations in the pleasant arts, are modes of cognition in the fine arts. Thus, only the fine arts contain aesthetic ideas.

Kant's disparaging comparison of instrumental music to wallpaper, overall assessment of music's conceptual poverty, and famous quip about its "lack of urbanity" ([1790] 1952, 536) would seem damning evidence for music's status in his aesthetic. Indeed, points in his argument like the following may appear to condemn music as incapable of inspiring any creative and spontaneous mental activity: If "we judge the value of the fine arts by the culture they provide, by which is meant the development of those faculties that must combine in the act of cognition when judgment is being exercised, then music is least amongst the fine arts, because it plays *merely* with the emotions" ([1790], trans. in Le Huray and Day 1981, 222, my emphasis). In the end, though, despite this low assessment of music, Kant cannot eliminate it entirely from the category of the fine arts.[9] As hinted at in the conclusion to this section of the Third Critique, and reaffirmed in Section 53, he does allow the "beautiful interplay of emotions" to constitute the basis of music, thereby granting it status, however low, in the category of the fine arts. The great philosopher Kant thus acknowledges, however grudgingly, that communication and generation of aesthetic ideas is possible in music. But the mere human Kant, whose own listening subjectivity was conditioned by the annoyance of his jailed but apparently quite musical neighbors[10] and the resulting affront to "the freedom of those who are not a party to the music-making" (223), suspects nonetheless we listen to music for sensual rather than intellectual stimulation (Neubauer 1986, 190).

Classicist Thomas Twining, on the other hand, goes far beyond Chabanon's, Diderot's, and Kant's assertions of music's abilities to stimulate the intellect. Almost presciently, Twining postulates an eighteenth-century listening subject who not just creates but maintains control over the meaning of a musical work or experience. The second dissertation accompanying his 1789 translation of Aristotle's treatise on poetry celebrates the interdependency of emotion and intellect in a musical experience, for together they constitute music's expressive power: "The whole power of music may be reduced I think to three distinct effects—upon the ear, the passions and the imagination: in other words it may be considered as simply delighting the senses, as raising emotions, or as raising ideas. The two last of these effects constitute the whole of what is called the moral or expressive power of music" (1789, 44). But the most intriguing idea in Twining's dissertation—that music raises some ideas "immediately" by "mere association"—stands outside of his primary argument, hidden within the lengthy footnotes. Ultimately Twining leaves this notion frustratingly underdeveloped, choosing to "pass over the effect of this principle, important and powerful as it is in music as in everything else" because it has nothing to do with imitation (44–45, note a).

He does, however, tantalizingly observe that "if to raise an idea of any object by casual association be to imitate, any one thing may imitate any other" (1789, 44–45, note a). At first glance, Twining may seem rather dismayed at the possibility of such a casual association between music and ideas. But eighteen notes later, referring back to the earlier footnote, he writes:

I observed that music is capable of raising ideas to a certain degree, through the medium of those emotions which it raises immediately. But this is an effect so delicate and uncertain—*so dependent on the fancy, the sensibility, the musical experience, and even the temporary disposition of the hearer,* that to call it imitation is surely going beyond the bounds of all reasonable analogy. Music here is not imitative, but, if I may hazard the expression, merely suggestive. But whatever we may call it, this I will venture to say—that in the best instrumental music, expressively performed, the very indecision itself of the expression, leaving the hearer to the *free operation* of his emotion upon his fancy, and as it were to the *free choice* of such ideas as are to him most adapted to react upon and heighten the emotion which occasioned them, produces a *pleasure* which nobody, I believe, who is able to feel it will deny to be one of the most delicious that music is capable of affording. (49 note s, my emphasis)

In this note, along with his clear appreciation of music's emotional and intellectual satisfaction, Twining embraces a startlingly postmodern conception of musical experience: not only may the associations the listening subject maintains for any given musical moment be grounded in happenstance, but the listening subject himself is free to construct the ideas generated by a piece of music. Indeed, Twining seems to suggest—just at the time when public concerts began to enjoy tremendous popularity—that musical meaning is not only situated within the listening subject, but in his control as well. Moreover, this freedom and control are the sources of the listener's pleasure, a crucial point to which we shall return in chapter 4.

What is striking about the aesthetic philosophies of these six Enlightenment aestheticians is just how fashionable many of their convictions sound at the beginning of the twenty-first century. All acknowledge the role the listener's mind plays in the construction of ideas during a musical experience, a stance that effectively denies the musical text as the location of meaning. A certain contingency of musical meaning follows logically, and at least Diderot and Twining heartily embrace the freedom of interpretation and the inevitable self-reflexivity that result from such contingency. By accepting an interpretive obligation on the part of the listener for music to be capable of imitating or expressing anything, Batteux and Twining go so far as to conceive of music as a system of signs. The eighteenth century thus emerges as the wellspring not only of modern thought but of many postmodern critical insights as well.

Twining's Subjectivity and Radical Intertextuality, Eco's Anxiety, and Eagleton's "Surrogate Discourse"

Despite their situations within critiques of imitation and thus constrained, perhaps, by philosophical abstraction, Du Bos's insistence on the listener's perception of sensation and Twining's observation that ideas may be raised in music by association align neatly with present-day theories of topical meaning in eighteenth-century music, theories that understand topics as semiotic codes and musical works as intertexts. For example, an eighteenth-century listener recognizes a brass tattoo in a symphonic first movement (a token) as a fanfare (a topic or type), associates its sound with the musical announcement of the arrival of a dignitary (interprets intertextually), feels emotions of respect, and thinks of noble authority (constructs a meaning). But Twining's qualification of such associations as "casual" and the effects of raising the emotions as "uncertain" also admits the unique and subjective experiences of the listener as not just an unavoidable but in fact welcome variable.

Adding, say, social status to this hypothetical listener's subjectivity, our example may become the following: the listener, through his personal experiences as a member of the servant class, associates the sound of a fanfare with the arrival of a dignitary, then feels—on account of his lower respective social standing—emotions of inferiority, and ultimately constructs in his mind an idea of deference. But we could just as easily imagine the listener who associates the sound of a fanfare with how his own presence is customarily announced to the court, then feels—on account of his social standing superior to those assembled—acknowledged and entitled, and ultimately constructs in his mind an idea of empowerment.

To be sure, there will be, within certain limits, remarkably similar responses to certain musical topics by those who share a cultural heritage, social situation, political orientation, national identity, religious affiliation, etc. As we saw in chapter 2, the structural intelligibility of late-eighteenth-century public instrumental music depends on the intersubjectivity of many intertextually constructed meanings. And yet Twining's celebrated endorsement of instrumental music rests on his recognition that expressive meaning is ultimately dependent on the *individual* subjectivity of the listener. Taken to an extreme, his "casual associations," in fact, anticipate a conception of musical semiosis as radical intertextuality. But we can also hear a note of anxiety in Twining's thought, as he realizes that such a model of musical expressivity and meaning ultimately threatens the integrity of a musical composition. If "any one thing may imitate another," then the expressive meanings of a piece of music are potentially infinite. The musical work is thus either reduced to a mere broker of intertextual relationships or, conversely, inflated to a text encompassing the cosmos of all possible intertextual meaning.[11]

Like Twining, present-day writers in many disciplines have expressed trepidation over the apparent license for interpretive anarchy implied by such theoretical models of meaning. Perhaps loudest among them is semiotician Umberto Eco, whose later work attempts to restrain the undisciplined application of a cornerstone of his earlier work—the "open work" (see Eco [1965] 1989).[12] Eco's call to delimit textual meaning to those "interpretations allowed by the context" (1994, 21) is echoed, reinforced, and practiced by music theorists Hatten and Agawu, among others (see Hatten 1994, 3–5, 1996; Monelle 2000, 152). Such a strategy effectively focuses inquiry upon interpreted meanings within a contextually legitimated notion on which the community of interpreters agrees. That is to say, interpretations are socially shared and therefore, at least to some degree, intersubjective.

But to limit contextualization, while perhaps prudent, creates as many theoretical questions as practical answers it provides. For one, limiting context draws firm boundaries around the text as well, sustaining the problematic text/context binary Jacques Derrida has famously deconstructed (1981, 41–42).[13] As Kevin Korsyn observes, one can "seek closure at the level of context as in the individual text, ascribing a kind of organic unity, for example, to a historical period or to a particular mode of social organization. . . . The appeal to context does not necessarily escape the ideological impasses of the search for 'the music itself'" (2003, 44–45). Moreover, by constraining context and allowing a text to embrace only "relevant" intertextual relationships,[14] the main mechanism of intertextuality itself—context becoming text—can ultimately fail to operate. While we may recognize a duly expanded text, a firewall is built around it nonetheless, securing its borders and fixing its content. What of this new text's intertextual relationships? Does this text have a context? Offering Russian nesting dolls as a metaphor, Korsyn explains "you can contract to a point in your desire to reach the essence of an individual composition, or you can expand to the edges of your mental universe in your quest for even larger contextual frames, but you're still moving within the series of . . . 'privileged contexts'" (44–45)—those "stereotyped" and "predictable" contexts historians prefer because they "constitute various ways of framing compositions to create historical narratives" (1999, 67–68).

Equally problematic is the question of who decides which "some" things outside of the text "ascend" to become part of the text. According to Eco, it is not who, but *what:* the context itself.[15] His personification of context at the expense of the interpreter, on the one hand, reflects his confidence in Peirce's notion of a final interpretant—the final idea, accepted by the community, that "successful" semiosis reveals.[16] But Eco's notion of the open work also heartily embraces an "indefinite multiplicity"—emphatically *not* an infinity—of possible interpretations, for the final interpretant may be, at best, an allusive and unattainable ideal. However, Eco also finds the assertion of a unique meaning for a text—one "guaranteed by some interpretive authority"—to be a "repressive idea."[17] Eco's call for context to be limited, then, is ultimately a cautionary note to the interpreter to avoid flawed interpretations. As he puts it, "to say that a text potentially has no end does not mean that *every* act of interpretation can have a happy ending" (1994, 6). The same motivation lies behind Hatten's and Agawu's reconstructions of only "plausible intersubjective interpretations" (Hatten 1994, 5)—"meanings dictated by . . . historical and theoretical limitations" (Agawu 1991, 5)—in their readings of late-eighteenth- and early-nineteenth-century instrumental music. Any "fanciful meanings that are likely to crop up in an unbridled discussion" (Agawu 1991, 5) are thus safely avoided.

But what, besides a "bad" or "fanciful" interpretation, is so dangerous about unlimited semiosis? Or, in eighteenth-century terms, just what is at stake if "any one thing may imitate another"? Terry Eagleton has argued that during the Enlightenment a reciprocal relationship developed between works of art and human subjectivity: the new bourgeois subject came to be modeled on the aesthetic artifact, and the work of art became a kind of subject (1990, 4). As a result, aesthetic discourse became a "surrogate discourse," one in which middle-class aspirations for autonomy—"a mode of being which is entirely self-regulating and self-determining" (9)—were bound up with the autonomy of the art work. Within this discursive model, once the freedom and integrity of the individual subject are transferred to the artistic object, unlimited semiosis threatens the unity of our own human subjectivity.[18] Beyond the mere misunderstanding of the historical object, a "bad" or "fanciful" interpretation imperils nothing less than the intact, modern sense of Self—that unified subjectivity that evolved alongside the aesthetic independence of instrumental music.

Perhaps because of this implicit threat either to our Selves or to our notions of subjectivity, an intersubjective approach to musical meaning remains the preferred strategy in interpretations of late-eighteenth-century music (see chapter 1). To a certain extent, the construction of plausible historical meanings is an unavoidably intersubjective enterprise, for these meanings are dependent on the situation of the musical object within appropriate (if "privileged") historical and cultural contexts, entities that are themselves socially shared and communally determined. But limiting meanings to *only* those allowed by the historical and theoretical contexts does not entirely remove subjectivity from the picture, for (heeding Eco's warning) the interpreting subject herself sets any historical and theoretical limits on context. An intersubjective meaning produced by constraining context is ultimately just as fanciful as a subjective one produced by the theoretically limitless semiotic processes of "unbridled" discussion.

Of course, only the naive interpreter believes it actually possible to park her own subjectivity on the doorstep of a theoretical time machine, return to the historical point of a text's origins, and strip away from it any and all meaning acquired during its "afterlife."[19] Moreover, fewer still would actually desire such a journey, for the insights we gain by interpreting texts within canonic horizons as well as historical ones are often too rich, revealing, and rewarding to discard or disallow.[20] All texts are intertexts, and the interpretive enterprise is inescapably subjective at every turn. But rather than finding this critical state of affairs an obstacle to be avoided if not overcome, we shall instead welcome it and, in an experimental first step, take it to a surprising but hopefully productive end. Just as we (re)construct such individual objects as musical texts and their communal contexts from the past, may we not (re)construct individual listening subjects? A certain amount of critical imagination and license is required here, to be sure. But if, as Eagleton argues, during the Enlightenment the bourgeois subject and the aesthetic object entered into a reciprocal relationship, just as the listening subject constructs musical meaning, so may musical meaning construct listener subjectivity.

Embracing the Fictive to (Re)Define the Listening Subject

Few practicing humanists would deny the presence of the fictive in historical writing in favor of a modern ideal of historical realism, so complete does the paradigm shift initiated by French and German literary theory seem today. By exploring the hermeneutic functions of Johann Gustav Droysen's three negatively conceived "illusions" of classical narrative history—a complete course of events, a clear beginning and end, and objectivity (1967)—and analyzing the use of fictional means in various historical writings, Hans Robert Jauss theorized a quarter-century ago the communicative role of the fictive in historical narrative. His purpose: to argue for the legitimacy of fiction in the writing of history. Crucially important to the risky interpretive experiment that follows here is his point that "when the novelist decides to construct a 'picture of the past' or 'the life and customs of his age,' and when the historian, because of the distance in time, is forced to construct an abbreviated account of some prior reality on the basis of a diffuse mass of sources" (1989, 27), the novelist and historian are equally dependent on fictive means. Noting differences among the expectations literary and historical writing arouses in their readers, he continues:

> The reader of Scott's *Quentin Durward* can enjoy the fiction of a prior world as fiction, without posing questions about actual truth and invention. On the other hand, the
> · reader who wishes to learn from Ranke how French history really unfolded in the sixteenth and seventeenth centuries can assume that the *res fictae* only serves to bring the *res factae* into view. These different attitudes toward the fictive or the factual aspects of a story can, of course, be reversed: *Quentin Durward* can also be read as a bit of medieval history (when the fictional parts are removed, a picture of the past remains that is replete with authentic details). Ranke's *French History,* on the other hand, can easily be regarded as a historical work of art and thus be enjoyed in the same manner as a Scott novel. (28)

Jauss's great concern here is to advocate fiction's "revelatory power" to make the "alterity of distant and alien worlds comprehensible and communicable" (29).

Jauss's "fiction" is a mode of writing, a particular way of "perceiving and representing historical experience" (1989, 4), not (necessarily) a literary genre. But what historical fiction and historical narrative share is a devotion to the probable, a notion that, like intertextuality and subjectivity, materialized (or rematerialized, as it is traceable back to Aristotle's *Poetics*) during the Enlightenment. Indeed, the Enlightenment's "discovery of a specifically historical time" necessitated the category of the probable as a mediator between fact and fiction for, as Jauss notes, "the fictional literature of the bourgeois era is no less involved in the discovery of the world as history than is the new discourse of historicism" (26–27). Henry Fielding, for example, in addition to framing his characters' subjectivity within a narratorial objectivity (Bender 1997, 3), explicitly defends his "species of writing"—the "new" novel of the eighteenth century—on grounds of its "Probability." In the "prolegomenous" of Book VIII of his historical novel *Tom Jones,* he writes: "We who deal in private Character, who search into the most retired Recesses, and draw forth Examples of Virtue and Vice, from Holes and Corners of the World, are in a more dangerous Situation. As we have no publick Notoriety, no current Testimony, no Records to support and corroborate what we deliver, it becomes us to keep within the Limits not only of Possibility, but of Probability too" ([1749] 1974, 402).[21] But it is perhaps Diderot's intentional blending of fact and fiction that speaks most directly to the postmodern questioning of the boundaries of the two categories. The letters "authored" by Diderot's fictional character Suzanne Simonin of *La Religieuse* to the real Marquis de Croismare provide but one example of Diderot's many "factional" transgressions.[22]

Resting on the Enlightenment's own distrust in the authority of facts (see Datson 2001) and taking cues from both Fielding and Diderot, the "factional" transgressions that follow here are intended as an experiment in music-historical writing, one that not only takes the role of the fictive for granted in historical narrative but embraces it unabashedly in a pursuit of plausible, if not probable, historical meaning. To explore the interdependence of musical meaning and listener subjectivity suggested by Eagleton's notion of reciprocity between the aesthetic object and the bourgeois subject, we shall undertake an undeniably "fanciful" project. We shall first delineate three historically grounded but otherwise fictional late-eighteenth-century listening subjects. Then, based on our sketching of certain significant life experiences, we shall consider plausible meanings each could conceivably construct during a first and only hearing of Haydn's Symphony in G Major, No. 88. As we shall see, the public instrumental music of the Classical style has great polysemic potential. Its meaning is not fixed in time or space but rather changes, even for the same hearer, based on ever-shifting contexts and conditions of the listening experience. Likewise, the listening subject changes: she is (re)defined by the meanings she constructs during her musical experience.

Hearing Haydn in Joseph II's Vienna

Among those in attendance at a December 1788 concert of the Tonkünstler Societät in Joseph II's Vienna would have been members of the landed first nobility. Our first listener is a member of this order, a wealthy count with considerable holdings in Upper Austria who lives permanently in his Viennese residence. After suffering years of interminable anxiety over his family lineage brought about by the birth of six successive daughters, our count is visibly relieved to have an heir in a newborn son. His two oldest daughters have disappointed him terribly by marrying men who are, to his way of thinking, far beneath them—a bourgeois court servant and, worse, a newly ennobled councillor. His approval of these unions was granted solely to expedite his daughters' leave of his residence.

In addition to his rising debt, caused at least in part by changes in the tax structure, compounding our count's anxieties about the status of his family are the reforms and bourgeois style of the emperor's court. Since Joseph only rarely holds court, the public has no opportunity to learn of the count's reception there. Moreover, the emperor no longer seems to grant men of his importance any favors. This new and strict fairness for all has, from the count's perspective, done nothing but punish men of status and encourage the social aspirations of men like those his daughters married—men whose decorum and ignorance only affirm their utter unsuitability for noble rank. Nostalgic for the "good old days" when those of the middling orders had no aristocratic pretensions, a gentleman's word was trusted, and nobles were duly respected and rewarded, the count worries openly that the social stability of his world is crumbling.[23]

Upon his grudging arrival at the Burgtheater and while the first symphony of the "widow's concert"[a] plays, our count makes his leisurely way with his guests upstairs to the box he rents by the year. Spying two barons seated below, he is secretly grateful that his eroding financial security has not yet forced him to join them in the *Parterre noble*.[b] While the count notes those in the *Parterre* to his guests, the concert's second symphony (Haydn's Symphony No. 88)[c] begins, its opening forte chords and dotted rhythms (Example 3.1a) serving not just to announce the opening of another instrumental composition but to remind the count to speak up a bit more so as to be heard over the grand and noble Allegro that surely follows. The lightly scored contredanse tune that appears in its place (at m. 17) first surprises and amuses the count, for he does enjoy the ball, and the season is just around the corner. But the echoing of the sounds of a hunt, confirmed by the horns joining the band (at m. 24), irks him, for he is loathe to invite men like his daughters' husbands, men he associates with the wildly popular contredanse, to join him in such noble diversions. Just when

a. The "Widow's Concert," as Count Zinzendorf casually referred to it in diary entry of 23 December 1787, was a public concert given by the Tonkünstler Societät, a society established in 1771 by Court Kapellmeister Florian Gassmann to fund pensions for wives and children of deceased members.[24] In his diaries, Zinzendorf gives the distinct impression that many nobles felt obliged to attend these concerts.[25]

b. The design of the Burgtheater, on the Michaelerplatz, was an oval-shaped house with boxes and galleries on two floors above. In 1748 the parquet was divided into two sections, the *Parterre noble* in front, which "was for the nobility and other 'distinguished persons' who did not have boxes," and the *zweyter Parterre* behind, for non-noble attendants.[26]

c. At the 22 December 1788 concert of the Tonkünstler Societät two Haydn symphonies were performed as the opening compositions. We do not know which ones, but two symphonies by Haydn (Nos. 88 and 89) were likely sold to Haydn's Viennese publishing firm Artaria by Johann Tost in 1788. While there is some evidence that Artaria may not have announced these two symphonies until early in 1789, we shall use Symphony No. 88 nonetheless for our hypothetical count's listening pleasure.[27]

Example 3.1.
a. Haydn, Symphony in G Major, No. 88, I, slow introduction, first group, and bridge
Continued on the next page

Example 3.1.
b. Haydn, Symphony in G Major, No. 88, I, in the development section
c. Haydn, Symphony in G Major, No. 88, I, beginning of the recapitulation

his half-listening has finally come into
good balance with his conversation, for
the band is playing more quietly now,
the count is startled into silence by a
surprising, but admittedly satisfying,
passionate turn of the contredanse tune

(at m. 129, Example 3.1b). An audible wave of excitement rushes through the theater, and the count enjoys sharing in the collective feeling of unrest generated by such a "stormy" musical moment. When the contredanse returns intact (at m. 180, Example 3.1c), which the count knows will happen presently, he has been won over, if only musically and momentarily, by the potential compatibility of that most middling of dances and an expression of higher passions. After all, the count, too, dances long after the minuets are over.[d]

The sheer beauty of the slow movement finds immediate sympathy in our count. Hearing in the melody's opening line (Example 3.2a) echoes of those sentimental songs sung by the most beautiful, sweet, and innocent women in Italian opera,[e] idealized memories of the courtship with his wife surface—for she, like the character amalgam who, oblivious to his presence, serenades him now, once embodied all that was pure and naive to win his heart and hand.[f] Indeed, again like the sentimental heroine whose "voice" the count hears, his countess, though noble in character, was not of noble birth. Only through their marriage did she attain her (rightful, in his opinion) noble status. The surprising but, like the unexpected passionate turn in the first movement, exciting and very satisfying interruption of the sentimental mood by the entrance of trumpets and drums (at m. 41, Example 3.2b) affirm the nobility of such sentimentality. Our count suddenly realizes the tune of which Haydn's new slow movement reminds him: that most exquisite melody sung by the Countess in Mozart's *Le nozze di Figaro* ("Porgi amor"), a song that likewise adds a touch

d. In the Viennese public ballrooms of the time, the minuet was the required formality, a nod to tradition and authority, danced first—two at a time, since the minuet is a couple dance—by the members of the aristocracy in attendance. The mostly middle-class attendants could then, after watching the nobles perform, move on to the more lively and popular *Deutsche* and contredanses, dances that could be learned without years of instruction from a dancing master.

e. Many commentators describe the slow movement of Haydn's Symphony No. 88 as "hymnlike." While the Largo tempo, steady quarter-note rhythms, and simple block-chordal accompaniment may certainly suggest a hymn, the combination of strophic, rondo, sonata, and variation formal elements, the appoggiatura sighing motives of the melody, and the increasing elaboration of the accompaniment—culminating in an Alberti pattern for the final reprise—also suggest a sentimental aria. Perhaps the tendency to hear stronger echoes of a hymn comes from a particular moment in this movement's reception history: Brahms reputedly commented, "I want my Ninth Symphony to sound like that."

f. The "sentimental heroine," as Mary Hunter has delineated her, is a character archetype of opera buffa whose sweet passivity and silent suffering mark her as noble, though she is typically not of noble birth. Marriage being the purpose of her life, the

Example 3.2.
a. Haydn, Symphony in G Major, No. 88, II, opening
b. Haydn, Symphony in G Major, No. 88, II, first interruption of the sentimental mood
c. Haydn, Symphony in G Major, No. 88, II, second interruption of the sentimental mood
to the end

Continued on the next page

Example 3.2.

of military flair (e.g., mm. 7, 9, 13–14) to its cantabile style and lovely sentimentality.[28] The next interruption (at m. 76, Example 3.2c), however, the count finds, while musically still very satisfying, a bit unsettling, for the disruption sentimental heroine's identity is defined entirely by her relation to other characters. Her only power is over the audience, and it is, as Hunter argues, a performative power: by singing ravishingly beautiful music in a state of total self-absorption, sentimental hero-of the sentimental mood sounds more tempestuous than martial. Thankfully, though, when the tune repeats (at m. 95) for what will turn out to be its last return, it "sings" more sweetly than ever, its natural melody thrown into relief by the busy (second) violins. The trumpets and drums that enter at the song's end (at m. 107) threaten no more: they serve only to affirm the nobility of our heroine's beautiful simplicity.[g]

The symphony's expected third movement minuet (Example 3.3a) transports our count to the Redoutensaal, where he asserts his aristocratic rank by demonstrating to the mostly bourgeois dancers in attendance his graceful and flawless execution of the minuet's intricate steps, tracing effortlessly the dance's pattern on the ballroom's beautiful floor. The extraordinarily countrified trio (Example 3.3b) pleases the count even more than the noble minuet, as he regards his elegant performance the perfect complement (and compliment) to an aristocratic ideal of pastoral life, blissfully unaware of the condescension underlying his vision.

The count's nostalgic image of pastoral simplicity is sustained well into the symphony's contredanse finale (Example 3.4a), as he finds its unassuming character, uncomplicated by any effort to be something that it is not, more appropriate for the hundreds of amateur dancers who crowd the ballrooms during Carnival.[29] He especially enjoys the dances in the Redoutensäle: since the rule that everyone be masked still applies at the court balls (even though there is, of course, no real attempt to hide one's identity), the count can safely shed, for the moment, the restraint and decorum expected of someone of his standing.[30] His "contredansing" ceases,

ines position the listener as "eavesdropper," a strategy which renders her performance uniquely effective and her character especially demanding of sympathy.

The music of the sentimental heroine "embodies song." Often strophic in form, pastoral in topic, and smooth and predictable in phrase structure, the typical sentimental heroine aria is "marked by touching cantabile lines that float above rhythmically active (and often carefully orchestrated) accompaniments." This type of music, Hunter notes, "draws attention to its own beauty, in part by being divorced from the stage action, in part by emphasizing the singing (rather than declamatory) qualities of the voice, and in part by displaying an unusually sensuous surface in the accompaniment." See Hunter (1999, 84–92).

g. The Enlightenment's new aesthetic concept of *noble simplicité* was a qualification of the expression of the noble passions. See chapter 4 for further discussion of this central idea in the aesthetics of the Enlightenment.

Example 3.3.
a. Haydn, Symphony in G Major, No. 88, III, first strain of the minuet
b. Haydn, Symphony in G Major, No. 88, III, first strain of the trio

however, once Haydn's finale departs from its dance strains (by m. 39, Example 3.4b), and he enjoys the intellectual challenge of keeping pace not just with the conversation in his box but with the music's transformation of the patently "popular" tune into something a bit more elevated. His notice of the canonic treatment of the tune (at m. 109, Example 3.4c) upon its later return especially pleases him, for it secures the

Example 3.4.
a. Haydn, Symphony in G Major, No. 88, IV, opening strain of the contredanse
b. Haydn, Symphony in G Major, No. 88, IV, first episode
c. Haydn, Symphony in G Major, No. 88, IV, developmental episode and retransition
Continued on the next page

Example 3.4.
d. Haydn, Symphony in G Major, No. 88, IV, end

count's sense of his own status as undeniably superior to those standing in the
zweyter Parterre (and even many in the
Parterre noble!) who, he assumes, still
imagine themselves to be dancing. The
military rhythms and drum tattoos at
the end (at m. 210, Example 3.4d) echo
his own court guards: after an evening
spent mingling with members of the
middling orders, his noble status is reaffirmed upon returning home.

Hearing Haydn in Post-Thermidorian Paris

Among the *nouveaux riches* attending a concert at the Théâtre Feydeau[h] in post-Thermidorian Paris would have been women dressed in the most extravagant attire and accessories who much prefer the theater, where one could still enjoy creating something of a spectacle in her private box, to the concerts, where the men seem to care more for the music than for them.[i] One Madame, our second listener, is just such a woman, and on a cold November evening in 1794 she is none too happy to be standing in a private box at the theater rather than dancing in a grand ballroom at a public ball. At least she is able to display her diamonds, fashionable silk tunic, and elaborately coiffed wig[j] before the insufferable silence of the concert itself descends on the hall.

The first notes of the of the concert's opening symphony (again, Haydn's Symphony No. 88) reverberate through the hall, bouncing off the ceiling and walls, and as calls to "hush" are heard throughout the audience, Madame notes wryly to herself how nice it is that the music also seems to have obliged (at m. 3, Example 3.1a). The simple dance tune (at m. 17) that has most in attendance—many of the women as well as the men—following each turn with rapt attention and greeting each orchestral swell with enthusiastic approval, fails to move our Madame. Although she has been instructed by her concert-loving companions that the listener's task is to discover and contemplate the image or emotion the great composer's music is depicting,[k] she endures the whole of the first movement largely indifferent to Haydn's

h. The theater on the *rue* Feydeau was opened in 1791 by a company dedicated to performing French comic opera, but by the mid-1790s came increasingly to specialize in Italian comedies. As such, it "quickly became the preferred theater for the new regime of ostentation" (J. Johnson 1995, 156).

i. Although *La Vedette* reported in 1797 that women attending the theater were "concerned only with making themselves noticed" and the *Correspondence des amateurs musiciens* noted in 1803 that women were "sometimes indifferent to the beauties of a Haydn symphony," by the end of the eighteenth century audiences were largely (and uniquely, it would seem) quiet at public concerts, listening attentively.[31]

j. After the Terror, men's and women's fashion became extravagant and flashy, if not also somewhat grotesque, as the "new aristocracy of wealth was eager to show off its fortunes. The private ostentation of the Old Regime gave way to public display" (J. Johnson 1995, 155).[32]

k. In French aesthetics, music's imitative imperative was particularly long lasting.

charms, noting only a passing likeness here and there to the sounds of military music (or so she hears) (e.g., mm. 39–44), echoes that summon feelings of patriotism for France's recent successes on the battlefield[l] while rekindling her aversion to the all too recent excesses of the Revolution. She also wonders why, at this time of war, Haydn's music should still be played in Paris—the Austrians are, after all, enemies of France.

The second movement, much to her surprise, Madame rather enjoys, for she hears a clear expression of tenderness in the serene, hymnlike melody, warm orchestrations, and relaxed pacing (Example 3.2a). But as musically exciting as the subsequent interruptions may be (at mm. 41 and 76, Examples 3.2b and 3.2c)—her companions have greeted the beating chords and outbursts of trumpets and drums most heartily—she finds herself dismayed by the hostile intrusion upon the tranquil mood. The sudden turns to an aggressive, martial tone remind her not just of military music again, but of those heavy-handed, revolutionary hymns heard so often in the theater during the past few years.[m] Surely this is not the meaning the esteemed Haydn intends, for Robespierre is gone, the guillotine stands silent, and the audience's reception of this movement is overwhelmingly positive.[n] But for our Madame, who associates the violence of the interruptions with the musical sounds of the Revolution and the Terror, Haydn's fortissimo chords and timpani rolls cruelly summon memories of her former and truest love, an unyielding revolutionary, if bourgeois, unfairly denounced and guillotined.[o] Much to her dismay, Madame's silent suffering is extended as the now rowdy audience demands that the movement be repeated.

Calls for precise depictions continue in music reviews well into the early nineteenth century, long after most writers in England and Germany had jettisoned imitation for more abstract notions of expression.

l. In the summer of 1794, France went on a new offensive, defeating the Austrians at Fleurus and advancing as far as Mannheim on one front and the Low Countries on another.

m. Music during the Revolution was conservative, reactionary, and decidedly simplistic: homophony was the rule; melodies were plain, predictable, and singable; harmony was unsophisticated; and brass and percussion secured orchestrational bombast. Weighty choruses and Revolutionary hymns in particular acquired new significance as a reflection of a people united through equality.

n. During the Revolution listeners expected an exactness of expression, to be able to envision just the scene or object, or to feel just the sentiment, the composer intended to depict.[33]

o. While the popular insurrection of the Paris Revolution was led by men and women of the working trades, some leaders seem to have been bourgeois and even aristocrats.[34]

The certain courtliness Madame hears in the following minuet (Example 3.3a) is as much a throwback to pre-Revolutionary days as a reflection of her current expectations for the proper decorum of all people—ex-nobles and ex-revolutionaries alike. Just as the bourgeois characters in French comedies learn much from their noble counterparts (and at their own expense), so too should wealthy women (such as herself) model behavior for the less fortunate.[p] While she cannot perform the minuet steps all that gracefully, her bourgeois upbringing having lacked such staples of noble households as the employment of dancing masters, she does not lament this shortcoming, especially since minuets were on their way to becoming passé in the ballroom well before the Revolution. In the trio (Example 3.3b) Madame hears the naiveté of life in a province far from Paris, country folk dancing solely for the pleasure it brings them. She envies the natural joy of country people, unaware, of course, that the innocence and simplicity of that lifestyle are constructions of urbanites like herself.

Like the rest of the audience, Madame receives the contredanse of the symphony's finale (Example 3.4a) enthusiastically—after all, she herself would still much rather be dancing at this very moment. While the first departure from the dance couplets (by m. 39, Example 3.4b) Madame greets with indifference, Haydn's failure to present the second strain intact upon the dance's return alienates her. She finds the learned presentation of the tune (at m. 109, Example 3.4c) unintelligible and, worse, entirely unsuitable for dancing. Despite the satisfying subsequent return of both couplets nearly intact (mm. 159–90)

p. Louis-Sébastien Mercier, author of the utopian novel *L'An 2440* of 1771, objected to the glorification of noble characters at the expense of the bourgeoisie in comedies performed at the Comédie Française, but observed that bourgeois attendants did not disapprove.[35]

and the obvious martial references at the end (mm. 210–13, Example 3.4d), Madame is perplexed (once again) by the everyone else's fervent reception of Haydn's symphony. Haydn's failure to paint images or sentiments unambiguously is beyond tedious. As her dearly departed revolutionary claimed, Haydn's music—like all symphonic music—is aesthetically suspect.[q]

q. See n.

Hearing Haydn in Haydn's London

Our third listener is an eminent merchant-banker who resides among the bourgeoisie in the City of London.[r] His prosperity has grown steadily during the past two decades, and his home, needs, aspirations, and pastimes emulate those of the gentry. When his only daughter was married to a member of the House of Commons, she was well prepared to oversee a household not all that different from the one in which she was born, raised, and tutored. A fine pianist and singer, she is able to enliven any conversation at the private Ladies Concert.[s] Our merchant-banker, however, is untutored in music, and although he is a seasonal holder of West End theater and concert subscriptions, he prefers to spend his time in coffeehouses engaged in political debates or discussions of literature.[t] And yet he finds his musical ear growing somewhat, no doubt due to his support for one of the City's own musical institutions, the Academy of Ancient Music, even though he finds its new air of exclusivity somewhat off-putting. But at least now he can distinguish not just street songs from concert arias but ancient music from the modern overtures.[u] Moreover, he feels increasingly able to participate in the lively aesthetic debates that frequently

r. According to Patrick Colquhoun's estimate based on the census returns of 1801 and the pauper returns of 1803, 2,000 "eminent merchants, bankers, &c." lived in Britain at the end of the eighteenth century.[36] Rudé suggests that about half of them resided within the City of London (1971, 43).

s. The Ladies Concert was a private subscription concert series that, at least by 1791, was separate from the Grand Private Subscription Concerts and was attended by the nobility and the gentry. Meeting on Fridays, it was in direct competition with Salomon's series.[37]

t. Coffeehouses were centers for intellectual and political discussion for the middle classes in eighteenth-century London.[38]

u. The Academy of Ancient Music was organized by wealthy merchants in the City of London and subscribed to primarily by dominate literary-club and coffeehouse conversation.

On a warm summer evening in 1791, the first movement of a Haydn symphony (No. 88 once more) is well underway when our merchant-banker, strolling in the Vauxhall Gardens with his wife, stops to take in some supper at a table near the "orchestra."[v] The sound of hunting horns (at m. 188, Example 3.1c,) reminds him of one of his favorite songs, "With Horns and with Hounds,"[w] despite the facts that (1) there is absolutely no resemblance between Haydn's music and the popular song, (2) he has never actually been on a hunt (or even to the countryside for that matter), and (3) he finds the activity itself rather distasteful. He may associate regularly with great men, in both business and pleasure, but still finds himself largely an outsider to their manners and culture. Respect for nobles and gentry he has, but envy none at all. As he scans the crowd ambling through the gardens, he appreciates its heterogeneity.[x] In fact, the combination of popularity and privilege he hears in Haydn's "overture" reflects the secret of his own professional and social success: tasteful accessibility to all.

Again only half listening to the music as the second movement gets underway, our merchant-banker relates to one of the gentlemen in his company a recent aesthetic debate from the coffeehouse, for he finds the songlike quality of melodies like the one he hears now the source of music's beauty (Example 3.2a). Perhaps he is just echoing the concert reviews he reads regularly in the newspaper, but simplicity, he argues, is what makes music expressive.[y] Thundering chords, amplified by trumpets and drums (at m. 41, Example 3.2b), in-

the moneyed middle classes. While serious Renaissance music was its original focus, by the 1790s not only was Handel the society's favored composer, but "modern" music (e.g., Haydn's symphonies) was programmed as well.

v. The "orchestra," here, refers not just to the band but also to the open-air building from which the performers played.

w. Thomas Warren, "With Horns and Hounds," in *A Collection of Catches, Canons, and Glees* (London: ca. 1765), 39. The song is also found in *Songs from a Colonial Tavern* (Williamsburg, Virginia: Colonial Williamsburg Foundation, 1964), 13.

x. At least one reviewer of the Vauxhall Jubilee of 1786, writing in *The Morning Chronicle*, describes the *"melange"* [*sic*] thus: "the cit and the courtier jostled each other with the usual familiarity; the half guinea was no repellant to the middling order; John Bull loves to shoulder his superiors in rank, his betters he'll not allow them to be; and where he pays as much for admission, he never considers them to be more than his equals."[39]

y. Music reviews in newspapers often echoed key ideas of aesthetic theories of the day, the notion of *noble simplicité* among them.

terrupt his case for the good sense of simplicity in all things. As the crowd of listeners voices approval, the merchant-banker's acquaintance comments smugly that simplicity is well and good but sublimity is surely the greater musical expression: music's purpose is to elevate as much as to please.[z] And so continues this light discussion of musical aesthetics—in essence a watered-down version of some current aesthetic issues. The points volley back and forth, nearly mirroring the alternating expressive states of Haydn's music.[aa]

In the third movement the merchant-banker hears a formal ballroom dance (Example 3.3a), the drums at the end of each strain (mm. 11–12, 41–42) affirming its high character. He enjoys the mixed company at the dances and takes secret pleasure watching nobles mix not just with the bourgeois and middling sorts, but even with men and women of working trades. Now that his business successes have established his family among the City's rich, his politics have shifted somewhat, but not in the way most would expect. Despite the increasing exclusivity of his social and occupational associations, and the recent political alliance between the City and Westminster and Middlesex, he secretly continues to support the radical candidates and their opposition to the Court and government. The trio's folk idiom (Example 3.3b) plays right into his sympathies for the lower orders, as he aligns the bucolic world of Haydn's trio with an idealized humility of the less fortunate. He does not realize, of course, that this urbanized affectation is every bit as patronizing as the behavior of the elites, whom he often criticizes for attending dances and visiting the gardens to enjoy

z. In late-eighteenth-century England, the category of the sublime embraced a surprisingly wide range of expressive stances, "from a grandiose Handel chorus to a threatening Haydn military movement." But all of them, as McVeigh notes, "step beyond everyday urban experience and comforting pastoral make-believe into a world of deeper emotions, whether spiritual, inspirational or anxiety-ridden" (McVeigh 1993, 155–56).

aa. The dichotomy of the sublime and the beautiful, a division well established in Britain by Joseph Addison's "Essay on the Pleasures of the Imagination" for *The Spectator* in 1712, was heartily embraced and commonly invoked in both casual and learned aesthetic discussion.

their superior social distinction as much as the entertainments.[bb]

bb. See note x.

The opening of Haydn's contredanse finale (Example 3.4a) reminds the merchant-banker of the sound of the dance bands that play at City banquets. As he continues eating and conversing, thoroughly enjoying his dinner music, he is struck suddenly by how much Haydn's overture sounds like Handel (so he hears) (at m. 109, Example 3.4c). But before he can comment to his companions (and thereby demonstrate his learned appreciation for the ancient master), the likeness dissolves into anticipation (by m. 142, Example 3.4c) of the dance's return. The clamor of trumpets and drums (mm. 210–221, Example 3.4d), while marking the end of this delightful dance, pleases our merchant-banker above anything else he has heard this evening. He hears them not just as marking the end of the symphony but as announcements for the next act which, according to the program posted at the bar, should be some most agreeable Scottish songs.

Admittedly indulgent to the imagination, unabashedly subjective on nearly every count, and undeniably "fanciful," these three hearings of Haydn's Symphony No. 88 are nonetheless grounded in the social, cultural, and political realities of their respective "privileged" historical listening contexts, as attested by the lengthy glosses provided. They were formed by associating the constructed personal experiences, musical and otherwise, of each fictional listening subject's plausible everyday late-eighteenth-century life with various salient features of the expressive surface of Haydn's symphony—features such listeners would have easily noticed during a first and only hearing of this music. These associations, along with the emotions and ideas stimulated by them in the body and mind of the listener, not only lie at the heart of musical expressivity in the aesthetics of the Enlightenment, but are also a primary mechanism of musical meaning in late-twentieth-century theories of topicality and expressive meaning in late-eighteenth-century music.

That such historically informed fictions may generate reasonably "safe" musical meanings, that is, meanings in tune with traditional historical narratives, suggests that the text has the power not just to influence and inform but even to construct a listener's beliefs, values, persuasions, passions, etc.—in short, his subjectivity. But, as Twining for one argues in his striking anticipation of the reader-response theories of the late twentieth century, the listener himself must still be empowered to make the "free operation of his emotion upon his fancy" and the "free choice" of ideas during a musical experience. As we shall see in chapter 4, it is precisely this power of the listening subject—whether she is contemporary, historical, or fictional—to construct meaning freely that assures the instrumental music of the late eighteenth century an ability to generate pleasure, aesthetic and otherwise, among its diversity of listeners.

4   Entertaining Pleasure

In late-eighteenth-century Europe, the most immediate purpose of public concert music was to entertain the listener. Composers were keenly aware that their audience was a cross section of the public—the "many-headed Monster of the Pit," to borrow Alexander Pope's image of the public theater audience (1737, line 305). Listeners were people of varying social status, musical literacy, and interest in the concert itself. Haydn's famous desire "to surprise the public with something new" with the *Paukenschlag* in the slow movement of his Symphony in G Major, No. 94 (Griesinger [1810] 1963, 33) and Mozart's pitching of his piano concertos, K. 413–15, so that not just connoisseurs but "the less learned cannot fail to be pleased" (Anderson 1966, 2:833) are but two among many such acknowledgments of a composer's intentions to please his listener, whomever he might be. And yet, conditioned by Romantic and modernist notions of the autonomy of art, most twentieth-century criticism of this music sidesteps (or even belittles) its original purpose to entertain its listeners, focusing its analysis instead on a work's form and content. As valuable as these analyses may be for those seeking a deeper understanding of the inner structural workings of concert music, many of the details revealed are unlikely to have been perceived by most listeners in eighteenth-century public concert audiences. Moreover, when a work was perhaps too successful in its original purpose—too accessible, "popular," or pleasing even to the lay listener—it is today often categorically dismissed as "mere entertainment," music whose structural attributes are unworthy of serious attention.

Only recently have we begun to reassess the public music of the late eighteenth century within an aesthetic of entertainment and pleasure. While the "pragmatic orientation" of this music—that is, its "ordering the aim of the artist and the character of the work to the nature, the needs, and the springs of pleasure in the audience" (Abrams 1953, 20–21)—is often acknowledged, even emphasized, in recent musicological discussion, questions of *how* instrumental music entertained its audience have hardly been addressed. The most significant consideration of music's situation within late-eighteenth-century entertainment culture is Mary Hunter's trailblazing study (1999) of opera buffa's poetics of entertainment. Her work, in turn, supplies much of the theoretical foundation for Webster's passionate defense (1998) of Haydn's long-disparaged symphonies between the *Sturm und Drang* and the mid-1780s, the only study of Classical instrumental music (of which I am aware) to address this music's accessibility within an aesthetic of entertainment and, consequently, in a positive light.[1] And yet, as smart and stimulating as Hunter's and Webster's studies are, both accept a bit too easily, I think, a definition of entertainment as simply "supplying [to its audience] pleasure and diversion of various sorts" (Hunter 1999, 4). Given the significance of pleasure as a philosophical construct and the sophistication of its various delineations not just in eighteenth-century aesthetics but in late-twentieth-century cultural and critical theories, our exploration of late-eighteenth-century public instrumental music as entertainment requires further consideration of the particular pleasures it supplies. As we shall see, entertainment and pleasure maintain less of an interdependent relationship than a dialectical one.

Aesthetic Pleasures

Joseph Addison, in the 27 June 1712 edition of *The Spectator*, articulates a conception of aesthetic pleasure that would become widely embraced and often reiterated throughout the eighteenth century: "the pleasures of the imagination . . . proceed from that action of the mind which compares the ideas arising from the original objects with the ideas we receive from the statue, picture, description or sound that represents them" ([1712] 1965, 59). His orientation clearly mimetic, Addison explicitly locates the pleasure experienced by the beholder of a work of representational art (as, of course, all art was expected to be at the time) within the subject's mind. The beholder's pleasure derives solely from the mental activity of judging the representational success of the artistic object. Like the separation of "good taste" from "desire," "lust," "the gratification of appetite," and "the pursuit of gain"—a separation advocated by such writers as Alexander Gerard and Edmund Burke to protect the fine arts from the perils of commodity culture (Gerard 1764; Burke 1756)—Addison's "pleasures of the imagination" sit in direct opposition to the "sensual" pleasures of the body.[2]

The pleasures of the imagination are routinely distinguished from the pleasures of the senses in the aesthetic philosophies of the eighteenth century. Kant, for example, in the "Analytic of the Beautiful" in the *Kritik der Urteilskraft*, delineated three distinct types of pleasure: that which is "pleasurable" gratifies the senses and satisfies a need, that which "pleases" is judged as beautiful in its formal purposiveness, and that which is "good" "pleases purely as a rational concept." Kant's foundational distinction between the first two categories—that which "gives pleasure" and that which "pleases"—rests on the same separation of sensory and cognitive pleasures put forward by Addison. In the case of the former category, a pleasurable reaction "has nothing to do with the character of the object. So anyone who has enjoyment as his sole aim (for that is what the word means that describes the inner core of satisfaction) will happily evade judging in any respect." Only that which pleases, an aesthetic experience not tainted by the subject's worldly needs, physical desires, or individual interests, is the product of "disinterested" judging (Kant [1790] 1952, trans. in Le Huray and Day 1981, 215–20).

While most philosophers of the nineteenth century, building on Kant's sturdy foundation, maintain aesthetic pleasure as disinterested pleasure,[3] the distinction between aesthetic pleasure and purely sensory or purely cognitive pleasures—"what the balance of thought and feeling in an aesthetic experience is or should be"—becomes a central concern only in the aesthetic philosophies of the twentieth century. Jerrold Levinson, for one, argues that aesthetic pleasure can also be experienced as a result of an artwork's traditionally conceived "nonaesthetic" aspects—its cognitive, moral, or political content, for example—as well its formal or gestalt qualities (1996, 3–4, 18–20). David Pole proposes that many of the aesthetic aspects of an artwork are in fact wholly conceptual rather than perceptual, particularly its political meaning (1957, 93–106). And for Scruton, the awareness of one's cognitive activity during the aesthetically pleasurable experience is essential, for his aesthetic requires the subject consciously to form mental conceptions of the artistic object (1979, 71–103; 1997, 369–79).

In the recent theorizing of pleasure, however, it is Roland Barthes who overturns the applecart of two centuries of aesthetic philosophy. Like Kant, he delineates distinct categories of pleasure, but unlike all other writers of either Kant's time or his own, Barthes embraces unreservedly the sheer physicality of the pleasure experienced by readers of texts. *Plaisir,* his first category, is produced culturally when the reader finds her identity confirmed by a text; *jouissance,* his second category, is produced physically when the reader experiences bodily pleasure in a text. While Barthes's earlier work (e.g., *Mythologies*) was concerned with distinguishing between nature and culture, and in particular how ideology informs the meaning of texts in culture, it is the physical *jouissance* that matters to Barthes in the end, for, as he argues in *The Pleasure of the Text,* the pleasure of a text is "the articulation of the body, of the tongue, not that of meaning, of language." His exposition of *jouissance* in cinema is also its exhibition:

> It suffices that the cinema capture the sound of speech *close up* (this is, in fact, the generalized definition of the 'grain' of writing) and make us hear in their materiality, their sensuality, the breath, the gutturals, the fleshiness of the lips, a whole presence of the human muzzle (that the voice, that writing, be as fresh, supple, lubricated, delicately granular and vibrant as an animal's muzzle) to succeed in shifting the signified a great distance and in throwing, so to speak, the anonymous body of the actor into my ear: it granulates, it crackles, it caresses, it grates, it cuts, it comes: that is bliss [*jouissance*]. (1975, 67)

Kant and Barthes constitute the two ends of aesthetic pleasure's spectrum: for Kant, aesthetic pleasure is entirely separate from sensory experience; for Barthes (or at least the later, hedonistic Barthes of *The Pleasure of the Text*), they are indivisible.

Informing not just Barthes's *jouissance* but indeed the whole category of pleasure in much late-twentieth-century critical writing is the psychoanalytic use of the term, originating in Sigmund Freud's "pleasure principle." According to Freud, the satisfaction of immediate needs and the avoidance of pain are primary and universal mental processes that guide instinctive behavior ([1911] 1989, 301–306). Laura Mulvey, for one, embraces Freud's pleasure principle in her essay "Visual Pleasure and Narrative Cinema" (1975). In this hugely influential feminist work, she argues that integral to traditional filmic pleasure is the voyeuristic-scopophilic look, specifically the masculine gaze at the female body. The effect of this look is to produce a masculine subjectivity in the viewer, whatever his or her actual gender. The typical Hollywood narrative cinema thus rewards the viewer with pleasure when he or she acquiesces to its patriarchal demands.

Any critical methodology grounded in the pleasure principle thus grants the text tremendous social and political power, for in Freudian psychoanalysis the desire for pleasure is an *unconscious* mental process.[4] The reader would seem to have little or no control over a text's meaning. As Mulvey argues is the case with traditional cinema, meaning may still reside in the reader, but since the text in effect determines her subjectivity, mainstream texts thereby align the reader's subjectivity with the dominant ideology. For Barthes, however, despite his own dependence on Freud's pleasure principle, aesthetic pleasure is ultimately subversive. While *plaisir* theoretically allows for the identity of a reader who opposes a dominant ideology to be confirmed by a text (by reading into a text codes of resistance, for example), *jouissance* is subversive because it evades ideology altogether. The sheer physicality of Barthes's *jouissance*—its residence in the body—positions this textual pleasure outside culture and therefore beyond ideological control.

John Fiske's pioneering study of television culture offers a compelling demonstration of the critical power of integrating various categories of pleasure, such as the aesthetic, the psychoanalytic, the social, and the physical, into a theory of how cultural texts mean. The variety of pleasures experienced while watching television, he argues, results from the variety of socially situated viewers. "For those in easy accommodation with the dominant ideology," he explains, "pleasure will be conforming and reactionary." While it might seem that the viewing subject in this case has been programmed (so to speak) passively to embrace meanings that reside within the television text itself, a viewing situation in which aesthetic pleasure would be theoretically impossible, Fiske argues that this is not the viewer's experience. Rather, the viewing subject feels that he is "voluntarily adopting a social position that happens to conform to the dominant ideology" (1987, 234). In other words, because the viewer's pleasure *feels* self-generated to him, it *is* self-generated and therefore genuine.

But for those who are not as easily accommodated by "the system," Fiske contends that "evasion, or at least a negotiation, of dominant ideological practice—the ability to shake oneself free from its constraints"—is an essential component of the viewer's pleasure (1987, 234). Indeed, a viewer's desire and ability to construct meanings of resistance speaks to the dialectical relationship between pleasure and power theorized most famously by Michel Foucault as a "perpetual spiral": "The pleasure that comes of exercising a power . . . kindles [a pleasure] at having to evade this power" (1978, 45).

The pleasures of television, then, experienced by conforming and resisting viewers alike, provide both homogenizing and heterogenizing forces within the culture and society that consumes it. As we shall see, the entertainment music of the late eighteenth century also contains "both tendencies in active contradiction" (Fiske 1987, 234). Similarly public though usually less "popular," public concert music empowered its original listeners to experience the pleasures of constructing meanings that vary along with their subjectivities, social situations, degrees of political enfranchisement, and shifting relationships to the various dominant ideologies of late-eighteenth-century Europe. The pleasures of this music could also be, however, agents of public disempowerment.

Taste, the Powers of Pleasure, and the Politics of Entertainment

In his "Most Humble Suggestion for the Improvement of the National Stage and Theatre in General," Tobias Philipp Gebler, imperial advisor to Joseph II, argues that a public sufficiently cheered by diversions from the hardships and unpleasantries of everyday life is more acquiescent to government control. He writes:

> Every subject who can give joy and pleasure in alternation keeps his spirits up and bears work and ill fortune patiently. Public dance-places, concerts, walks, [and] especially good plays are the means to make the public cheerful. He who tries to keep his fellow citizen in good humor lightens the burden of government for the Regent, since it will be easier to rule his subjects in this cheerful condition than [it would be] if they were discontented. (Quoted and trans. in Hunter 1999, 52–53)

Entertainment, for Gebler, wielded considerable political power. Through its potential to keep a citizenry in good spirits, and therefore content or at least distracted, the "joy and pleasure" inspired by certain leisure activities could purportedly prevent public unrest and possible uprisings. Like Du Bos's, Diderot's, and Twining's anticipations of certain aspects of postmodern critical theory, Gebler's recognition of the political power of entertainment prefigures what is arguably the central tenet of late-twentieth-century cultural studies: cultural processes underwrite structures of social power. To be sure, Gebler's purpose is practical rather than analytical, prescriptive rather than descriptive. But his direct linking of concerts for the public with the government's control over its subjects invites our investigation into the social forces of this music's political power.

Chief among the socially homogenizing forces of late-eighteenth-century concert music is its appeal to listeners of "good taste." In eighteenth-century Europe, taste as much as wealth or title became a decisive sign of social standing, the one essential attribute required in the "distinguished," "refined," and "sociable man" of "polite culture,"[5] Voltaire's *homme de goût*. While the definition of taste was widely debated by contemporary critics and philosophers,[6] the "fine or elegant arts"[7] were categorically understood as "objects of taste" whose purpose was to excite the "pleasures of the imagination." Burke's formulation is typical: "I mean by the word taste no more than that faculty, or those faculties of the mind which are affected with, or which form a judgment of, the works of imagination and the elegant arts" ([1756] 1958, 13).

In accordance with the egalitarian ideals of the Enlightenment, taste was widely considered a gift of nature, present in everyone (see, e.g., Hume [1757] 1965). But the social and political reality was quite different, as taste could be developed only "if assisted by proper culture" (Gerard 1764, 1). Simply put, taste was more easily acquired by the wealthy and prosperous, particularly the financially independent.

The issue was philosophical, not practical, however, for in theory anyone who could afford the ticket had access to culture and could partake of the cultivation offered by the fine arts. The wealthy, however, could more readily adopt the disinterested perspective that critics and philosophers maintained was necessary for aesthetic judgment—the ability to evaluate works of art unbiased by personal needs, desires, or inclinations. As John Brewer explains, "Not required to work for a living, not economically dependent on others, [the independently wealthy] were considered to have unbiased and impartial views" (1997, 90). "Taste" thereby easily became code for "refinement." But this stance is, of course, a smokescreen, for the valuing of unbiased evaluation is itself biased.

Precisely because the aesthetic values of good taste were at the time presumed universal, Pierre Bourdieu's critique of taste, and especially his economic metaphor of "cultural capital"—both formulated to operate within the late capitalist democracies of the present Western world—translate quite well to late-eighteenth-century Europe (see Bourdieu 1980, 225–54; 1984). In a nutshell, Bourdieu's primary argument is as follows: cultural capital—the ability to read and understand cultural codes—is distributed unequally among social orders; like material wealth, cultural capital serves to perpetuate a stratified society; those people with "good taste" who appreciate the "higher" forms of culture are members of the dominant classes and strive to control a society's culture just as they control its wealth. Particularly applicable to the late eighteenth century is Bourdieu's claim that as subordinate classes gain in material wealth, cultural differences emerge to reinforce and sustain otherwise diminishing class distinctions. It is no coincidence that the rise of the aesthetic category of the fine arts—the culture of noble tastes and sophistication—accompanied the rise of the middle classes during Europe's Enlightenment. For the aspirational middling orders, for whom the nobility served as the model of behavior, social refinement and good taste became as essential to acquire as economic capital—perhaps even more so. But as bourgeois taste approached noble taste, the aristocracy responded by creating new and more exclusive cultural forms and forums, which the middle classes, in turn, again strove to emulate.

As the wish to better one's social standing was nearly universal among the public of Enlightenment Europe, the edification one sought in "proper culture" became a powerful agent of social homogeneity. Middle-class citizens self-consciously consumed, when possible, the same cultural products as did the noble and wealthy. The diary of Anna Larpent, an English woman, neither noble nor poor, provides compelling testimony to the bourgeois conviction that developing a proper appreciation for the arts was the means to gaining social traction.[8] Aspiring to what she called "a refinement which can only be felt in the pure pleasure of intellectual pursuits," Larpent found her everyday activities of attending plays and concerts and reading literature, poetry, and philosophy "edifying rather than amusing." Noting the "fashioning of a refined persona" as the "overriding concern" in her diary, Brewer offers Anna Larpent as his archetype for "a cultured lady of late eighteenth-century London" (1997, 57). For Larpent, the cultivation of taste—the means to acquire greater cultural capital—was tantamount to social promotion.

The pleasures of the imagination thus supplied a powerful centripetal political force for the state, as clearly implied by one of the first published guides to the arts in London: "The cultivation of the polite arts is justly deemed an object of the highest importance in every well-regulated state; for it is universally allowed, that in proportion as these are encouraged or discountenanced, the manners of the people are civilized and improved, or degenerate into brutal ferocity, and savage moroseness" (Brewer 1997, xix). The resemblance to Gebler's "humble suggestion" to Joseph II could hardly be more striking. To be sure, the control Anna Larpent maintained over the meaning of her cultural experiences—that they were to educate, elevate, and provide moral instruction—may have made them distinctly pleasurable to her as she fashioned her refined persona. But from the government's perspective, the principal value of such diversions was political: an entertained public was a polite public, and a polite public, passive.

At the same time, however, the cultivation of taste had a concomitant opposite social effect. The notion that the boundaries between social orders may be somewhat porous, at least culturally, generated a fixation on status, especially in Vienna where the actions, climate, and expansions of the court encouraged the noble aspirations of the upper bourgeoisie (see Bruckmüller 1985, 240–41, 286, and esp. 321–39; 2003, 206, 216–17, and esp. 229–30). As the hitherto "uncultured" acquired cultural capital, the increase in the attention paid to the stratification of society by titled and untitled alike bolstered the division between the two classes. The old nobility hardly accepted the newly ennobled as equals, and the middle class remained, at least in principle, dependent on the court and the monarchy (Bruckmüller 2003, 336). The homogenizing pleasures of the imagination thus also served to sustain the underlying social heterogeneity of the European public. As social aspiration in the eighteenth century could, for the most part, be acted out culturally, such pleasures generated tangible centrifugal social and political forces as well.

The particular nature of taste and its concomitant social force depend wholly on the meanings the beholder creates during her experience with the fine and elegant arts. And these meanings, of course, hinge on her subjectivity. Pondering the question of why "the whole world [doesn't] love chamber music," Christopher Small reflects:

> Whatever our position in society may be, we shall espouse values that support our sense of worth and self-esteem. If that position is elevated or privileged our values will be those which justify that position. This is not necessarily a conscious choice, just our sense of the proper order of things. On the other hand, those in a lowly position may either espouse values that make them feel just as good as the elites, or else they may accept their position as part of the given order of things. (2001, 347)

Despite the philosophical argument to the contrary current in the eighteenth century, beholders of the "proper culture" at that time, whatever their status, could hardly jettison their own interests, particularly on social and political matters, any more than we can today. For those in real or imagined positions of political, social, or economic power, hearing codes of stability in public concert music could reinforce the security of individual status. For the comparatively disempowered, conversely, hearing codes of resistance could encourage transcendence of political, social, and economic subordination. The pleasure experienced in the former instance, whether aesthetic or not, would be the pleasure of power; in the latter, the pleasure of subversion—or at least the evasion of power, to use Foucault's model and terminology. To experience the various pleasures of concert music in the late eighteenth century, then, was an active process, one that excited the listener's imagination to construct meaning that best served her personal needs.

The acceptance of a position of lesser power and privilege, on the other hand, results in a more passive listening experience, one in which the listener does not assume the degree of control over meaning he does in an distinctively pleasurable cultural experience. Much like Mulvey's film viewer whose masculine subjectivity is constructed by traditional Hollywood narrative cinema, the listening subjectivity of the person "merely" entertained by public concert music in the late eighteenth century would be, to a certain extent, determined by the musical work itself. The pleasure that such a listener could experience might feel self-generated, but the meanings he constructed would conform to the demands of the dominant ideology, even if he were disempowered by that ideology. While Fiske would maintain that this listener nevertheless experiences genuine pleasure, the text's power to disempower suggests otherwise. The listener, merely entertained, relinquishes his control over music's meaning, rendering him politically inert, just as Gebler advised.

Public concert music, then, in its capacity to entertain its audience, was potentially a powerful political agent. The cheerfulness Gebler contends would ensure a readily governable citizenry is a direct result of the passivity of the entertained listener, whatever his social position. But Gebler's "humble suggestion" may also be surprisingly effective for those listeners who, not easily accommodated by the dominant ideology, take real, active pleasure in constructing musical meanings that oppose or evade the sources of their disempowerment. Such listeners may spend their subversive energy in the concert hall rather than save it for the coffeehouse or perhaps even the street. In this sense, late-eighteenth-century public concert music may be theorized as carnivalesque: its pleasure resides within the expression, but not the activity, of resistance. The status quo reaffirmed, public musical entertainment remains "merely" entertaining.

To begin our exploration of the mechanisms of entertainment and pleasure in late-eighteenth-century concert music, we shall now consider how meanings constructed for the same music could operate as both centripetal and centrifugal political forces in Enlightenment Europe. Minuets from Haydn's and Mozart's symphonies, works composed for both private and public audiences, will serve as our proving grounds, for not only were minuets arguably the most readily "readable" symphonic movement type in the eighteenth century, but their noble affect and certain association with the aristocracy made the dance particularly amenable to political interpretation. Although we shall not delineate (or fantasize) individual listeners as in chapter 3, the readings offered below, despite their apparent projection as intersubjective meanings, are dependent on the notion of an individual listener subjectivity shaped by his or her personal experiences within the social and political realities of the time. They also assume the immediate structural intelligibility of the dance.

The Noble Minuet

Among classical instrumental movements, the minuet was unique. Because its title revealed its subject as the widely known court and ballroom dance, the minuet movement of the concert hall possessed a "fixed generic identity."[9] Upon hearing the three equally stressed beats of its measure and the *pas de menuet*'s two-bar groupings, listeners in eighteenth-century public concert audiences would have immediately recognized the minuet. From their own experiences in Europe's fashionable ballrooms, most listeners would also have been familiar with the late-eighteenth-century minuet's hierarchical and symmetrical phrase structure. While theorists of the time considered the minuet's two-reprise form—usually presented in the I–V, X–I key-area plan (or i–III, X–i for those few dances in the minor mode)—archetypal,[10] amateur players and other music enthusiasts enjoyed composing new minuets with musical *ars combinatoria* dice games (Ratner, 1970). So crystallized were the basic melodic, rhythmic, and harmonic patterns of the minuet in the late eighteenth century that even lay listeners, from their countless encounters with the binary dance form, would have been able to follow a minuet movement's formal scheme without difficulty.

In the last quarter of the century, the minuet's affect had grown stately and quite serious.[11] An exaggeration of the dance's characteristic gestures, the result of which was a revised, slower tempo, dispassionate disposition, and introduction of a motto rhythm (♩♪♪♪♪),[12] developed most likely to ensure correspondence between the dance's affect and its reputation of refinement and association with nobility. Indeed, "noble" was the word of choice among eighteenth-century critics to describe the Classic minuet's affect. Jean-Jacques Rousseau, in his widely circulated *Dictionnaire de musique*, describes the minuet as a dance of "elegant and noble simplicity" ([1768] 1969, 277).[13] Similarly, Johann Georg Sulzer, in his influential encyclopedic general theory of the arts, *Allgemeine Theorie der schönen Künste*, characterizes the minuet's expression as having "a noble and charming deportment, but combined with simplicity" ([1771–74] 1967–70, 3:388).[14] Capturing the Classic minuet's patrician spirit, he continues: "The minuet is universally well known, and deserves preference over the other social dances on account of its noble and charming nature. . . . It appears to have been invented by the Graces themselves, and is more suited than any other dance for assemblages of persons who distinguish themselves by a fine manner of living" ([1771–74] 1967–70, 3:389, quoted and trans. in Allanbrook 1983, 33).[15] To the mid-eighteenth-century dancing master C. J. von Feldtenstein, the minuet was "the queen of all dances" (quoted and trans. in Allanbrook 1983, 33).

Both Rousseau and Sulzer, however, temper their characterizations of the noble minuet by also noting its simplicity, a clear reflection of the Enlightenment's new aesthetic concept of *noble simplicité*. Although the notion of *noble simplicité* would seem to embody contradiction—the elevation of nobility combined with the lowliness of simplicity—Matteson, for one, instructs readers of his influential *Der vollkommene Capellmeister* not to misunderstand simplicity "as something stupid, absurd, or common, but rather as something noble, unembellished, and quite unique" ([1737] 1981, 149).[16] In this sense, *noble simplicité* is not a combination of two conflicting concepts but, despite the order of its adjective-noun construction, a qualification of the expression of the noble passions. Moreover, as revealed by the many references to classical art in eighteenth-century aesthetics—Mattheson describes the "beautiful simplicity" of the "strong features, majestic faces and emphatic postures" of ancient painting, sculpture and engraving, for example (149)[17]—"simplicity" also presumes a certain neoclassical directness and authenticity of emotion. As Ruth Katz and Carl Dahlhaus put it, "The bourgeois conviction that a 'genuine' emotion manifests itself simply, and that simplicity guarantees the 'genuineness' of an emotion was the central thesis of the aesthetics of the Enlightenment" (1989, 114). The late-eighteenth-century minuet, then, as a dance of "noble simplicity," ironically acquired a certain sincerity through its pretense of a lack of pretension.

While general character and intertextual relationships with other types of music were, for eighteenth-century lay listeners, key to discerning musical affect, the affective foundation for critics, as mentioned above, rested on the classical division of rhetorical styles into three degrees of dignity, "lofty," "mean," and "humble," transmitted in seventeenth-century French aesthetics. Although the high style was widely considered a heritage from the motet style of the Baroque, Scheibe, in the 20 August 1737 issue (No. 13) of *Critischer Musikus,* argued that it was not limited to evocations of an earlier—read polyphonic—musical tradition. He warned, "In general, one has a false conception of the high style. One calls high only that which is extraordinarily artificial and contrapuntal, or that which produces altogether eccentric, incomprehensible, or stirring sounds" (1745, 126).[18] Scheibe, who defended the new Classical style as it was developing, considered "the natural" and "the clear" to be the true signs of good style (126),[19] two values clearly opposed to the "artificial" and "indistinct" style of fugal writing and counterpoint (274).[20] In light of his argument for "a return to simplicity, to an imitation of nature and to an emphasis on persuasive melody" (Buelow 1980, 600), the galant or free style was, in the new musical aesthetic he advocated, an essential component of his conception of high style: "The magnificence and emphasis [of the true high style] is now achieved when the harmony is full, when all ideas are carried though, when all voices progress in an impassioned pursuit at the same time or in unison. The melody must be rich in ideas, new, lively, and grand" (1745, 126).[21] Later eighteenth-century critics, in particular Ernst Gerber, reiterated such delineations of stylistic level as Classical aesthetic values peaked in musical composition (1799, cols. 292–97, 305–12).

During the second half of the eighteenth century, the minuet was the last of the French court dances still being danced. As a nod to tradition and authority, or in Allanbrook's words, the "primary representative of the *ancien régime, . . .* the epitome of choreographic elegance and refinement" (1983, 33–35), the minuet was a dance of utmost dignity. The affected humility of its *noble simplicité* imparts further sincerity. As Sulzer informs us, "the minuet was generally considered superior to all dances of this style. There [was] hardly another dance invented that combine[d] so much elegance, a noble deportment, and the highest, most pleasing nature" ([1771–74] 1967–70, 4:505).[22] Although he does not list specific dances, the minuet would surely belong in the highest category of theatrical dances as profiled in the "Tanz" article: "The fourth class includes the dances of serious, higher character, as required by the tragic stage. They consist of either solo dances that portray only great and serious characters, or whole actions with fixed content. Here must come together all figures and movements that the art has the ability to present for the expression of great passions" (506).[23] As the most dignified of the eighteenth-century social dances, appropriate, as Scheibe prescribes, for the portrayal of "heroes, kings, and other great men and lofty spirits" (1745, 126),[24] the minuet is clearly in the high stylistic register. We may therefore capsulize its expressive content, reflecting the terms and categories established by eighteenth-century critics and theorists, as the courtly (i.e., galant), as opposed to the ecclesiastical (i.e., learned), high style.

Is this also how the many lay listeners in the public concert audiences of the time would have heard the minuet? Certainly most listeners would have immediately recognized a minuet upon hearing a dance movement's first strain, if not just its opening measures. Dancing had become an increasingly fashionable form of entertainment and socializing for the middle as well as the upper classes, and the minuet was the obligatory first dance of every evening in the late-eighteenth-century ballroom. But since most bourgeois dancers would have lacked the training required to execute the minuet's intricate steps, the dance's courtly status and association with nobility was affirmed at every public ball by the effective exclusion of all but those dancers who had access to formal dance instruction—that is, the noble or wealthy. Moreover, as the minuet was a couple dance (danced "solo," so to speak, by only one couple at a time), many balls began with the middling orders watching the aristocratic dancers display their training—and therefore also their privileged position in the social order. Only after the minuets were danced would the ballroom floor become crowded with middle-class dancers enjoying the "middle-class" *Deutsche Tänze* and contredanses, dances with rustic and common associations that were danced by all couples at once or as a group, respectively. Based largely on their contact with minuets in public ballrooms, and perhaps strengthened by their experiences hearing the highest characters portrayed by minuets in the theater, most lay listeners in late-eighteenth-century concert audiences would have heard the minuet just as the noble dance described by music critics and theorists.

Reviews in the increasingly popular music magazines, publications aimed at middle-class readers and often disparaged by more learned music theoreticians and critics, reveal that listeners of the time understood instrumental music intertextually—in terms of associations and musical references to other types of music. In a review of *Six Simphonies* by Friedrich Schwindl for Johann Adam Hiller's *Wöchentliche Nachrichten*, for example, the author acknowledges his recognition of a surprising reference in the second movement as well as the expected dance that follows:

> The first movement was pleasant and passionate; the varied shadings and the modulations were effective. But then came a stiff, sluggish Andante, which did have some

movement in the middle voices, but was so monotonous from beginning to end that it went nowhere. We did not know what to make of it until we finally realized it was a varied chorale. What? A chorale? In a symphony? Yes indeed, a chorale, followed by a right jolly minuet. . . . In short, Herr Schwindl has sought out the waggish and adventurous too much to please reasonable ears with his symphonies. (Hiller 1766–70, 3:33, 160; trans. in Morrow 1997, 79)

So too did listeners hear references to dance and other topics in vocal music, suggesting that recognition of a reference to a minuet in the context of a public concert was not simply a result of having been conditioned to expect one as the third movement of a symphony. Thomas Busby, for example, criticizes Handel's use of the "slow and graceful movement of a minuet" at an inappropriate moment in *Alexander's Feast* (1819, 2:386; quoted in Allanbrook 1983, 334n44) and French critic Laurent Garcin finds "Jommelli ridiculous, when in his air *Già di nubbi, etc.*, after having made the threat thunder in the mouth of an angry king, he finishes it off with a lovely little minuet on the words 'If you want to find shelter from the storm, you, you indeed, know how to do it'" (1772, 310; quoted and trans. in Allanbrook 1983, 334n45).

From these comments in popular music magazines it seems that contemporary listeners, if we may accept the reviews as both representing and informing lay listeners, not only recognized the minuet in various musical contexts but also possessed a keen sense of the dance's status and affect. Schwindl's minuet movement is too jovial, and Handel and Jommelli, despite the dance's aptness for the character depicted, compromise dramatic integrity by using the minuet inappropriately at moments that require a tempestuous rather than dignified expression. From the prescriptive treatises of Mattheson aimed at the composer and potential capellmeister to the music reviews in music magazines addressing music enthusiasts among the general public, the minuet was understood by *Kenner, Liebhaber,* and lay listener alike to be a noble dance of utmost dignity and elegance.

The "Minuet Filter"

Since the great majority of late-eighteenth-century symphonic third movements were minuets, and nearly all of those by Austrian-Bohemian composers,[25] audiences of the time would have expected the dance in the third position, even though concert programs of the time did not list movement titles. But the expressive content of a minuet movement does not always agree with its title, whether stated or implied. The expected minuet topic may be qualified or challenged by other topics and styles. In Haydn's symphonic minuets, for instance, uncontested agreement between title and topic is in fact quite rare. And yet, when listeners of the time expected or perceived a minuet, they heard that movement, regardless of its actual expressive content, within the frame of reference of the dance—through a "minuet filter," so to speak, those expectations conditioned by the stylistic conventions and expressive categories outlined above.

That such a minuet filter might operate presumes the existence of an "ideal minuet," a normative abstraction that forms the foundation of a listener's expectations. As Leonard B. Meyer has argued regarding memory and musical structure, "we tend to remember themes as being simpler than they really are and . . . we remember forms as 'ideal types' rather than as particular things. For as recollections of similar types, whether of parts or wholes, become regularized in the memory, they tend to be grouped into classes, thus forming the norms which are the basis of stylistic perception and expectation" (1956, 89–90). Quoting Kurt Koffka on Gestalt psychology, Meyer notes that "we possess within our store of traces [left in the memory by experience] many systems which, through a process of condensation and assimilation form the basis for 'class' perceptions, for the 'normal' and 'unusual'" (Koffka 1935, 476; Meyer 1956, 90). The "normal" minuet, then, is not just an abstraction generated by the Enlightenment's inclination to categorize all knowledge for practical reasons. It is also a construction of individual listeners, distilled from their experiences of certain musical realities. The existence of the minuet-generating *ars combinatoria* dice games both suggests and reinforces something of an agreement among musical amateurs, not just professional critics, theorists, and musicians, as to what a normal minuet was. As such, the abstraction of a normal minuet, one in which every stylistic and expressive feature would pass freely through the minuet filter, plays a vital role in a particular minuet's expressivity. It forms the topically consonant end of an expressive spectrum, the theoretical minuet norm required for a listener's perception of any topical troping or other expressive play.[26] The minuet of Haydn's Symphony in F Major, No. 67 (1775), for example, with its three even beats, unqualified "menuetto" tempo, regular phrase structure, appearances of the motto rhythm (in the second strain), and stately triadic melody, offers little or no topical challenge to such a minuet ideal (Example 4.1). Because it corresponds with the listener's constructed stylistic and expressive expectations of a normal minuet, its topical consonance suggests an uncontested nobility.

How a late-eighteenth-century listener heard the minuet's musical expression of nobility, however, depended largely on that listener's station within the social order of the time, along with, of course, his or her (unknowable) personal experiences, musical and otherwise. For instance, a member of the landed first nobility may have easily identified with the patrician character of the dance and interpreted a topically consonant minuet movement accordingly—as a public musical affirmation of his aristocratic status. Likewise, a wealthy upper-bourgeois citizen, or

Example 4.1.
Haydn, Symphony in F Major, No. 67, III, first strain of the minuet

even an aspirational member of the middle class who looked to the nobility as model and goal, may have heard the minuet's character as an expression of taste—something to be admired and acquired. Listeners disenfranchised by the status quo, on the other hand, may have easily heard a topically consonant minuet as a musical representation of the agent of their subordination. Not "their" music, minuets of uncontested noble character offered these listeners little opportunity for interpretations of identification or resistance. Meanings for minuet movements uncomplicated by other topics or affects, then, tacitly endorsed the stratified societies of late-eighteenth-century Europe. Their political forces were likely centripetal and socially homogenizing.

Moreover, for the listener of any social status, a topically consonant minuet would have likely encouraged a passive listening experience. Just as traditional Hollywood narrative cinema constructs the masculine subjectivity of Mulvey's film viewer, a minuet whose noble character remains unchallenged endorses and tacitly sustains the socially status—whether dominant or subordinate—of the late-eighteenth-century public concert-goer. Of course, following Fiske's argument, the listener may have experienced his interpretations as self-generated and therefore also as decidedly pleasurable. But as the meanings he constructed conformed to the dominant ideology, even the aristocratic listener would ultimately be denied the pleasure of power over his interpretive activities. The minuet's nobility simply corroborated his own, and his listening experience remained simply entertaining.

Tropological Meanings in Learned Minuets

Expressively enriched minuets, most frequently produced by topical troping, on the other hand, encourage a more active interpretive process. Topical troping occurs when two distinct topics meet, often unexpectedly, and through their interaction inspire the listener to hear new and distinct meanings.[27] When eighteenth-century listeners heard minuet movements in which certain stylistic features did not pass unchecked through the minuet filter, the imagination was excited to construct new meanings not just for those features but also for the dance that contains them. When the listener's control over meaning yields interpretations that serve her personal needs and interests, the listener experiences the pleasures of entertainment. (Whether that pleasure could be categorized as aesthetic pleasure depends, of course, on one's philosophical orientation: for Kant, absolutely not; for Pole, absolutely.)

Arguably the most expressively striking tropes in Classical minuet movements occur when the composer experiments with canons and other learned techniques. In light of the expectation that minuets, even stylized ones, should be constructed of balanced, symmetrical phrases and periods so as to be danceable,[28] a learned presentation—one not dependent on periodic phrase punctuation—obliges the listener to consider the combination of two dissonant expressive elements. In some minuets, the composer may even seem to invite the listener to hear the trope as an undercutting of the presumed sincerity of the dance's noble character.

The two canonic minuets in Haydn's symphonies, the dance movements of Symphony in G Major, No. 3 (by 1762), and Symphony in G Major, No. 23 (1764), for example, generate extended moments of topical troping as the minuet's requisite periodicity attempts to accommodate the strictest articulation of the learned style. In addition to the salient expressive conflict, there are several musical "incongruities of canonic procedure in a dance-related movement," as Gretchen Wheelock lists: "A linear and seamless continuity of overlapping imitation provides an unlikely medium for steps that rely upon clear metric and phrase patterns reinforced by regular melodic and harmonic articulations. Then too, the overall tonal structure of the minuet imposes formal constraints on canonic procedure: modulation, clear cadences, dominant preparation for tonic return—above all, the internal repetitions indigenous to the minuet scheme" (1992, 64). The accommodation of the minuet's formal requirements within the rigid contrapuntal demands of the canon presented Haydn an opportunity not only to display some clever musical craftsmanship (as we all know, Haydn loved a good compositional gimmick), but also to play with the potential meanings of the dance.

Haydn's listener could hardly miss the undisguised learned presentation in the minuet movement of Symphony No. 23 (Example 4.2). The minuet is a strict two-part canon at the octave at the distance of one measure; the trio a three-part canon, first at unison and then doubled at unison and the octave, at the distance of two measures. In addition to the octave interval and one-measure distance of imitation, arguably the most audible type of canon, several additional musical details in the minuet proper suggest Haydn's concern to ensure the listener's notice of the learned presentation: an opening gesture with duple subdivisions on beats 1 and 2 but not 3, rhythmically distinctive and quite unusual in a minuet; repeated two-measure gestures in each voice, forcing four one-measure statements of the same figure in a row (mm. 3–6); duple and triple rhythmic subdivisions that shift at distances of two or four measures, allowing the second voice to echo one rhythm before the first voice changes it; divergence from these two- or four-measure intervals only at the end of a strain, generating one beat of two against three in preparation for the cadence; and sparse scoring and crucial rests—particularly in the opening measures of each strain—in the horns, the only free voices in the movement. In the trio Haydn likewise draws attention to the canonic procedure, although listeners would hardly need encouragement, having been alerted to expect a learned presentation by the preceding minuet. For example, there are similar two-measure repetitions, shifts back and forth between duple and triple rhythmic subdivisions, and occasional beats of two against three. To be sure, the reiterations that draw attention to the canon also generate the minuet's two-measure phrase structures and anchor the dance's formal and harmonic design; changes in rhythmic subdivision heighten momentum toward the cadence at the end of each strain, thereby intensifying the sense of arrival;[29] and the anticipatory turns in the upper voice of measures 7 and 22 are not repeated in the lower voice, rendering the top voice just slightly superior. (Of course, one might also argue that trills in the lower voice are implied by the imitation.) But, despite the successful accommodation of both the canon's and the

Example 4.2.
Haydn, Symphony in G Major, No. 23, III, minuet

minuet's structural and harmonic requirements, the sustained salience of the learned style charges this minuet with topical dissonance. Haydn demands the listener's participation to construct expressive meanings for this extended trope.

By hearing this dance movement intertextually within the context of eighteenth-century music, the listener may interpret the turn to the learned style as an attempt to raise the dignity level of the minuet, for, as Scheibe tells us, polyphony is a hallmark of high style. But should she acknowledge that the noble minuet's status is already high, the infusion of learned elements may more readily shift the minuet's expressive content on a different stylistic axis, so to speak. By moving the dance from the free style to the strict style, its courtly associations may be substituted for ecclesiastical ones, suggesting a move from the general expressive category of the comic (or "nontragic," as Hatten suggests this broad expressive category is more appropriately named)[30] to the more specific category of the exalted. As such, it becomes a highly marked value,[31] an expressive situation that may encourage further interpretive activity in the listener. Should she hear this minuet's new exalted status as questioned by the long-standing conflict between dance music and sacred music, the steadfast audibility of the canon questions the dance, while its situation within a dance questions the canon. In other words, the trope may affectively jeopardize the integrity of both galant and learned elements. The exalted status of the noble minuet becomes only illusory in this case, and the listener may interpret the movement, for the moment anyway, as an instance of musical parody.[32]

When the listener remains in control of this minuet's expressive meaning, she may choose, whether consciously or not, to stop at any point along this interpretive path (or perhaps even chart a course entirely different from the one we have considered here). Determining the meanings that result from such interpretation, of course, is her subjectivity as listener. Those listeners who experience pleasure in the heightening of (or the attempt to heighten) the status of the aristocratic dance may find their own high status reaffirmed; those who experience pleasure noting the fundamental incompatibility between the secular and the "sacred" styles may find their religious convictions and practices either challenged or upheld, depending on whether the expressive meaning constructed for the trope stops at mere inappropriateness or progresses to parody. Musical parody itself may then be interpreted socially as well as religiously, suggesting the interpretive pleasures that result from adhering to or evading the dominant political ideology implied by the dance's aristocratic status. And so on . . .

That the listener's political or national identity, for example, would have been an important decisive factor in interpreting expressive tropes of the kind found in the minuet of Haydn's Symphony No. 23 is revealed in the implicit threats the North Germans in particular heard in certain stylistic mixtures. First, many North German critics heard the mere inclusion of the minuet in the context of a symphony as a breach of decorum, a musical and aesthetic opinion that likely found its roots in the North German national identity. As Wheelock suggests, "traditional associations of the minuet with the courtly manners of the *ancien régime* may have sat uneasily with the social and moral values of German burghers, as well as with the emergent nationalism in [Johann Adam] Hiller's day. . . . [I]n the context of a lofty (and 'manly') symphony, the minuet [may have] called up images of artificial and effete manners at the French court" (1992, 45). To demonstrate the depth of these critics' disdain, Wheelock offers up such delightful quotes as this one from one of Hiller's reviewers: minuets give symphonies "a foppish appearance and interfere with the manly impression that an unbroken succession of three related and more serious movements always makes" (Hiller [1766–70] 1970, 1:243; quoted and trans. in Wheelock 1992, 45). The simultaneous presentation of the solemnity of the learned style and a certain Austrian triviality heard in the minuet would have been even more offensive. In 1768 Hiller himself complained that "Minuets and trios placed between larger movements give to the whole an air of gaiety, which is better suited to symphonies than if a man wants to display his art inopportunely with retrograde canons and other harmonic artifices" (3:107; quoted and trans. in Wheelock, 43). For Hiller, as Wheelock notes, "the inclusion of a minuet movement in the symphony appears to offend . . . less than the use in such movements of learned techniques appropriate to the serious style" (43). Some critics sustained such protestations even through the end of the century. Johann Gottlieb Karl Spazier, for example, contended in 1792 that minuets "simply recall at the wrong time the realm of dance, and thus misuse music; and if they are caricatured, as is often the case with those by Pleyel and Haydn, they provoke laughter. If this latter be the case, there can no longer be any question of whether minuets are appropriate in lofty symphonies" (Reichardt 1792, 91–92; quoted and trans. in Wheelock, 45). The expressive troping clearly caused the greatest offense.

While the canonic procedure seems especially salient in Haydn's Symphony No. 23, in the minuet of Symphony No. 3 the counterpoint is deftly disguised by the end of the second strain,[33] suggesting different and perhaps even richer interpretive possibilities (Example 4.3). Not only does the first strain's entire length of ten measures provide for the *pas de menuet's* required two-measure units, but it would also allow an eight-measure canon (the length of the archetypal minuet strain) at the distance of one measure to run its full course. But Haydn does not leave the canonic procedure so exposed. Although the canon's melody in the first strain divides neatly into two phrases, the first four measures long and the second six, its phrase structure is in fact even closer to that of the dance: two parallel four-measure phrases, with a two-measure extension in the *middle* of the second phrase. In the reprise at the end of the second strain, however, the phrase structure of the melody has magically become the 4+4 archetype. The device that allows Haydn to pull off this sleight of hand is the voice exchange set up by the identical rhythms and pitches in the third and fifth measures of the canon. Because the melody repeats itself two measures later, the upper voice's melodic content of measure 3 is actually heard four times in a row when the melody is combined with itself at the distance of one measure. Thus it follows quite smoothly when Haydn slips in an extra repetition of this measure at the end of the second strain, forcing the voice exchange that in effect cuts out a measure. One more measure needs to be cut to create a 4+4 phrase structure, and Haydn eliminates it by starting the canon with the lower voice at the return of the A section. When the lower voice enters with the $\hat{5}$ to $\hat{1}$ descent, we now hear this line not as melody but as retransition. It sets

Example 4.3.
Haydn, Symphony in G Major, No. 3, III, minuet

up an authentic cadence, providing both a root-position tonic chord for the upper voice's entrance and a satisfying sense of arrival for the first time in the movement. Although Haydn uses striking musical elements (for example, trills and much repetition) that might call attention to the canonic procedure, by the end of the minuet we cannot hear the two voices as equals. The lower voice clearly functions as support for the upper voice during the reprise (mm. 20–28), creating a deceptively homophonic-sounding texture. While the canonic procedure nearly eclipses the dance in the first strain, the dance subsumes the canon in the reprise.

In addition to returning to a homophonic texture and archetypal minuet phrase structure at the end of this minuet, Haydn includes several of the dance's characteristic rhythmic gestures. For example, the minuet's three even beats are established in the second measure by the accented, straight quarter notes (which, of course, are then repeated by the lower voice in the next measure). In the parallel measure of the second strain, the same rhythm appears, but this time on the same pitch for all three notes, inhibiting a light execution of the dance. Haydn also uses the minuet's motto rhythm in the third and fifth measures of the melody of the second strain, setting up the four successive statements of that gesture (mm. 13–16). In fact, every measure of the second strain contains either three accented quarter notes or the motto rhythm, if not the two in combination. Finally, along with providing harmonic support in the background, the horns (again, the only free voices) articulate a drum tattoo rhythm in the fourth measure of the reprise of the A section (m. 24), evoking a military style and affirming the minuet's noble character. (We might also hear the movement's many dotted rhythms as military tags, but because they are so prevalent in the galant style of the early Classical period, we must be careful not to exaggerate their expressive significance.)

The remarkable degree to which Haydn accommodates the formal requirements of the minuet dance type within the rigid contrapuntal demands of the canon suggests a different possible ending for an interpretive course similar to the one charted in the minuet of Symphony No. 23. Regardless of the successful accommodation of the structural requirements of both the canon and the dance, once alerted to the canon's presence by the salient learned presentation the listener can hardly ignore it, even when the imitation is expertly disguised in the reprise. The learned style, no matter how cleverly integrated, cannot easily or comfortably masquerade as a dance movement in the Classical style. But, of course, it is unlikely that this movement would have been heard by its eighteenth-century listeners as an act of musical deception. Because Haydn's musical argument in the end softens the trope's conspicuous topical dissonance, the potential for parody is lessened.

The following conversational trio, lacking even a hint of the learned style, may seem for the moment to reinforce the minuet's underlying courtly character and usual dignified expression. But the movement ends, of course, with the minuet da capo—the audible canon and its subsequent compromise. For listeners who hear the second strain temper any parody suggested by the first strain, the dance's return to galant phrase structure and a "homophonic" texture may sound a conciliation. The movement's end may therefore suggest tolerance—if not wholehearted acceptance—of expressive difference. While it is, perhaps, too early in the century (as well as Haydn's career) to argue persuasively for a full-fledged musical statement of enlightened values, this movement would certainly allow, if not outright encourage, such an interpretation.[34] But any meaning of this kind would, of course, depend on the listener's political leanings, moral education, and familiarity with recent trends in philosophical thought.

To be sure, the possible meanings offered for these two minuet movements require somewhat sophisticated processes of interpretation and therefore rest on the presumption of attentive, knowledgeable, and reflective listeners. That these works may have enjoyed such listeners rests, in turn, on the circumstances of their composition and the makeup of their original audiences. Composed in the early 1760s for courtly audiences, these two symphonies can hardly be considered "public" music. No. 23 is an early Esterházy symphony, and No. 3, though the reason for its composition and first performances are unknown, is unlikely to have been written for any purpose other than a courtly performance. Stylistically they have much more in common with Haydn's chamber works of the time than do his later "public" symphonies. Canonic experimentation in minuets, for example, to choose the stylistic feature most relevant to the present discussion, is not at all unusual in mid-century chamber music; in orchestral works, however, it is a rarity.[35] Intended, then, for the private use of a noble patron, these symphonies are not aimed at the diversity of listeners Haydn would find for his later symphonies. Not surprisingly, perhaps, once his audience became a cross section of the middle and high orders of the European public, he abandoned learned techniques in his minuet movements for a more direct expressive course, one that extended the individual listener an easier invitation to construct the meanings—many of them social if not explicitly political—that would best suit him.

But Mozart, however, employs a salient learned presentation in a symphonic minuet movement as late as 1788, in the "Great G Minor" Symphony K. 550. Though we do not know why Mozart composed this symphony (or its two companions, Symphony in E-flat K. 543, and the "Jupiter," K. 551)—they were not commissioned, no explanation appears in his correspondence, they were not published during his lifetime, and no documentation survives to determine where, when, or even if these works were performed before his death[36]—it is highly unlikely that he had anything in mind other than public performances on subscription concert series in Vienna or perhaps London, a trip that never materialized.[37] Despite the lack of historical information, Mozart's intended listeners were almost certainly the concert-going European public. What, then, might conspicuous learned techniques mean in a "public" symphonic movement that, despite its artful presentation, was expected by critics, theorists, and listeners alike to echo at least somewhat faithfully the ballroom dance?

The metric complexity with which the Menuetto (Example 4.4) begins puts the listener on immediate alert: this will be no ballroom minuet. The hemiola in (what sounds like) the melody, played by the violins and doubled at the octave by the flutes, accomplishes several compositional goals in the space of the movement's two opening measures. First, it prevents a normal articulation of the *pas de menuet*'s archetypal two-measure phrase structure, as the first "bar" is effectively in $\frac{3}{2}$, not $\frac{3}{4}$.

Example 4.4.
Mozart, Symphony in G Minor K. 550, III, minuet
Continued on the next page

The result is a limping two-measure minuet step, an effect heightened by the minuet motto rhythm's repeated attempts to assert a pattern of metric normalcy at the end of each hemiola "bar." Meanwhile, the "accompanying" parts (but the lines are actually contrapuntal) articulate the minuet's regular $\frac{3}{4}$ meter, conforming in three-measure phrases to the structural demands of the hemiola. The phrase structure is consequently loaded with rhythmic and metric tension, as both domi-

Example 4.4.
Mozart, Symphony in G Minor K. 550, III, minuet

nant and subordinate lines can claim accordance with the rhythmic and metric demands of the dance while in fact disrupting its regular patterns: the "melody" presents the archetypal two-measure phrase structure, but the metric weight of its measures is unequal—$\begin{smallmatrix}3\\2\end{smallmatrix}\begin{smallmatrix}3\\4\end{smallmatrix}+\begin{smallmatrix}3\\2\end{smallmatrix}\begin{smallmatrix}3\\4\end{smallmatrix}$; the "accompaniment" keeps a steady pulse in $\frac{3}{4}$ but groups into three-measure phrases. Though measuring an archetypal eight measures in length, the second half of the first strain (mm. 7–14) maintains its distinctively un-minuet-like phrase structure. The hemiola that opens its antecedent phrase does not return for the consequent phrase, as the repetitions of the motto rhythm (mm. 8–10) force the music to remain in $\frac{3}{4}$. But the damage to the dance's phrase structure has been done, yielding an eight-bar period that suggests at least two possible phrase rhythms: $\begin{smallmatrix}3\\2\end{smallmatrix}\begin{smallmatrix}3\\4\end{smallmatrix}+\begin{smallmatrix}3\\4\end{smallmatrix}+\begin{smallmatrix}3\\4\end{smallmatrix}\begin{smallmatrix}3\\4\end{smallmatrix}\begin{smallmatrix}3\\4\end{smallmatrix}$ or $\begin{smallmatrix}3\\2\end{smallmatrix}+\begin{smallmatrix}3\\2\end{smallmatrix}\begin{smallmatrix}3\\4\end{smallmatrix}+\begin{smallmatrix}3\\4\end{smallmatrix}\begin{smallmatrix}3\\4\end{smallmatrix}\begin{smallmatrix}3\\4\end{smallmatrix}$. Mozart has thereby denied any easy imagining of the *pas de menuet*, the dance's emblem of grace.

Second, the metric tension generated by the hemiola forces a 6–5 suspension in the dance's second measure (as barred in $\frac{3}{4}$), lending sudden salience to the movement's learned presentation. No longer can we hear the accompanying parts—especially the bassoon, viola, and cello/bass lines—as harmonic support, for their move to the dominant pitch on what is effectively the second half of the melody's second beat (in m. 2) asserts their rhythmic if not melodic independence. As the previously "supporting" parts (oboe, viola, cello, and bass, plus flute; and also clarinet in Mozart's rescoring) lead with the melody in the second strain (at m. 15), their independent status is confirmed. The dramatic appoggiaturas in the violins (in mm. 16, 19, 22), arguably the feature to which the listener's ear is most drawn, accentuate the movement's contrapuntal construction.

But Mozart leaves for the return the strictest application of the learned style—a canon at the fourth at the distance of one $\frac{3}{4}$ measure (at m. 28). As if the minuet's phrase structure were not already challenged and obscured by metric complexity, the canon flirts with total metric meltdown. As we observed above in the two Haydn examples, in a dance movement canonic procedures present the composer real structural challenges. Whereas Haydn normalizes the listener's impression of phrase lengths through voice exchanges and other clever compositional tricks, Mozart's exaggerations effectively bar the listener from entertaining any illusions of minuet normalcy. Though the second canonic voice now measures the minuet's archetypal eight-bar period, Mozart employs no clever device to shorten the first voice to prevent the canon from requiring nine measures to run its course. Then, while his immediate following of the first $\frac{3}{2}$ hemiola measure by another $\frac{3}{2}$ measure (rather than by a measure of $\frac{3}{4}$, as in the first strain) may suggest a four-bar phrase in $\frac{3}{2}$, a seemingly "normal" minuet phrase structure, the switch back to $\frac{3}{4}$ after the third measure of $\frac{3}{2}$ (in m. 33), combined with the rhythmic conflict generated by both the second canonic voice and the viola and cello/bass lines, prevents the audibility of even a hint of such a regular structure. In the canon's meter of $\frac{3}{2}$, the second voice enters not at the distance of a measure (as, barred in $\frac{3}{4}$, it would appear) but at the half measure—that is, one-and-a-half beats. The viola and cello/bass lines, meanwhile, remain solidly in $\frac{3}{4}$. After such metric upheaval, the codetta (mm. 37–42) sounds an apology. As if to compensate for the chaos of the preceding period, Mozart offers the listener six bars in which neither phrase structure nor texture is challenged. The melody, though still marked by hemiola, remains the dominant line and presents unequivocally two symmetrical and balanced phrases, heard as either 3+3 in $\frac{3}{4}$ or 2+2 in the "limping" $\frac{3}{2} + \frac{3}{4}$.

While the meanings generated by the expressive troping in Haydn's earlier canonic minuets are dependent on a certain compatibility—or at least the momentary appearance of compatibility—of expressively opposed topics, Mozart's trope presents an unyielding expressive collision. Before considering how Mozart's listeners may have heard and interpreted this collision, the extraordinary tension generated by the rise in metric and textural complexity and resulting increase in expressive dissonance begs at least brief consideration of the composer's intended meaning, no matter how unknowable that might ultimately be. The two topics brought together in the dance movement of the "Great G Minor" Symphony have, by this point, specific and long-established associations. As discussed above, the minuet topic is a direct reference to the social dance, an aristocratic entity understood during Mozart's lifetime as a symbol of the *ancien régime*. The learned style, particularly the strict imitative procedures of canon and fugue, refer to sacred music, especially its more archaic styles. Both topics, then, summon evocations of an established authority—the Austrian Empire and the Catholic Church, respectively.

Despite nearly two centuries of attempts to render Mozart an apolitical being—from the earliest biographies to Milos Forman's film *Amadeus*—evidence culled from Mozart's music, letters, and personal loyalties suggests at least some subversive tendencies if not outright revolutionary affinity.[38] The social and political content and commentary in Le nozze di Figaro are, of course, undeniable. Not only did Mozart himself choose for his opera Beaumarchais's banned revolutionary play[39] but, as Allanbrook has brilliantly demonstrated, Mozart's music restores much of the play's subversive content omitted from the opera to get the libretto approved by the imperial censors. The subversive attacks on both Austrian nationalism and Catholicism in Die Zauberflöte suggest Mozart's commitment to the enlightened ideals espoused by the Freemasons.[40] Moreover, Mozart's commitment to Freemasonry, the subject of debate for decades, "extended far beyond commonplace economic and recreational motivations." As Maynard Solomon argues, Freemasonry "surely exercised a powerful ideological pull upon Mozart that stemmed from its humanitarian and enlightened aspirations, its ideals of equality, liberty, tolerance, and fraternity, and its vision of salvation through love and reason" (1995, 330–31). Further, several comments in his correspondence—for example, his admiration of the freedom of the English (Anderson 1966, 2:828); his low regard for the "stupid Tyrolese custom . . . that no one may hit a nobleman, no matter what right he may have to do so" (2:757);[41] and his near-verbatim echoing of Figaro's lines in Beaumarchais's Le Mariage de Figaro[42]—reveal a man not just interested in contemporary politics but one with a subversive and perhaps even revolutionary agenda.

The clashing combination of musical symbols of the two greatest political authorities of his time suggests that Mozart may have had in mind a politically subversive meaning for the dance movement of the "Great G Minor" Symphony. Despite its situation within a minor-mode symphony, a minor-mode minuet is expressively marked before any other topical elements enter the field. Not only is every surviving dance minuet proper by Haydn and Mozart, with one exception (Haydn, Hob. IX:16, No. 18), in the major mode, but those minuets in the few minor-mode "public" symphonies of the late eighteenth century are almost always presented in the tonic major, as in, for example, Haydn's Symphony in G Minor, No. 83, composed only three years before Mozart's G-minor symphony.[43] Set in the minor mode, then, the expressive troping of the minuet's courtly high style and the ecclesiastical learned style yields not the exalted expression we observed in Haydn's canonic minuets but rather the more specific and highly marked expressive world of Passion, the musical evocation of personal suffering encountered most frequently in religious drama. While it may be more comfortable for the interpretive path to end here, as I would argue it should in Haydn's minor-mode symphonic minuets of his so-called Sturm und Drang period,[44] the escalation of the movement's topical tension to outright expressive dissonance in the metric contortions of the canonic return threatens to undermine the sincerity of both courtly and ecclesiastical domains, thereby effectively challenging their authority. While blatant satirical intentions may be too much to claim here, Mozart's flirtation with parody may explain the somewhat sheepish codetta.

What Mozart may (or may not) have intended and what his listeners likely heard, however, are two very different things. By this point in Mozart's compositional career, his reputation as a "difficult" composer was beginning to precede him.

Gerber, for one, notes in 1790 that "an unpracticed ear finds it difficult to follow his works. Even more experienced ones," he continues, "have to hear his things several times" ([1790–92] 1966–69, 1:383; quoted and trans. in Solomon 1995, 425). If Mozart's tendency to write "too many notes," as Joseph II famously quipped, challenged even the most dedicated and experienced connoisseurs, how might the mere *Liebhaber* and lay listeners in his public audiences have heard the demanding minuet of the "Great G Minor" Symphony? Certainly most listeners would have noticed the hemiola that disrupts the minuet topic's three even beats in nearly every phrase of the minuet proper. And the learned presentation, too, particularly in the return, would likely have been easily perceptible to many if not most listeners among the concert-going public. But what of their interaction and the resultant expressive troping? On their first and likely only hearing of this work, it is probable that most of Mozart's listeners would simply be unable to hear past the movement's difficulty. Indeed, the learned style in the context of this minuet may actually present itself as a "topic of difficulty," Sisman's term for a "category of 'rhetorical' topics whose effect depends on the effort of understanding them" (1997, 53). It is even less likely that in the real time of a first hearing many of Mozart's listeners would have been able to discern and interpret the musical devices driving the escalating expressive conflict. If the musical surface, then, throws up such an impenetrable veneer, the irony here is that the authoritative stances of both court and church are ultimately sustained. Their rights to authority remain unchecked, as the listener relinquishes his interpretive power—his control over musical meaning. This surrender may explain the real *dis*pleasure so many of Mozart's contemporary critics felt when confronted with his work, as its meaning ironically became the listener's *inability* to construct meaning.

Tropological Meanings in "Common" Minuets

In Haydn's later music, a learned presentation seems not to have challenged listeners to the same degree, if at all. In fact, writing in 1790 Gerber even connects Haydn's broad accessibility to his ability to render contrapuntal passages "pleasing": "Every harmonic artifice is at his command, even those from the Gothic age of the grey contrapuntists. But instead of their former stiffness, they assume a pleasing manner as soon as he prepares them for our ears. He has a great gift for making a piece sound familiar. In this way, despite all the contrapuntal artifices therein, he achieves a popular style and is agreeable to every amateur" ([1790–92] 1966–69, 1:610; quoted and trans. in Kirkendale 1979, 150). The attitude of the German critics has certainly shifted from the earlier disapproving stance against such compositional cleverness. But the contrapuntal passages in Haydn's symphonies to which Gerber refers must be primarily those encountered in the development sections of Haydn's first movements and finales, for the expressive troping in the dance movements of Haydn's later public music is of a sort entirely different from that generated by learned techniques in his earlier courtly symphonies.

In the minuet movements of his later symphonies, particularly the "London" symphonies, Haydn experiments with popular dance topics, folk influences, and humor, rarely leaving the minuet topic unchecked. But unlike the expressive troping in Mozart's "Great G Minor" minuet, the easy accessibility of Haydn's added expressive elements invite even the most casual and inexperienced listener on an interpretive journey. The composer may serve as guide, but the listener may safely and comfortably embark on her own, for the expressive terrain and structural landmarks are entirely familiar. In fact, as we shall see, Haydn's stylistic deviations from the now staid minuet norm proactively empower his listeners to construct meanings that serve their own personal, social, and political interests in the real time of a first hearing.[45]

Haydn's use of popular and folk-dance topics in the minuet movement was a decided turn from away from the noble dance's long-established high stylistic status. As Scheibe indicates in his lengthy description of the low style, rustic elements, and indeed most dances, are in the lowest stylistic register.[46] Haydn's occasional humorous turns likewise undercut the minuet's lofty status, as Gerber's emphasis on the accessible and comedic aspects of the low style indicate. Writing in the *Allgemeine musikalische Zeitung* in 1799, Gerber specifically includes in the low stylistic category "that which is more popular and widespread than noble, more merry and trifling than clever, and on the whole everything pertaining to comedy and caricature" (1799, col. 296).[47] Unlike the layered expressive experimentation in the canonic minuets, in which the listener might hear the learned style either replacing the courtly and high comic with the ecclesiastical and tragic, or pretending to heighten the dignity of the dance but instead, through a fundamental incompatibility of expression, in fact lowering it, Haydn's engagement with the low style in the "London" minuets is direct. Late-eighteenth-century listeners, from the most knowledgeable of connoisseurs to the least experienced of lay listeners, would have immediately recognized the popular *Deutscher Tanz* as the defining topic of most of Haydn's minuet movements. How they interpreted the expressive troping of courtly minuet and common *Deutsche,* however, likely varied considerably from listener to listener according to his or her individual and subjective needs, desires, and aesthetic values. The celebrated pleasure the listeners in Haydn's public audiences experienced in his music bespeaks their ultimate control over its meaning.

By 1780 most of the minuets in Haydn's symphonies are expressively enriched by rustic and popular dance topics, if not completely subsumed by the *Deutscher Tanz* itself. As if to ensure proper performance and communication of affect, Haydn consistently indicates a tempo of Allegretto or faster for movements with a rustic or popular expression and leaves the title "Minuet" unqualified, or occasionally even indicates a slower tempo, for those few movements that remain true to the aristocratic dance. The contrast between the two emergent expressive types is easily observed in the minuet movements of the "Paris" symphonies. The minuet of Symphony in C Major, No. 82, "*L'Ours*" (1786), for example, marked simply "Menuet," retains the minuet topic's three even beats, straight quarter-note gestures, and motto rhythm, which, played by the horns, trumpets, and timpani, easily punches through the orchestral texture (Example 4.5a). It begins squarely on beat 1 (as does the other "Paris" minuet lacking a tempo indication other than the title "Menuet") and makes no attempt toward humor or surprise. In contrast, the minuet of Sym-

Example 4.5.
a. Haydn, Symphony in C Major, No. 82, "*L'Ours*," III, first strain of the minuet
b. Haydn, Symphony in G Minor, No. 83, "*La Poule*," III, first strain of the minuet

phony in G Minor, No. 83, "*La Poule*" (1785), marked Allegretto, begins with an upbeat (as do all of the "Paris" minuets marked Allegretto), and in the second measure, the slurred eighth-note gestures on beats 1 and 3 throw the triple meter slightly off balance (Example 4.5b). Hints of a waltzlike accompaniment throughout the movement, especially when played at Haydn's specifically indicated Allegretto tempo, suggest the metric pattern of the *Deutscher Tanz*, while the wide leaps and many passages of continuous eighth-note activity infuse the melody with countrified spirit. For added insurance against too noble a deportment, several sudden changes in dynamic level compromise the minuet's usual dignity.

The two expressive types become even more sharply defined in the "London" symphonic minuet movements. One need look only to the opening measures of the Allegro molto of Symphony in G Major, No. 94, "Surprise" (1791), and the Moderato of Symphony in G Major, No. 100, "Military" (1793–94), to hear their respective characteristic metric patterns. The *Deutsche's* oom-pah-pah accompaniment places

Example 4.6.
a. Haydn, Symphony in G Major, No. 94, "Surprise," III, opening of the first strain of the minuet
b. Haydn, Symphony in G Major, No. 100, "Military," III, first strain of the minuet

the pulse of the minuet in No. 94 at the measure (Example 4.6a) while the emphatic two-beat quarter-note gestures place the pulse of No. 100 squarely on the beat (Example 4.6b). Almost all of the "London" minuet movements are boisterous *Deutsche Tänze,* and the rare movement that clings to a minuet topic now sounds reserved and conspicuously tame by comparison. As Haydn's audience came to anticipate a rowdy or rustic affect in place of the dignified and noble minuet, the courtly expression became the marked entity.

In the *Deutscher Tanz* movements, the expressive content may seem to shift directly from the courtly high style to the popular low style. But as most listeners of the time would have maintained for the minuet a fixed generic identity, firmly established by their familiarity with the conventions of the ballroom dance and the concert symphony, the expressive course from high to low is not necessarily as uncomplicated as it would seem. Heard through a minuet filter, kept in place by both composer label and audience expectation, such dance movements may sound twice bracketed: an "aristocrat" masquerading as a "commoner" masquerading as an "aristocrat." While this expressive path suggests that a minuet's assumed popular style is a pretense, the underlying challenge to its sincerity prevents it from retaining its courtly status.

The minuet movement that preserves a courtly style, however, may be expressively no less complicated. Thrown into relief by a listener's anticipations of a *Deutsche,* the dance movement whose expressive content remains true to its original topic can appear all the more conservative, restrained, even pompous. Its air of refinement and noble character may now sound exaggerated and forced, suggesting that the dance, like the *ancien régime* itself, is in jeopardy of collapsing under the weight of its own presumed importance. Its courtly status questioned by the seeming omnipresence of the masquerading "aristocrat," the dance's discernible strain in keeping up appearances reveals its underlying vulnerability. In retaining its courtly status, the minuet has sacrificed its expressive hallmark: its *noble simplicité*.

In playing with this moment of crisis in the minuet's social identity, Haydn created symphonic movements certain to accomplish his repeatedly articulated goal for the "London" compositions: to please his public audience, an audience that contained a striking diversity of listeners.[48] By exploring divergent avenues of expressive troping and topical enrichment, the "London" minuet movements invite the listener not just to hear in them expressions of various social and political situations but to experience the distinct pleasure of choosing the expressive path that best accommodates the needs, desires, and values of his own social status and political identity.

In the dance movement of his Symphony in E-flat Major, No. 99 (1793), for example, Haydn sits on the fence between the two expressive types delineated above, a masquerading *Deutscher Tanz* and a self-conscious minuet, challenging the listener not to take the expressive content of the movement at face value. Indeed, the expressive troping of this minuet offers the listener a ready invitation to chart his own interpretive course. The Allegretto marking suggests the faster tempo of the rustic dances, but the dominant gestures of the opening period—descending arpeggiated antecedents followed by stepwise consequent answers—articulate only the three even quarter-note beats of the minuet topic (mm. 1–8; Example 4.7). Where one listener may hear an unusually energized courtly minuet, another may hear a socially ambitious *Deutsche*. But the hesitancy in this opening period, communicated by the *piano* dynamic of each antecedent phrase, encourages the listener not to commit to any one expressive meaning too soon. In each consequent phrase, the patrician constituency may find reassurance in the *forte* dynamic and the addition of winds, brass, and timpani to the instrumentation, the tutti effect reinforcing the minuet's aristocratic style and lofty status. But for those partial to the *Deutsche,* the timidity imparted by the opening "solo" instrumentation may undermine the minuet's confidence nevertheless, just as its identity is being established.

Following an extension and development of the minuet's arpeggiated figures (mm. 9–17), a boisterous *Deutscher Tanz* emerges (at m. 18) to conclude the first strain just at the point the minuet seems to gain traction. Its identity entirely secure, affirmed by sforzandos on the downbeats, an oom-pah-pah accompaniment, and continuous rhythmic activity in the melody, the *Deutsche* overtakes for the moment the minuet's expressive momentum. After the repeat of the noble minuet's abdication to the more common dance, the developmental second strain brings back the opening topic (at m. 27), but it is transformed into an unsettled, ascending outline of a dominant-ninth chord (or an enharmonic vii$_7^0$ of ♭VI in V), its identity and status undermined by the poaching *Deutsche*. A sequence of deceptive cadences, anchored by a chromatically ascending bass line, follows, and the minuet finally lands, *forte,* in an agitated G minor (at m. 37). A sleight-of-hand pivot chord (m. 44) brings the dance nearly unawares back to the tonic for the reprise of the first strain, ending abruptly the movement's expressive tug of war between the courtly high and low styles.

Example 4.7.
Haydn, Symphony in E-flat Major, No. 99, III, minuet
Continued on the next page

Example 4.7.
Haydn, Symphony in E-flat Major, No. 99, III, minuet
Continued on the next page

Example 4.7.
Haydn, Symphony in E-flat Major, No. 99, III, minuet

The minuet's descending arpeggiated figure returns intact (at m. 45), now tutti, *forte*, and thoroughly confident. Victorious over its own insecurity, as well as perhaps the *Deutscher Tanz's* implicit challenge, the courtly dance celebrates with hemiola (mm. 52–56) to end the first period. Moreover, where the bold and boisterous *Deutsche* took over in the first strain, in its place now stands the most graceful phrase in the movement (mm. 57–62)—a nod, perhaps, to the dance's ideal decorum. The minuet proper closes with the most assertive minuet figure yet, the transformation of the hesitant opening phrase into a triumphant fanfare (mm. 62–68).

The meanings Haydn's listeners would have constructed while hearing this dance movement depend, of course, on each individual listener's social situation, political orientation, cultural preferences, personal experiences, and myriad other and unknowable circumstances. But considering only one facet of a listener's subjectivity, his fairly easily identifiable social status, we may at least theorize several interpretive possibilities. A nobleman who identifies with the social status of the aristocratic minuet but whose wealth and prominence are waning may hear the plebeian *Deutscher Tanz* as socially threatening, while a commoner who favors political reform may find it affirming and potentially liberating. A more aspirational member of the middling orders, on the other hand, may identify musically with the *Deutsche* but find the minuet's sophistication and taste something to be acquired for upward social mobility, thereby complicating his expressive alliances. The listener's pleasure here resides primarily in his ability to identify with one of the two broad expressive stances and to interpret Haydn's musical argument according to the needs and desires of his own personal situation.

Political forces, then, both centripetal and centrifugal, are put in play when the listener adopts—consciously or not—either an enlightened, bourgeois perspective or a patrician, conservative one. As the *Deutsche* that closes the opening strain is conspicuously absent at the end of the second strain, its common expression wholly displaced by the triumphant fanfare, the minuet proper of Haydn's Symphony No. 99 may be heard to empower courtly authority by silencing the common voice. If such a silencing, in turn, inspires political activity, the result may be just the opposite—an empowering of the common voice. But then, should such subversive energy be spent in entertainment rather than civic venues, Haydn's minuet again silences by becoming carnivalesque—reinforcing the status quo by entertaining its overturning. The pleasure Haydn's listener experienced while listening to his music resided within her individual sense of control over her interpretive activity, whatever the ultimate effect—political, social, or otherwise—of her constructed meanings.

5   Pleasure and Meaning in Haydn's Symphony in D Major, No. 93

Haydn's ostensible turn toward accessibility around 1790, particularly in the compositions for large forces and public performance, is one of the most well-trodden paths in Haydn scholarship. Even in his own time contemporary critics and commentators, along with Haydn himself, noted this cultivation of a popular style, suggesting that it was a direct result of the composer's desire to secure the approval of his increasingly public audience. Diarist and English Haydn enthusiast Charlotte Papendiek, a sometimes unreliable source, provides the most widely quoted evidence for the motivations behind Haydn's stylistic adjustment. She writes:

> Haydn, immediately on his arrival, told Salomon that he should stay the summer in England, and that as he heard there were to be twelve concerts and two benefits during the season there would be ample time for him to compose his first symphonies after he had had an opportunity of studying the taste of the English. He was determined that his first production should both amuse and please the musical public and rivet him in their favour. (1887, 290)

There is no reason to doubt Mrs. Papendiek's report, for Haydn himself acknowledges his rapport with his listening public. In a letter to Mme Genzinger written ten months after his arrival in London, Haydn notes that "[his] credit with the common people has been firmly established for a long time" (Haydn 1959, 120).

While the need for such public approval was undoubtedly motivated by practical, personal, and artistic reasons, underlying all of them are the dramatically shifting political and social forces of Haydn's time. As Charles Rosen notes, Haydn's "movement towards a 'popular' style must certainly be related to the republican enthusiasm of the latter part of the eighteenth century" (1997, 330). And yet within Haydn's celebrated accessibility is almost always an inner sophistication, something to appeal to the connoisseur as well as the lay listener. This "artful popularity or popular (intelligible, penetrating) artfulness," as Johann Karl Friedrich Triest described Haydn's style in 1801 (*AMZ*, 11 March 1801, col. 407; quoted and trans. in Gotwals 1963, 199), or "pretension . . . to simplicity," as Rosen echoes (1997, 163), reflects not just the diversity of Haydn's public audience but its confluence of social aspirations and political persuasions.[1] Many members of the middle classes may have been committed to enlightened and even republican ideals, but the significant aristocratic contingent of the late-eighteenth-century public complicates political hearings of Haydn's public music. While many nobles may have likewise embraced republican ideals, a democratic reality would threaten both the social status and economic stability of the aristocracy. Also complicating political hearings of Haydn's music are the undeniably noble aspirations of many middle-class citizens, especially those socially ambitious members of the professional classes who looked to the aristocracy for models of decorum and taste. Haydn's ability to amuse and please not just *Kenner* and *Liebhaber* but commoner and king alike rests on the distinct pleasure his music affords its listeners. The sophistication of its accessibility empowers the listener to construct meanings aligned with the needs of his own social, political, and personal situation.

To explore how the pleasure of Haydn's public style rests on the individual listener's control over musical meaning, in this chapter we shall "hear" Haydn's Symphony in D Major, No. 93, as its original English audiences might have heard it. This symphony, composed at least six months after his arrival in London, was the first Haydn composed having had the opportunity to study English audiences. Unlike the fanciful exercise of chapter 3, we shall not invent listeners or imagine the largely personal meanings such individuals could have constructed while listening to Haydn's music. Rather, we shall limit our analytical engagement to only those structural and expressive details that listeners in Haydn's original London audience could have easily noticed on a first hearing of the symphony and confine our interpretive activity to embrace only those meanings inspired by obvious echoes of the immediate cultural surroundings, musical and otherwise. As we shall see, the expressive echoes are often unambiguous, but their meanings may easily be aligned with more than one social agenda or political orientation.

The danger of setting such restrictions on the interpretive enterprise is to eliminate a degree of sophistication from our musical readings. But if we are to consider how Haydn's public music accommodated a variety of meanings, thereby enabling his original eighteenth-century listeners to construct the ones most accommodating to their individual needs and desires, we cannot expect to observe the same types of musical details as would present-day musically trained, score-equipped analysts. (Analysts today, however, are equally as concerned with controlling musical meanings; musical analysis is a source of great pleasure for many of us.) Moreover, in attempting to hear this music from the perspective of unknown listeners in a known historical audience, we risk reducing our theoretical listeners to caricatures—listener types defined by only a handful of traits. But in conceiving of our theoretical listeners primarily in terms of social status, we reflect the principal category for self-definition in late-eighteenth-century Europe. As Thomas Munck observes, "most people thought in terms of a fundamentally static hierarchical social structure in which the rich hereditary elite was always at the top, and (to use terminology customary in England at the time) the 'mean' or 'industrious' labouring sort somewhere towards the bottom." Indeed, "eighteenth-century society was built on the inescapable premiss of engrained inequality" (2000, 195–96). The secret to Haydn's accessibility and public success, particularly in England, was to provide some listeners a musical corroboration of Europe's stratified society while offering others a momentary, if imaginary, musical escape from this inescapable premise.

Salomon's Audience

Haydn's Symphony No. 93 premiered on 17 February 1792 in London's Hanover Square Rooms to the unanimous praise of every music critic present.[2] In addition to the usual accolades for the concert's novelty vocalist and Haydn's "extraordinary" music, the *Morning Herald* notes the "very elegant audience" (quoted in Landon 1976, 3:134). Undoubtedly the majority of those in attendance would have been London's most fashionable citizens, "the Nobility and Gentry" to whom Salomon's concert announcements were addressed. But the question of just how socially broad the audience was at subscription concerts remains open. Landon, among others, suggests a direct link between the rise in public concerts and middle-class patronage (3:23). As the prices for single tickets to all of London's public concerts of the time reflect both a desire for and dependence on middle-class patronage, it seems likely that listeners from a reasonably wide range of social, economic, and political strata enjoyed an evening of musical entertainment in London's West End. As Thomas Milligan points out, such entertainments were beyond the means only of the working class (1983, 13–14).

But Salomon's concert series were subscription series, the most prestigious concerts of modern music in London. Even allowing for the sale of single tickets and the admission of subscribers' friends (Salomon allowed this in 1793), Simon McVeigh argues that middle-class attendance at West End subscription concerts should be limited to "the 'big bourgeoisie,' such as Haydn's friend the banker Nathaniel Brassey, and to wealthy professionals." Moreover, he adds, "it is by no means clear that the less-aspiring middle classes frequented the Hanover Square Rooms, even when they could afford to do so" (1993, 20–21). In any event, since no audience lists survive, we can only speculate about the social composition of Salomon's audiences.[3] For our present purpose, then, we shall presume the listeners in attendance at the first performance of Haydn's Symphony No. 93 were predominantly London's high society: members of the nobility and gentry, the leisured wealthy, and perhaps a few members of the middle classes who embraced noble tastes and aspired to join polite society.

Given the rave reviews and spontaneous encore of the second movement (both the first and second movements were encored at the second concert given a week later), Haydn's audience, however mixed, was undeniably entertained by his symphony. But did this new work inspire individual listeners, whatever their social status, to experience pleasure, as we have defined it here, while hearing this music? With neither a time machine nor a surviving account of an individual's immediate and reflective response, we cannot know. But given Haydn's legendary financial success in London, enduring popularity among public and private audiences, and near-permanent status on concert programs given anywhere from the most exclusive private houses to the pleasure gardens, Haydn's symphonies must have provided not merely entertaining diversions but meaningful experiences for many among the diversity of his listeners. Indeed, without the capacity to accommodate a multiplicity of interpretations, it is unlikely that Haydn or his music would have been so uniquely and universally celebrated throughout Europe during a time of considerable social volatility and political turbulence.

The hearings that follow explore both how and what Haydn's Symphony No. 93 may have meant to its first listeners. Since a precondition for the construction of meaning in this context is a certain degree of structural intelligibility, the immediacy of this music's formal communication—the ability of the listener, whatever her degree of musical initiation, to follow the music's structural argument in the real time of a first hearing—will be incorporated, as needed, into the interpretations.

Haydn's Symphony in D Major, No. 93

Adagio–Allegro assai: Salient Juxtapositions of Status

Inviting sociopolitical readings of this symphony are its unusually frequent and salient juxtapositions of stylistic registers, points of contact between high, middle, and low musical expressions that would have been clearly audible and immediately apparent to Haydn's late-eighteenth-century listener. The symphony's opening measures set the stage (Example 5.1): a sentimental melody (mm. 3–6) follows the grand gesture with which the first movement opens (mm. 1–2), extending an immediate invitation for the listener to hear cultural resonances of her own subjectivity within a complex web of musical signs and echoes. The status of the electrifying fortissimo and tutti unison is unequivocally high, an echo of the customary sounds of courtly and theatrical commencement. The status of the sentimental style, however, commonly aligned with middle-class values and placed in the middle stylistic register by eighteenth-century critics and theorists, depends on the listener's own social positioning.

The sentimental mode, as Mary Hunter analyzes it in the context of opera buffa, may seem "to offer an occasion for the breaching of social barriers, and for the creation of a middle space that characters . . . can occupy 'on the merits' of their sentiments rather than on the basis of their social space." But on stage, at least, it can also "redefine the relation between gender and class, linking the expression of sentiment with women, with naturalness, and with an upper-class sensibility" (1999, 146–47). As the expressive meaning of instrumental music at this time is greatly dependent on its echoing of other forms of entertainment, musical and otherwise, the meaning of Haydn's immediate turn to sentimentality in the third measure of his symphony depends on each individual listener's unique experience with and subjective relationship to the sentimental mode. Haydn's London audience would likely have been especially sensitive to musical expressions of emotionalism or moral sensitivity, for bourgeois sensibility was championed in such fashionable publications as Lawrence Sterne's *A Sentimental Journey,* Richard Steele's plays, and Joseph Addison and Steele's periodicals the *Spectator, Tatler,* and *Guardian.* As Robert Markley argues, "in cultural terms, sentimentality stakes the claim of the middle class to playing the role of England's moral conscience. Sentiment

Example 5.1.
Haydn, Symphony in D Major, No. 93, I, slow introduction

thus represents the bourgeois usurpation of and accommodation to what formerly had been considered aristocratic prerogatives" (1987, 217). Where, say, a middle-class, socially aspirational woman in Haydn's audience may hear in the expression of sentimentality evocations of her own virtue and inner nobility, a conservative, aristocratic man and head of household may find such sentiment feminizing, weak, and ultimately threatening to his authority in both domestic and public arenas. The expressive meaning, then, of Haydn's juxtapositioning of the grand, theatrical opening gesture and the sentimental mode that immediately follows at the beginning of Symphony No. 93 depends entirely on the individual listener's relationships to the two expressive stances. An expressive alignment of the splendid opening and subsequent sentimentality affirms the values and tastes of the middle; an expressive incongruity, on the other hand, exaggerates any difference in expressive status. As Haydn maintains the temporal proximity of these two styles throughout the slow introduction (for example, the sentimental sigh following the tattoos, mm. 16–

18), it becomes the listener's pleasure to construct meanings for these stylistic juxta-positions most agreeable with his or her social station and even gender.

Like the activity of the ballroom, the two dance tunes in the Allegro assai are great social equalizers (Examples 5.2a and b). Both $\frac{3}{4}$ allemandes that immediately establish extended moments of structural stability, neither approaches the rowdi-ness of Haydn's countrified minuet-trios or the ballroom dance itself. While we should not make too much of the "assai" marking qualifying Haydn's Allegro tempo, the reduced scoring, dynamic subtlety, smooth articulations, and lack of an overly assertive downbeat temper somewhat the first dance's popular spirit. The resulting air of restraint greatly affects this movement's possibilities for expressive meaning. First, there is less chance for an ironic relationship between the weight of the introduction and the accessibility of the following allemande. Whether one hears this dance as relaxed nobility, a cultured middle class, or even self-consciously controlled boisterousness, the introduction cannot be heard to introduce a subject too far below its own status. (As we shall see, this expressive ploy Haydn reserves for the symphony's minuet-trio.)

Moreover, the restraint of the first allemande ensures an expressive descent to the second allemande, whose popular spirit, though likewise contained, is asserted more forcefully by stronger downbeats, pizzicato and staccato articulations, motoric broken-chordal accompanimental patterns, oom-pah-pah rhythms, and the dis-tinctive dance-band orchestration in the repeat of the strain (mm. 85–95). In ad-dition to continuing the descent of broad expressive stances within the movement, the slightly lower status of the second dance, reflecting not just the order of dances in the ballroom but its spirit of democracy as well, provides for an easy accommo-dation of both bourgeois and aristocratic subjectivities. Indeed, Haydn invites the listener to take an active role in determining the expressive meaning of the second allemande by delaying the start of the second group with a two-measure scalar climb from the new tonic pitch to the starting pitch of the second dance tune (the climb spans a twelfth; mm. 74–75). While this two-measure "introduction" sets the dance off from the preceding material, drawing attention to its separate iden-tity and expressive difference, it also prevents an alignment of the arrival in the new key and the commencement of the new tune. The listener's sense of structural resolution at this important strategic event is thereby tempered, undermining, if only slightly, her sense of the second allemande as a destination.

The expressive meaning of the level of discourse becomes more of an issue, however, in the Allegro assai's development. The second ending of the exposition plunges the listener into another expressive world altogether, one defined by the minor mode, contrapuntal textures, relentless and driving eighth notes, and up-ward sequences of anxious sigh motives (Example 5.3). The abruptness of the dra-matic shift in expressive stance would alone be enough to trigger the listener's sense of unease at the beginning of the development, but the duration of our visit to this stormy and stressful place, combined with some salient topical dissonances, secures both structural and expressive significance of the extended instability.

The invertible double counterpoint, the controlling texture and topic for more than half of the movement's development, forces a stylistic juxtaposition between

Example 5.2.
a. Haydn, Symphony in D Major, No. 93, I, first theme
b. Haydn, Symphony in D Major, No. 93, I, second theme

Example 5.3.
Haydn, Symphony in D Major, No. 93, I, development section
Continued on the next page

Example 5.3.
Haydn, Symphony in D Major, No. 93, I, development section

a high stance and something lower (just how much lower depends on the listener's individual interpretation). A new subject whose defining expressive feature is the downbeat sigh heard previously in both the introduction (see Example 5.1, m. 18) and the second dance of the exposition (see Example 5.2b; mm. 77 passim) (though it is unlikely that Haydn's listeners would have heard such thematic connections)[4] is set in two-part counterpoint with a line of driving eighth notes (mm. 111–53). The learned style is the reining topic here, and its elevated stance—already ensured by the abrupt shift to the minor mode and the stormy expression—becomes only more imposing as the texture thickens when Haydn adds a line of parallel thirds (and tenths) above the driving eighths (mm. 115–22). The learned style does eventually disintegrate into the popular style with the appearance of the exposition's second dance tune (at m. 161), but four bars into the dance Haydn commences a clearly audible (and necessary, since the dance tune is one step off target, in C major instead of D major) modulation, effectively delaying the listener's shift back to a relaxed listening modality. Attentive listeners may well have been aware that our arrival was off target, as the familiar dance tune is the "wrong" one—this dance is from the second group, not the first.

But while the development's climax and retransition may offer conspicuous juxtapositions of otherworldly and terrestrial passions (esp. in mm. 146–64), the combination of styles that make up the counterpoint itself provides for the richest interpretative possibilities. At issue is the expressive meaning of the sigh motive of the development's new subject (mm. 111–12). Landon notes "a curious and very strong feeling that this five-note figure is well known to us" (1976, 3:519), a feeling that at first is likely caused not by any motivic connections to earlier themes but rather by the ubiquity of the sigh as a generic motivic type with a specific expressive meaning in late-eighteenth-century music. A trademark gesture of the *empfindsamer Stil*, sighing figures impart that undeniably personal, intimate quality to the sentimental mode. But divorced from their contrapuntal treatment, especially when leading into and out of the development's snippet of dance (mm. 153–56, 169–77), the sighs shift to a more popular expression in that Haydn uses them comically, suggesting an expressive kinship between sentimentality and popularity. While musically this expressive closeness may seem somewhat surprising, the alliance makes good political sense: the middle-class values of the sentimental style align with the democratic spirit of popular dance.

The expressive meanings of the learned style/sighing figure trope, then, are largely contingent upon the meanings individual listeners maintain for the sigh itself. On the one hand, the sentimentality of the sigh may work in expressive tandem with the counterpoint it creates, especially should the sentimental mode find subjective resonance in the listener and the stormy affect be heard as an expression of intense subjectivity. On the other hand, the sentimentality of the sigh may generate expressive dissonance within its contrapuntal context if the listener lacks the means or desire to identify with either its musical source or associated social values. But once the sighs lean more comic than sentimental in the first anticipatory passage (mm. 122–28), the expressive makeup of the trope may shift. Rather than an intense feeling generated by the combination of sentimentality and subjectivity, or an unrest spawned by the uneasy mixture of the elevated and the embarrassing, the expressive incompatibility of the tempestuous and the trivial may ironically lend the following contrapuntal passage (mm. 128–53) even more tension. When we keep in mind that Haydn had his sights clearly set on a public audience, his turn, albeit brief, to an unchallenged popular style to set the stage for retransition is a brilliant expressive move: the allemande again functions as social equalizer. Regardless of the listener's politics or social status, the democratic spirit of the dance prepares the grand style/popular style trope that follows (mm. 169–80). With the sigh motive now inverted and accompanied by brass and drum tattoos, the trope's expressive meaning secures its strategic function: to generate an unequivocal sense of anticipation for the most significant structural event in the movement—the beginning of the recapitulation.

Structurally, as Brown notes, "Haydn treats the recapitulation in a surprisingly regular manner, with the elimination of 1T (m. 53) and 2K (m. 105), the expansion of 1K, and the addition of 2Py (m. 256) as part of a short but effective coda with a fanfare" (2002, 253). But despite the formal regularity, a design structure that would seem to provide little opportunity for further development of the movement's expressive meaning, Haydn's orchestrational changes and additions appeal increasingly to popular taste. To the repeat of the strain of the first allemande, for example, Haydn adds a countermelody in the first violins (Example 5.4a). While strategically this addition may serve to distract the listener from thematic changes that keep the dance from modulating, the countermelody itself—marked by the continuous rhythmic activity of the countrified dances so popular in late-eighteenth-century ballrooms—lowers slightly the dance's stylistic register. To be sure, this first

Example 5.4.
a. Haydn, Symphony in D Major, No. 93, I, repeat of the allemande strain in the first theme of the recapitulation
b. Haydn, Symphony in D Major, No. 93, I, second theme of the recapitulation

allemande retains its distinctive air of restraint, but in the second strain, depending on the orientation of the listener, its status is either complemented or compromised. In either case, Haydn's countermelody affects a subtle but significant localized expressive descent. This expressive descent is continued in the second allemande, a tune that as noted above is already at a slightly lower stylistic level. Here Haydn's orchestrational changes—the bassoon doubling of the melody in the first strain and the shifting of the accompanimental "pah pahs" from staccato strings to horns in the second—sharpen the timbral reflection of a popular dance band (Example 5.4b, mm. 215–28). The overall expressive trajectory of the recapitulation, then, is a descent through subtle shadings of a popular style, a descent that mirrors the downward shift of the exposition but charts a smoother path.

While concluding tattoos and fanfares supply a grand conclusion for the Allegro assai, the largely conventional closing group composed of stock cadential material does invite some modest expressive questioning. The closing group, rushing full steam ahead, hits a speed bump: two measures of dotted-half notes in the melody that stall the busy strings' eighth-note activity (Example 5.5, mm. 247–49). Harmonically, this two-measure chromatic interruption recalls exactly the $vii^{\circ6}_{6}/V$–iv^6–V^7 progression of the penultimate measures of the slow introduction (Example 5.1, mm. 18–20), the very measures that introduce the sigh motive of the second allemande and development. Although Haydn's original listeners, enjoying this symphony for the first and perhaps only time, were unlikely to hear this resemblance and would therefore presumably also have missed the musical "pointer" to the sighs, we may glimpse in this undeniable harmonic connection something of Haydn's expressive intentions. Perhaps with this subtle reference Haydn sought to interject into the closing group's grand and ceremonial style a touch of middle-class sensibility, the same stylistic juxtaposition that offered rich expressive possibilities in the introduction.

Whatever Haydn's intentions, and however undeniable this instance of cyclic integration as Webster has defined it in Haydn's music,[5] it remains doubtful that any but the most musically literate, attentive, and devoted eighteenth-century listeners would have noticed a harmonic connection between this movement's closing group and its introduction. But where Webster finds the passage "unmotivated" (1991a, 162) were it not for the motivic link to the introduction, more sensitivity to the needs and orientation of Haydn's first listeners reveals an entirely practical motivation as well for this unexpected harmonic and rhythmic turn. While the closing material of the recapitulation must offer the listener a greater sense of conclusion than the parallel point in the exposition, it must not provide too strong a sense of finality. There are, of course, three more movements to hear. Haydn's speed bump, which consists of more than just its chromatic harmonies and stalled rhythms, provides the means to balance these two contradictory forces. The listener certainly feels an unexpected change in momentum, but the accompanying tattoos in the brass and drums impel the music forward nonetheless. The sudden but small loss of stability is easily—and necessarily—resolved by a few more stock cadential figures, an addition that nearly doubles the length of the closing group, providing the additional weight needed to close not an exposition but a whole

Example 5.5.
Haydn, Symphony in D Major, No. 93, I, ending

movement. Among the cadential figures, however, is another recall, one more likely to have been noticed by Haydn's eighteenth-century listeners: the ascending arpeggios from the first group of the exposition (mm. 256–58), figures that were omitted from the recapitulation in the telescoping of the transition passage. Just as these ascending arpeggios served to heighten anticipation and signal strategic change in the exposition, echoes of that purpose may invite the listener to look forward as they bring Haydn's first movement to a close.

Even with the possibility of some sentimental tempering, the grand style of the concluding tattoos and fanfares, together with the weight of the introduction's exordium, provide a lofty frame for the movement's predominantly popular subjects. The appeal of this expressive picture to a public audience of mixed social standings and political persuasions, not to mention personal experiences, tastes, and degrees of musical initiation, rests on the multiplicity of possible interpretations—the two extremes, perhaps, being the elevation of the common and the compromising of the patrician. But given the widespread republican enthusiasm of the time and the democratic ideals of the English nobility and gentry in particular, it is likely that Haydn's first listeners heard a certain leveling of status in this subtle but salient framed expressive descent, the listener's control over his position within such a leveling the source of his listening pleasure. The spontaneous encore of this movement demanded at the symphony's second performance suggests that Haydn's audience was indeed pleased with the interpretive possibilities this music afforded them.

Largo cantabile: Salient Juxtapositions of Voice and Style

The second movement of Symphony No. 93 is another study in stylistic juxtapositions. As such, its form has challenged critics to find a category that adequately accommodates the structural manifestations of its stylistic eccentricities. Sisman hears an "ABA design with a central *minore*" (1993a, 170); A. Peter Brown finds it "rondo-like" (2002, 253); and Landon describes a "combined variation with rondo form," suggesting that the "fascinating hybrid . . . would be called 'variation rondo form' if [Haydn] had composed more examples of it and made it more popular" (1976, 3:520). The listener of Haydn's time, however, despite the difficulty we may have placing it comfortably in any formal category, would have had little trouble following its structural argument in the real time of a first hearing. Heard linearly and without too much concern for how what is heard "now" relates to what has been heard already or what will be heard soon, this movement gains the listener's trust early with a delightful melody whose internal symmetry, regular period structure, and unambiguous pastoral topic would immediately put the listener at ease (Example 5.6). Because Haydn takes great care to guide his listener through the somewhat unconventional formal design with unambiguous structural signposts, unexpected turns may excite and surprise but never threaten the listener with structural incoherence. Localized structural tension is resolved by imparting a familiar rounded-binary formal strategy (mm. 23–26); unison and solo textures prepare for thematic returns (mm. 40–43, 58–60, respectively); wind and brass tattoos generate forward motion and anticipation (mm. 30–34); and rhythmic activity is suspended, generating a change in the flow of musical time, at points where the harmonic rhythm slows en route to a crucial cadence (mm. 66–71, 73–80).

But either of the two salient stylistic juxtapositions—one of voice and one of style—could threaten the Largo cantabile with expressive incoherence were it not for the social meanings Haydn's listeners would have likely heard in them. The first and more subtle juxtaposition places the "ravishingly beautiful oboe solo," as Landon perfectly describes it (1976, 3:520), increasingly closer to the pastoral theme. The distance between the two "voices"—the oboe's individual and the pastoral

Example 5.6.
Haydn, Symphony in D Major, No. 93, II (complete)
Continued on the next page

Example 5.6.
Haydn, Symphony in D Major, No. 93, II (complete)
Continued on the next page

Example 5.6.
Haydn, Symphony in D Major, No. 93, II (complete)

theme's community—is twice mediated by authoritative textures. After the first solo excursion (mm. 31–36) a unison texture, reflecting perhaps the power of individuals united in a common purpose, redirects the music back to the pastoral theme with escalating intensity and volume as all the instruments in the orchestra, including the oboes, join the collective call for return (mm. 40–43). After the second oboe solo (mm. 53–56), Haydn turns to a solo texture—tiptoeing violins whose sound shrinks to pianissimo—to lead into the return of the theme (mm. 58–61). The delivery may seem timid, but the message is backed by the support and sanctioning of the community—the rest of the band. The location of the third oboe solo suggests a different relationship between this individual voice and the movement's communal theme. Instead of placing the solo oboe in the episodes between thematic statements, Haydn clears space for its presence within the theme itself as harmonic motion stalls and the melody pauses (mm. 66–70). Moreover, the first violins join in unison with the solo oboe (m. 70) as a I–IV–I$_4^6$–V^7–I cadence returns the music to the pastoral theme. Only here, in their final appearance in the movement, do the oboes join the band to present the first and only full tutti statement of the pastoral theme (m. 71).

It is difficult to speculate about just what Haydn's listeners may have heard in these varied juxtapositionings of the individual beauty of the solo oboe's voice and the serenity of the pastoral theme's community. As the pastoral governs the movement as a whole—the Handelian outbursts discussed below offer the only significant affective contrast—the expressive meaning of the juxtaposition is unlikely to stem from the listener's discernment of any subtle expressive differences between the solo episodes and tutti themes. Rather, the sheer and inescapable beauty of the oboe line as it first emerges from the orchestral texture underscores its solo status, while the authority of many voices joined together in unison points to the communal identity of the movement's theme upon its first return. Indeed, Haydn's striking opening orchestration—four solo strings in quartet arrangement—would have already drawn attention to the individual voices that work in concert to form this pastoral community. The interpretation of this contrast of voice—albeit one that requires more attentive listening and sophistication from the listener than others offered here—rests on eighteenth-century constructions of the individual self. Unlike the later Self of German Romanticism, in which the individual is defined inwardly through personal freedom, self-consciousness, the rhythms of the body, and most significantly a struggle to overcome or transcend the Self, the enlightened self of French rationalism is defined outwardly through its sympathetic relationships with the world around it. In the realities of the world, this self finds itself reflected (see Burnham 1995, esp. ch. 4; Lyons 1978, esp. ch. 1).

With the enlightened self as the philosophical backdrop, Haydn's listener may hear the eventual integration of the oboe into the orchestral collective as the completion of an organic complex. As a solo bassoon and a solo flute have already joined the pastoral collective, the oboe may be heard as the last voice needed for completion, one that once added secures the inclusion of all categories needed for the community's definition. By joining the pastoral collective, then, the oboe may be heard to achieve its own individual identity. It is also possible, of course, to hear the ultimate inclusion of the oboe in the pastoral theme as an assimilation, one that effectively silences the individual's "ravishingly beautiful" voice and sacrifices its personal freedom. While such an interpretation, in its conflation of beauty and freedom, may seem aligned with the values and ideals of the Enlightenment,[6] it also rests on a later Romantic conception of the Self. As plausible as such a reading may seem today,[7] it is unlikely that Haydn's listeners would have heard such a plot in this movement. In fact, any assimilation would likely have been interpreted in a positive light: just as the oboe's beauty complements the pastoral world, the pastoral world contains the oboe's beauty. The easy enjoyment of this music suggests only a carefree existence within Haydn's idyll.

By forcing a meeting of the humility of the pastoral mode and the pomp, grandeur, and sublimity of the ancient style (mm. 17–22, 80–83), the second and more flamboyant of the Largo cantabile's two stylistic juxtapositions begs the listener's active participation in the construction of its meaning. To be sure, representations of the pastoral in late-eighteenth-century music are rarely as uncomplicated as the contemporary critical discussions would lead us to believe. As Sisman argues, "there is no reason to assume that composers were not aware of the breadth of the pastoral—the range of pastorally tinged music, the versions of idyllic poetry, pastoral drama, and realistic pastoral, its eighteenth-century critiques, and even the central idea that it always involves 'the recognition of a contrast, implicit or expressed, between pastoral life and some more complex type of civilization'" (1997, 78). But experienced in the real time of a first hearing, this slow movement opens with a simple and uncomplicated evocation of a pastoral world. Haydn's listening public would have hardly greeted such an idealized space braced for an early and abrupt intrusion by that reality. Haydn clearly expected the sudden appearance of the ancient style to be shocking: he uses the same strategy—a forte/fortissimo tutti following a pianissimo repetition of an opening strain—to jolt his audience in the slow movement of his next symphony, No. 94, the "Surprise." And just as in that work, after the dramatic intrusion the tune nonchalantly returns to conclude in its opening expression.

The listener, however, cannot simply dismiss the disruption and continue amiably in the pastoral mode, for the meaning of both styles and their juxtaposition is now a pressing interpretive concern. For the English audience in particular, the ancient reference was undoubtedly Handelian, and its meaning here hinges on its sincerity. Is Haydn's reference a parody of the ancient master's style? A statement of homage? A simple gimmick to ingratiate himself to the English public? The listener's reading of the ancient style is entirely dependent on the musical and cultural echoes he chooses to hear in it. His personal and social relationships to both ancient and modern orchestral music are particularly significant, for in late-eighteenth-century London correlations between these two musical styles and the listener's social status were often a conscious decision. Moreover, they were in constant flux. In the late 1780s the English public showed an unprecedented enthusiasm for new symphonic music that led to a broader social range of listeners at many public concerts, perhaps even at the most exclusive subscription concerts. McVeigh suggests that this new diversity inspired two responses from the aristocracy: first, the aristocracy "[withdrew] from the public concert life they had helped to create, in favour of their own select private soirées"; and second, they founded the Concert of Ancient Music as a "serious-minded alternative to modern concerts" (1993, 7). While a clear alignment of musical taste and social class may be inferred from these two developments, the subsequent middle-class emulation of the new (or renewed, as it were) aristocratic taste complicates the picture. For example, the City-supported Academy of Ancient Music, founded in 1726 for its largely upper-bourgeois members to gather and sing "ancient" madrigals and motets, changed its repertoire and mission by the late 1780s to resemble the aristocratic Concert of Ancient Music's devotion to the music of the high Baroque.[8] Handel, then, became the favored composer of both societies.

With the inevitable "barbed satires mock[ing] middle-class pretensions to musical taste," the politics of concert life took on even more complexity. McVeigh summarizes the social concert scene in late-eighteenth-century London as follows:

> Ambivalence towards the values of fashionable modern concerts . . . resulted in a certain independence of taste even among the higher reaches of the middle classes. In particular they showed a continuing commitment to Handel, resulting in a strange alliance of interest. On the one hand were aristocratic connoisseurs, deliberately adopting the high artistic ground at the Concert of Ancient Music; on the other were the sober-minded middle classes of the Academy of Ancient Music, less conscious of their role, but naturally conservative and admiring of the frugal virtues of Baroque music. (1993, 13)

McVeigh even argues for a blatant political purpose to the Handel centenary in 1784: "an excuse for an elaborate Commemoration on a massive scale, which gave public expression to [the artistic] leadership [of the aristocracy]," who saw themselves as the "responsible guardians of the nation" (7).

An obvious Handelian reference heard within a new symphony in 1792 in London, then, carried an inescapable political charge. But Haydn's genius here is not just that the polarity of this charge varies with the listener and his individual social standing and political leanings but that it also demands his conscious control over its direction. It might be safe to assume that a listener choosing to attend Salomon's concert could hardly be opposed, aesthetically or politically, to the modern orchestral style, a stance that might suggest Haydn's Handelian interruption as a parody of the ancient style. But it is also difficult to imagine London's most fashionable citizens, many of whom would have also subscribed to the Concert of Ancient Music (McVeigh 1993, 22–27), reveling in an overt lampooning of the very music they presumed to hold highest. Likewise, any middle-class listeners attending Salomon's concert might have aligned aesthetically more with the social and musical accessibility of the pastoral mode, but, as supporters of the Academy of Ancient Music if not the Concert itself, they may also have been sympathetic to Baroque musical values. It becomes the listener's imperative, then, to determine for himself the meaning of Haydn's Handelian reference. The musical and social contexts leave it ambiguous.

We may even guess that this ambiguity of meaning was intentional on Haydn's part, as the bassoon outburst (m. 80) which precedes the return of the ancient style near the end of the movement suggests. In what turns out to be the Largo cantabile's final return to the pastoral theme (which, played by the full band, would immediately sound like a final return), Haydn suspends time in the second phrase by stretching the most conclusive of harmonic progressions—I–IV–I$_4^6$–V–I—over seven measures (mm. 75–81), sitting on the subdominant alone for what feels like a very long two measures. Just as the listener's anticipation approaches the breaking point, despite the gentleness with which it is generated, a fortissimo bassoon "fart" (m. 80), as Brown colorfully names it, comically voices the listener's impatience, waking perhaps inadvertently the ancient style from its apparent slumber (mm. 80–83). The incongruous pomp of the ancient style does not last, however, and as the dotted rhythms fade and the triplets expire, the listener is led to the pleasant and tender conclusion required of the movement's reigning pastoral topic (mm. 83–88).

Haydn rarely indulges in such "Rabelaisian humour" (to quote Landon's more polite description [1976, 3: 520]), a fact that makes this striking moment in the Largo cantabile demand interpretation from his listeners—both then and now. By supplying the missing subdominant harmonic anchor, the fortissimo bassoon outburst may sound the voice of the pastoral mode's frustration as the tune stalls, apparently unable to cadence. Its waking of the Handelian style, then, may be heard to rescue the pastoral mode from its own disintegration, just as the high artistic and moral values of the Ancient Music societies were, to a certain extent, intended to rescue music from the disintegrating values of modern music. But the bassoon outburst is also undeniably comic, suggesting a vulgarity that could comment on either musical world. If it is heard as originating in the pastoral world, the grandeur and seriousness of the ancient style may return taste to the music of this movement. If, on the other hand, the bassoon transgression is heard as belonging to the ancient style whose return it initiates, its vulgarity may suggest an overblown, clumsy, and bloated Handelian "giant," one easily and thankfully knocked over by the unaffectedness of the pastoral mode and the implied naturalness of the modern instrumental style. Both of these interpretations, of course, have obvious social and political overtones. That Haydn's first listeners derived such tremendous pleasure from this movement suggests their sense of control over its ultimate meaning.

Menuetto: Plotting Status and Identity

The dance movement as a type would present the listener of Haydn's time few structural difficulties, its binary forms and da capo presentation entirely familiar from both the ballroom and concert hall. As discussed in chapter 4, there existed a "minuet norm" in the late eighteenth century, one so crystallized as to allow "new" minuets to be generated by *ars combinatoria* dice games. Most if not all listeners in Haydn's audience would have expected the great majority of this movement's structural details, from binary phrase structures to the lengths of strains, from the number and order of repeats to the quasi-development in the B sections. Less expected would be the often noted thematic connection between the minuet's closing material and the second dance tune of the first movement (Example 5.7; see Landon 1976, 3:520–21; Marx 1976–80, 1–19; Webster 1991a, 200). (Incidentally, the second dance theme of the finale also links motivically to these two themes.) It is unlikely, though, that many listeners in Haydn's first audience would

Example 5.7.
a. Haydn, Symphony in D Major, No. 93, I, melody at the beginning of the second theme
b. Haydn, Symphony in D Major, No. 93, III, melody at the beginning of the third phrase of the minuet
c. Haydn, Symphony in D Major, No. 93, IV, melody at the beginning of the second dance theme

Example 5.8.
Haydn, Symphony in D Major, No. 93, III, minuet proper

have noticed this thematic link between movements as such, especially after the impact (and encore) of the second movement. Attentive listeners might have perceived the parallel stylistic shift downward from an energized aristocratic dance (Example 5.8, mm. 1–6) to a stylized peasant one (mm. 7–10). But, as we shall see, Haydn reserves the most memorable expressive play for the trio. Even those only half-listening could not fail to notice the trio's startling incongruity between style and location as insistent fanfares supplant the trio's traditionally countrified spirit (see Example 5.9). The surprises in this movement are all expressive ones.

The minuet movement of Symphony No. 93 contains one of Haydn's most direct engagements with the musical representation of status and identity. But again, it remains for the listener to determine the "plot" dramatized by the characters depicted. The minuet proper (Example 5.8), with its boisterous Allegro tempo,[9] Ländler-like melodies, particularly in the B section (mm. 25–28), broken-chordal and motoric accompanimental patterns (mm. 7–10, 38–43), and harmonic rhythm that settles on one change per bar by the end of each strain, may be a *Deutscher Tanz* in all but name. But this presentation of the wildly popular dance contains a few hints of the minuet's traditional nobility lurking just beneath the surface. While the tattoo and minuet tag rhythm ($\downarrow \downarrow\downarrow\downarrow$) (mm. 37–38, 41–42) serve as certain reminders of the minuet's presence, the unison with which the movement begins sounds a communal voice of authority, the learned textures that mark the "development" imply a more elevated status (mm. 15–20), and the pianissimo but prominent timpani solo in the second strain (mm. 31–38) lends the dance a touch of gravitas. It is up to the listener, of course, whether the character defined here is a masquerading aristocrat, a commoner with a touch of "uncommon" dignity, or even a "character" at all.

In the trio, however, Haydn gives his listener comparatively little interpretive choice, at least as to the representation of status. The "plot," however, may still be somewhat in the listener's control. Throughout the trio, a loud and dramatic fanfare in the winds, brass, and timpani nobly announces each phrase of a rustic dance (Example 5.9). While the fanfare's customary opening function may be aligned with its structural location at the beginning of each period in the trio, its strategic function to promote the listener's anticipation of stability is ultimately undermined by the dance's constant play with expressive incompatibility. Right from the start, such emphatic stateliness is expressively incongruent with a trio's typically rustic style. Having been conditioned to expect a dance of lower social status by the long tradition of framing a countrified dance with an urban dance,[10] Haydn's listeners would likely have heard this opening fanfare as expressively, and therefore also strategically, out of place. The fanfare's expressive and structural purpose is further compromised by its position *after* a dance that yields to a more common expression. Most damaging to the fanfare's imposing affect, however, is the simple dance tune it persistently introduces. With each inflated announcement the unassuming rustic dance tries a new tactic to harmonize with the gravity implied by its pompous introduction.[11] It first considers the minor mode (mm. 51–54). But rather than raising the trio's level of dignity by moving its expressive content to the high-style category of the tragic, the surprising turn to the relative minor in fact has the opposite effect. It reduces the dance to low tragedy—to bathos, the ironic category of incongruity. In the next phrase (mm. 59–62), the dance simply recovers its misstep. It returns to the major mode where it "should" have remained, moving the trio's expression from bathos to buffa. At the same time, however, the appearance of the tune in the subdominant reinterprets retroactively the preceding fanfares (mm. 47–50, 55–58) as the tonicizing agent within the dance's tonal space,

Example 5.9.
Haydn, Symphony in D Major, No. 93, III, first strain of the trio

emphasizing all the more their annunciatory purpose. But the *piano* dynamic and understated delivery reveal both the dance's underlying discomfort and incompatibility with the repeated, overstated introduction. It is not until the last phrase of each strain (mm. 67–72, 93–98) that the dance finally asserts its own status and identity, ironically with rustic but entirely conventional closing material. With a doodling melody in steady eighth notes and an oom-pah-pah accompaniment, the *Deutsche,* at the end, seems to revel in its common expression.

As in the second movement of this symphony, the political implications of the trio's expressive trajectory are potentially volatile. Although it is quite possible that the predominantly noble and wealthy listeners in Haydn's first audiences could have heard the bourgeois dance's attempts to conform to the dignity level prescribed by the high-flown military gestures as a social failure, it seems more likely that, given the stuffiness of the minuet and popularity of the *Deutscher Tanz* in the ballrooms of the time, these listeners, regardless of their own status, would be expressively aligned with the musical commoner in this case. While I would propose that this second interpretation approaches not only the meaning most contemporary listeners would have constructed while hearing this trio but also Haydn's intended one, his listeners of course remained in control of just how far beyond the concert hall's "ballroom" any political implications might reach.

*Finale: Presto ma non troppo: Structural Intelligibility and
Expressive Descents*

The recent critical reception of Haydn's finale for Symphony No. 93 has been somewhat mixed, thanks largely to reservations expressed by Haydn himself shortly after the symphony's premiere. In a letter to his dear friend and confidant Mme Genzinger, Haydn explains:

> I cannot send Your Grace the Symphony which is dedicated to you . . . because I intend to alter the last movement of it, and to improve it, since it is too weak compared with the preceding movements. I was persuaded of this myself, and by the public as well, when I produced it the first time, . . . notwithstanding which it [the symphony] made the most profound impression on the audience.[12] (Quoted and trans. in Webster 1991a, 183)

Because the autograph is lost and only one version of the finale survives, we cannot know if Haydn ever made his intended revisions. Most commentators, however, find little to complain about in "this dashing piece," as Antony Hodgson labels it (1976, 128), for as Webster asserts, in agreement with Landon, "in its present form the finale does not seem in any way inadequate" (1991a, 183). But Brown, at least, is troubled by its formal ambiguity. He writes: "For a sonata form, there is no development, and for a rondo, no real second episode. Although Haydn was a specialist in synthesizing the basic forms of the late-eighteenth century and was always clear as to which one controlled the larger structure, in [the finale of Symphony No. 93] one is never certain which model is the controlling factor. This Finale's problems stem from the lack of clarity at the larger level" (2002, 256).

Given Haydn's celebrated accessibility despite his penchant for formal hybrids, I would suggest that Brown's reservations stem from the present-day inclination toward spatial conceptions of musical form. It is unlikely that a listener in Haydn's first audience, whose only experience of the form of this finale was one of temporal unfolding in real time, would have found its structural processes to suffer the "lack of clarity" Brown hears. Indeed, with no indication of any revisions, no hints as to what types of revisions Haydn intended to make (or perhaps did make), and no evidence beyond Haydn's letter to Mme Genzinger that the public's reaction was anything other than the overwhelmingly positive reception reported in newspaper reviews of the concerts, there is little to suggest that listeners in Haydn's first audiences were challenged in any way by the structure of this finale.

In fact, as in the Largo cantabile, Haydn's finale provides the listener a ready roadmap of expressive conventions with which to navigate any unconventional formal processes she may encounter. Periodic dance strains secure varying degrees of structural stability throughout the movement (mm. 1–16, Example 5.10a; 43–50, 118–32, Example 5.10b; 172–87, 238–52, Example 5.11). The energy and urgency of string tremolos generate anticipation in transitional passages (mm. 70–80, 112–16). And forceful unison textures consistently redirect the music to important strategic events: measures 32–34 prepare for the reprise of the contredanse theme's first strain; measures 96–97 interrupt a disintegrating learned-style passage to focus all

Example 5.10.
a. Haydn, Symphony in D Major, No. 93, IV, first dance theme
b. Haydn, Symphony in D Major, No. 93, IV, second dance theme

energy on the ensuing anticipatory passage; measures 132–38 lead straightaway into a transitional passage; measures 229–32 (see Example 5.11), the most insistent unison in the movement, relieve an extended moment of instability in preparation for an expressively significant thematic return; and measures 252–60 and measures 280–84 (see Example 5.12) lead directly to closing material.

When we keep in mind that Haydn's first listener would be following primarily the expressive events of the structural argument, with little concern for what this finale "should do," "could do," or even "might do," much of the formal ambiguity vanishes. For example, it becomes irrelevant whether we label the return to the first dance tune in measure 172 a recapitulation or a reprise. The listener following the movement in the real time of a first performance simply hears the music acquiesce to the sudden demands of the tutti and fortissimo upbeat figure whose instance has risen with its pitch (see Example 5.11, mm. 163–87). Likewise, without questioning the structural significance of the ensuing transitional passage (mm. 188–237) laden with disruptions in the musical flow, thematic fragmentation, dramatic shifts in the expressive surface, and more upbeat anticipations, Haydn's listener need only follow the lead of the forceful unison (mm. 229–32) out of the extended instability to the stability of a dance strain. It matters not that the tune Haydn offers (mm. 238–52) is the second contredanse tune and not the first (or, put in formal terms, that we are hearing the second subject of a recapitulation rather than the reprise of a rondo), for as long as the material is presentational and (preferably) known at this point in the movement, a listener will experience the expressive stability necessary to find the music structurally intelligible. It is just as easy to hear the first dance tune emerging intact from the immediately preceding upbeat gestures, for it has done just that at several previous points in the finale. Of course, there is expressive significance in the presentation of the second tune in this location which we shall consider presently, but all that is required for the integrity of the structural argument at this point is the securing of the listener's sense of momentary stability. Either dance tune could perform that task effectively.

As in this symphony's slow movement and minuet-trio, the sounds of a higher expressive world inhabit a more common one. But while the Handelian references in the Largo cantabile and the persistent fanfares in the trio seem designed to inspire expressive meanings through pointed stylistic disparity, the moments of greatest stylistic contrast with the contredanse finale's popular style—learned-style passages and brief touches of *Sturm und Drang*—are more concerned with articulating strategic function. Haydn encourages the construction of expressive meaning in the finale rather more subtly: by including among the echoes of the musical soundscape of the listener's everyday life a few expressive echoes from this very symphony.

A stylistic descent from the first subject's popular dance style (Example 5.10a, mm. 1–8) to the second subject's slightly lower one (Example 5.10b, mm. 118–32) echoes the expressive trajectory of the first movement Allegro assai. While one might rightly argue that such expressive descents define the expressive course of most movements in sonata style, Haydn's use of strikingly similar musical means to establish a subtle drop in stylistic register in each movement suggests an intentional parallel: a motoric broken-chordal accompanimental pattern slows the harmonic rhythm while securing a more relaxed listening modality, and a salient orchestrational shift that foregrounds the winds evokes the distinctive sound of an even more rustic band. To be sure, only attentive listeners may have heard this descent specifically as an expressive echo of an earlier event, but few in Haydn's first audience would have found such expressive descents unfamiliar. They were nearly unavoidable in eighteenth-century musical life. In its movement toward the lowest common denominator (and here it is important to remember that many if not most nobles enjoyed a rowdy contredanse alongside common dancers), the slide to increasingly more accessible expressive stances reflects the humanistic ideals and democratic spirit of the Enlightenment.

The second appearance of the second dance tune (Example 5.11, mm. 238–52) is the location of the finale's second expressive echo. Following the longest and most topically varied anticipatory passage in the movement (mm. 188–237), the simple appearance of the dance tune itself would relieve the structural tension. But

Example 5.11.
Haydn, Symphony in D Major, No. 93, IV, return of the first dance theme, transition, return of the second dance theme

Continued on the next page

Example 5.11.
Haydn, Symphony in D Major, No. 93, IV, return of the first dance theme, transition, return of the second dance theme

Haydn's reorchestration of the dance inspires a particularly significant expressive meaning. By reducing the oboe-bassoon octave doubling of the melody in the dance's first appearance to a solo oboe in the second, Haydn encourages his listeners to hear an echo of the "ravishingly beautiful" oboe solo in the second movement. As both oboe solos "curve gracefully" (Landon 1976, 3:520) over an orchestra playing nothing but chords in repetitive motoric rhythms, the melodic lines emerge as the most beautiful and natural melodies in their respective movements. While the second movement, with its chamber opening and prominent solos, considers the situation and meaning of the self within the greater society, the finale may suggest an answer. Rather than the individual sounding a common expression, as in the Largo cantabile, the common expression here may yield the sounding self. In this intersection of identity and affectation of common musical values the student of the Enlightenment may hear musical expressions of equality. Listeners less sympathetic with the Enlightenment project may simply hear the individuated voice of the commoner. On a more practical level, however, hearing such beauty in a common expression may suggest to the middle-class listener his own nature and inner beauty, while the aristocrat may hear such common beauty as affirming the social value of mixed company.

This second expressive meaning would be reinforced by the finale's third expres-

Example 5.12.
Haydn, Symphony in D Major, No. 93, IV, first half of the coda

sive echo. The timpani roll and following tattoos (Example 5.12, mm. 269–80) that mark the symphony's ending clearly recall similar events in the minuet. Just as an exposed timpani roll anchors expressively the anticipatory passage that leads to the closing period of the minuet proper, so too does one impart a ceremonial and elevated tone to the finale's last anticipatory passage. The musical similarities are striking: both rolls hold an extended, pianissimo, unaccompanied tonic pedal, while winds, scored in wind-band thirds, converse with strings by tossing back and forth two-measure melodic fragments featuring leading-tone motion. Even if the reference to the earlier musical event were not recognized consciously, the finale's timpani roll would likely have sounded oddly familiar to Haydn's listeners, attentive and inattentive alike.

The tattoos that follow both rolls, however, relate differently to the movement that contains them, so the expressive meaning listeners may have heard in them would likely differ also. At the end of the minuet, the understated tattoos and brass punctuations hint at an elevated expressive stance, thereby serving as subtle reminders of the dance's underlying noble spirit. The tattoos and fanfares at the end of the finale, on the other hand, conclude a bourgeois dance with peasant origins. It is a big step up, then, from the contredanse's common stance to the stateliness implied by the ceremonial flourishes. To be sure, the fanfares serve an important strategic function, not just in this movement but in a great many symphonies of the late eighteenth century: to punctuate the end of a movement or symphony with a lofty flourish, one that reinforces or reinstates the grand and elevated style audiences expected of the symphonic genre.[13] Here, however, the closing fanfares, played only by the winds, brass, and timpani, alternate with the transformation of the contredanse's opening figure into a closing one, played only by strings. In an obvious echo of the trio, Haydn extends his listeners one more invitation to construct personal and perhaps political meanings for this symphony's juxtaposition of patrician and common expressions.

6   Old Entertainments, New Pleasures: Meanings of Late-Eighteenth-Century Public Instrumental Music in Contemporary American Culture

Lisa Simpson, the sensitive, politically correct, intelligent, seven-year-old conscience of the Fox cartoon sitcom *The Simpsons,* joins Mensa. Three ordinary high-school students and soon-to-be kidnappers knock on the door of their nemesis, the condescending teacher Mrs. Tingle, in *Teaching Mrs. Tingle.* Pet detective Ace Ventura, in *Ace Ventura: Pet Detective,* crashes a party hosted by one of Miami's billionaires. Ben Stein prepares to risk more of his own money as a "common" contestant on Comedy Central's game show *Win Ben Stein's Money.* These four recent and seemingly random American screen happenings all are tracked by what is now, undeniably, Mozart's greatest hit—*Eine kleine Nachtmusik* K. 525, composed in Vienna in 1787. The repeated use of this ubiquitous classic to accompany cinematic situations that involve affluence, superior intelligence, and especially "civilized" behavior renders Mozart's ever-current hit the most recognizable sound of the elite in American media.

Despite music requirements in education, the wide availability of the classical "Top 40," and the heightened marketing of classical recordings, the popular media, along with the incessant soundtracking of life, introduce most Americans to Western art music. For the average American—who watches several hours of television a day, goes to the movies at least every few months, and is subjected to tens of thousands of media advertisements a year—the construction of meaning for classical pieces takes place primarily during experiences with visual media: Hollywood films and prime-time television.[1] For decades classical music has accompanied countless moving images, enhancing our filmic experience and acquiring for itself new associations and compounded signification. But the meanings a listener constructs during such visual experiences may be reinforced, contradicted, preempted, altered, or otherwise informed also by those meanings she constructs while hearing classical music in waiting rooms, hotel lobbies, elevators, fine restaurants, when on hold on the telephone, and in many other everyday situations—in other words, within the soundscape of her daily life.

As we shall see in this final chapter, the postmodern listener of today shares much with the enlightened listener of the late eighteenth century. For both, the meanings of late-eighteenth-century instrumental music are determined within intertextual echoes of the listener's contemporary culture, especially its entertainment. But, of course, this process of signification can be argued for much if not most music in both the art and vernacular traditions of Western music. What seems unique about the public music of the late eighteenth century is that its first listeners are connected to its most recent ones by their respective abilities to hear this music, on the one hand, as entertaining resistance, a principal source of this music's pleasure, and on the other, as merely entertaining, a means to listener subordination and even control. In either case, the instrumental music of the Classical style occasions decidedly political meanings.

After a brief exploration of how classical music in general acquires and inspires meaning in American media, we shall return to questions of why and especially what late-eighteenth-century public instrumental music in particular means to Americans in the contexts of both American entertainment and the broader contemporary culture.

From Cinematic Meanings to Musical Meanings

Even before the advent of soundtracks, pieces of classical music participated in the viewer's construction of cinematic meaning during a viewing experience. In the silent era, movie-house pianists and orchestras mined the works of Mozart, Beethoven, Tchaikovsky, Verdi, and Wagner—music not protected by copyright—to find appropriate mood music. Like the musical clichés that came to accompany silent films, excerpts from a Mozart concerto, a Beethoven symphony, or a Verdi opera were deemed suitable for certain dramatic situations. Once the classics made their way into cue sheets alongside original cues, certain quotations were heard again and again, accompanying film after film. As Max Winkler, inventor of the cue sheet, reveals quite colorfully in apparent confession, Beethoven's "Sinister Misterioso," J. S. Bach's "Adagio Lamentoso," and Tchaikovsky's "Weird Moderato" were completely transferable.[2] Although much classical music, particularly the nineteenth-century operatic repertory, was still quite familiar to Americans at the time, certain pieces became widely known because of their frequent use as cinematic accompaniment. Such musical passages entered the public imagination connected with a particular kind of scene, and cinematic associations for these pieces were reinforced during subsequent film experiences. We may understand the mechanism of musical meaning that results from the cultural appropriation of these excerpts as metonymic troping: as viewers learn to associate specific types of cinematic situations with certain musical styles, the music eventually assumes that cinematic expressive meaning on its own, independent of a particular filmic moment.

With the advent of film scoring and ultimately synchronized sound, we begin to have, for the first time on screen, a fixed and permanent association between music and image. When the same piece of music is used in widely varying cinematic contexts—a relationship opposite to that between silent images and cue sheets—the interpretation and meaning of soundtrack music becomes a wonderfully messy affair. Consider, for example, the striking diversity of associations viewers of different generations maintain for Wagner's *Ride of the Valkyries*. In

1915 *Ride of the Valkyries* became suddenly repugnant for many liberal-minded Americans, as it was difficult to erase the image of the Ku Klux Klan rushing in, summoned forth by Wagner's call, in D. W. Griffith's ground-breaking film *The Birth of a Nation*.[3] For baby boomers to thirty-somethings, *Ride of the Valkyries* is good fun, recalling the silly self-admonition "Kill the wabbit" immortalized by Warner Bros.'s cartoon character Elmer Fudd in *What's Opera, Doc?* (1957). For others of this generation, *Ride of the Valkyries* may evoke a more serious meaning by suggesting the flight of attack helicopters over Vietnam, an association etched permanently in many a viewer's mind by Francis Ford Coppola's film *Apocalypse Now* (1979).[4] For teenagers to twenty-somethings, *Ride of the Valkyries* tracks mindless game-show entertainment (despite its class coding, to which we shall return presently), concluding their chances to *Win Ben Stein's Money* (1996–2002). Several of these associations undoubtedly coexist for some viewers, and any meaning Wagner's rousing tune may hold is further complicated by their interactions. *Ride of the Valkyries*, in the context of American media, assumes great polysemic potential.

This additive process of signification and resignification presents a particular challenge for filmmakers who use preexisting music in a soundtrack, as Stanley Kubrick, for one, clearly acknowledged. Defending his decision to replace Alex North's original score for *2001: A Space Odyssey* (1968) with the music of Richard Strauss, Johann Strauss, Jr., Khachaturian, and Ligeti, Kubrick remarked: "Don't underestimate the charm of *The Blue Danube*. Most people under thirty-five think of it in an objective way, as a beautiful composition. Older people associate it with a Palm Court orchestra or have another unfortunate association and generally, therefore, criticize its use in the film" (quoted in Manvell and Hartley 1975, 254). Kubrick was clearly aware of the different individual perspectives and experiences viewers would bring to his film. But now, perhaps ironically in light of Kubrick's comment, early-twenty-first-century viewers' experiences of these pieces include their use in *2001*. When many of us hear *The Blue Danube*, we don't simply hear a beautiful composition or envision Vienna, Nazis, or the Palm Court crowd waltzing on a ballroom floor. We see ships and stations waltzing in space, as *The Blue Danube* has acquired a permanent association with Kubrick's *2001*. But undoubtedly for many Americans, *The Blue Danube*, along with Richard Strauss's *Also Sprach Zarathustra* and Ligeti's *Atmospheres*, are not just associated with *2001*, but originate in *2001*.[5] Any meaning this music may have for such viewers begins with their *2001* viewing experiences.

There are striking differences between how, where, and when American listeners, particularly those of different generations, come into contact with pieces of classical music. When we take into consideration the social implications of the consumption of classical music and other forms of "high culture," a situation that bears striking resemblance to the cultivation of taste and the acquisition of cultural capital in late-eighteenth-century Europe, the use of art music in such popular cultural contexts as film and television soundtracks complicates the picture further. In the mid-nineteenth century, classical music was enjoyed by a great many Americans, not just members of the elite classes as it tends to be now and has been throughout most of the twentieth century. Presented in performance styles, contexts, and venues that suggest it not as high art accessible only to the privileged few but rather popular entertainment for anyone who could afford the ticket, certain "public" genres of classical music, in particular opera and symphony, were mutable mainstays of everyday American culture. But, as Lawrence Levine explains, in the first quarter of the twentieth century "the masterworks of the classic composers were to be performed . . . on programs free from the contamination of lesser works or lesser genres, . . . free from the distractions of the mundane; audiences were to approach the masters and their works with proper respect and proper seriousness, for aesthetic and spiritual elevation rather than mere entertainment was the goal" (1988, 146). In this new purpose for classical music, echoes of Anna Larpent's "edifying rather than amusing" cultural experiences could hardly ring clearer.[6] By the advent of film scoring and synchronized sound in motion pictures, the "sacralization of culture," in Levine's words, was fully realized. The use of classical excerpts to track America's "merely entertaining" moving images is now loaded with social significance.

By the late 1930s through the '40s and '50s, when Leopold Stowkowski conducted Walt Disney's *Fantasia* and Carl Stalling and Milt Franklin used classical music as quotations and source material in their cues for Warner Bros. *Merry Melodies* and *Loony Tunes* cartoons,[7] the American public again heard operatic and symphonic masterpieces in an accessible, popular cultural context. But whereas in nineteenth-century America classical music was, in some form or other, for everybody's everyday consumption,[8] throughout most of the twentieth century and into the twenty-first this has not been the case. Art music, like other forms of high culture, now belongs to the affluent and the educated—that is, those with social power (see Bourdieu 1980, 225–54). To be successfully parodied in cartoons, the high social status of classical music must be both intact and clear to viewers, most of whom undoubtedly rank lower in the social order than the elite consumers of high culture. Such a viewer may not be able to spot the composer of *Ride of the Valkyries*, to use our previous example, but much of the humor in *What's Opera, Doc?* depends on her recognition of this music as "classical" and then reading the cartoon text socially: dimwitted Elmer Fudd is singing *opera*, lampooning all pretensions to such "high" art.

Coppola's viewers too likely heard the music of *Ride of the Valkyries* as high art. After all, the sounds of operatic voices accompanied by an orchestra (even if blaring out of a helicopter) are unmistakable. But for many, if not most, late-twentieth-century viewers, this tune was familiar not because they knew Wagner but because they knew Elmer Fudd, an association that lends an ironic touch to its bombast in the skies over Vietnam.[9] Twenty years on, *Ride of the Valkyries* is still familiar to the Comedy Central viewer: she's heard it before in cartoons, films, commercials, and video games, and here it is again, back in its "cultured" (i.e., full orchestral) version, as the end credit music of *Win Ben Stein's Money*.[10] Precisely because it so often encountered, *Ride of the Valkyries* has the power to grab the attention of the viewer and encourage new and compounded meanings, whether such meanings are intended or not. As Robynn Stilwell argues (while defending temp-tracking and the use of preexisting music in film scores), "relying on these meanings for effect is not a cheap stunt but is the very reason why the text presents itself for use, because, in contrast to the concept of the autonomous art work, it is impossible for the text *not* to have accumulated cultural connotations, since the text is actually a nexus of cultural processes" (1997, 569).[11] What was "Wagner's music" to Griffith's audience is now ubiquitous media soundtrack music, ripe with accrued cultural and social meanings and primed for more.

From Cinematic to Cinematic
(via Musical and Cultural) Meaning

Beyond musical code, that is, solely musical signification, music in filmic and televisual contexts sounds as cultural code and cinematic code (Gorbman 1987, 3). It is often assumed that music within a film or television program typically sounds as cultural code first, for the cultural associations individuals bring to the viewing experience encourage particular meanings for soundtrack music.[12] Claudia Gorbman provides clear examples of this phenomenon: "We all know what 'Indian music,' battle music, and romance music sound like in the movies; we know that a standard forties film will choose to introduce its seductress on the screen by means of a sultry saxophone playing a Gershwinesque melody" (3). But where do these associations come from in the first place? Most viewers have likely not heard much Native American music; the battle music on screen did not sound during the Vietnam War, the Gulf War, the Iraq War, or any other recent military conflict; and amorous encounters typically don't involve an anonymous saxophone player noodling in the corner. These associations come not from "real" experiences, but from the real experience of filmic and televisual representations of such events.[13]

But, then again, echoing Barthes on intertextuality, such real experiences are perhaps never accessible anyway. They exist only in the interrelations between texts: the units of the code "are so many fragments of something that has always been *already* read, seen, done, experienced; the code is the wake of that *already*" (1974, 20). As Fiske interprets, "a representation of a car chase only makes sense in relation to all the others we have seen—after all, we are unlikely to have experienced one in reality, and if we did, we would, according to this model, make sense of it by turning it into another text, which we would also understand intertextually, in terms of what we have seen so often on our screens" (1987, 115). Applying this theory to soundtrack music, cultural codes are interdependent with cinematic codes. All codified by the viewing experience, "Indian music," battle music, romance music, and seductress music are topics in film music defined by processes of metonymic troping akin to those that during the silent era invested cues sheets with transferable musical meanings.

As Americans consume more popular media content than ever before, we experience an increased frequency of contact with not only music composed specifically for use in a soundtrack, but preexisting music as well, from pop tunes to the "classics" of classical music. Like the signification of "Indian music" et al., meanings we construct for preexisting music within the context of cinematic and televisual events are brought to other musical encounters in subsequent film and television experiences. Because these experiences now come, quite often, in seemingly rapid-fire succession, music, both individual pieces and generic types, sounds in a feed-back loop that generates its own self-reinforcing cycles of signification, just as topics came to do in late-eighteenth-century music. This signification exists in the space between viewing experiences and ultimately echoes beyond filmic and tele-visual contexts. With the same expressive potential and power of the surface features of public instrumental music in the late eighteenth century, this feedback sounds the meanings of music in media-saturated contemporary American culture.

The Pleasures of "Mozart" in American Media

In Alfred Hitchcock's 1958 thriller *Vertigo*, Midge visits Scottie after his nervous breakdown and plays a record—the slow movement of Mozart's Symphony in C Major K. 338. She explains that Mozart is "a broom that sweeps the cobwebs away." In *Vertigo* Mozart's music functions as cinematic code. Its placement in the film and role within the story suggest to the viewer a specific meaning: Mozart represents health and well-being.[14] Of course, Mozart's music also has cultural associations and meanings viewers themselves bring to the film, based on their previous experiences with the composer. But in this case, while the filmic and cultural codes may perhaps complement one another (or not), the notion that Mozart's music is therapeutic is established through spoken dialogue and its status as source music. We hear Mozart's symphony this particular way because Hitchcock's film assigns it a distinct meaning. This meaning also seems to apply to Mozart's slow symphonic music only within the context of *Vertigo*, as it is not reinforced (to my knowledge) by similar and immediate subsequent use in another film or popular cultural context. Perhaps a few people in *Vertigo's* original audience, if they were undergoing music therapy involving classical music, would have had a distinct cultural or even medical association with Mozart. But most viewers, like the characters in the film, would have heard Mozart's music mostly on records, and then only when they chose to play it. Unlike American film and television audiences of the last thirty years, for whom Mozart, Tchaikovsky, and Pachelbel mingle with advertising jingles, news music, sit-com theme songs, and video-game soundtracks to form the constant din of daily life, audiences of the mid-twentieth century would have heard pieces of classical music, for the most part, only when they chose to hear them. In other words, while the viewer may hear cultural echoes, there is no subsequent reinforcing of this specific cinematic meaning of Mozart's slow symphonic music in general or this symphonic slow movement in particular.[15]

Mainstream American film and television productions of the late twentieth and early twenty-first century rarely tell us so explicitly, through spoken dialogue for example, what soundtrack music should mean or how we should understand it. Rather, for those more recent soundtracks that incorporate classical music, meaning is much more dependent on the cultural associations contemporary American audiences maintain for it. And viewers construct these meanings largely through their contact with classical music in their daily lives, much of which occurs during experiences viewing various media. Such cultural associations are then further codified and capitalized on by those in the business of music and sound in Hollywood. As we shall see, once we enter this feedback loop we become increasingly conditioned to hear certain styles of classical music—in particular comic-style instrumental music—as a musical sign for the elite class.[16]

Despite the widely touted (and equally doubted) late-twentieth-century "discovery" known as the "Mozart Effect,"[17] an instance of vertical intertextuality that produces deafening feedback, the alignment of high culture with America's elite class is certainly nothing new. Indeed, as mentioned above, Levine locates the emergence of a cultural hierarchy in the United States in the late nineteenth century. Moreover, he explicitly links this hierarchy with exclusivity and the adoption of certain codes of behavior:

> There can be little doubt that the creation of the institutions and criteria of high culture was a primary means of social, intellectual, and aesthetic separation and selection. Here one learned not only how to appreciate art but also how to *behave* while doing so. . . . What was invented in the late nineteenth century were the rituals accompanying that appreciation; what was invented was the illusion that the aesthetic products of high culture were originally created to be appreciated in precisely the manner late-nineteenth-century Americans were taught to observe: with reverent, informed, disciplined seriousness. (1988, 229, my emphasis)

What does seem relatively new, however, emerging sometime in the last half of the twentieth century, is middle America's sense that the code of conduct of the elite class is not always genuine. Rather, the "initiated," as Levine calls them, "those who had the inclination, the leisure, and the knowledge to appreciate [high culture]" (1988, 230), that is, the wealthy, the educated, and even the (merely) intellectually gifted, are affecting not only their appreciation of high art but the whole of their manners. In short, they are phony. It should not be at all surprising, then, that the music of Mozart, the composer "who had become a symbol of divine artistic genius and a purveyor of cultivated taste" (Levine 1988, 230), is used most often to track artificially civilized behavior.

In Peter Wier's film *The Truman Show* (1998), for example, protagonist Truman Burbank lives in a quaint seaside town full of exceptionally friendly people. The weather always is nice, his wife is pleasant in all ways, and everyone, especially Truman, seems entirely content with his or her existence. But Truman's world is inside a giant television studio, and the townspeople, including his wife, are hired Hollywood actors. In a cruel joke, all in the name of nonstop reality TV, everyone knows this but Truman. He believes that his life—all but his physical existence entirely synthetic—is genuine.

Mozart is integral to the soundscape of Truman's artificial world. We first hear Mozart's music, the third movement of the Piano Sonata in A Major K. 331, on Truman's car radio as he heads to work. Initially we might hear some resonance with *Vertigo*'s therapeutic Mozart or expect the sense of well-being promised by the Mozart Effect: Truman feels suddenly apprehensive, having just seen part of an "airplane" (actually one of the ceiling lights of the soundstage) fall from the sky, and the classical radio dee-jay, concerned as everyone else in *The Truman Show* to quiet Truman's slightest suspicion, plays Mozart "to calm [him] down." But Mozart doesn't stay on the radio. It shifts from its original status as diegetic music to non-diegetic music. The piano sonata starts out as source music coming from the radio but continues after Truman is out of his car. As Truman has the most good-humored interactions imaginable with several "townspeople," Mozart tracks not Truman's but the *viewer's* introduction to Truman's world. Although the dee-jay suggests Mozart as an active agent—it will calm listeners down—Mozart's music is ultimately a passive backdrop to the artificially civilized world of *The Truman Show*. Through this filter, our filter, Mozart's music may be heard as the soundscape of synthetic civility.

In Hollywood, where the entertainment industry keeps its finger on the pulse of its audience—middle America's opinions, beliefs, politics, values, and tastes—caricatures of feigned civilized behavior are typically caricatures of affluence and snobbery as well. In John Hughes's 1986 comedy *Ferris Bueller's Day Off*, for example, cultural associations that middle America may already have for classical music, established through myriad media experiences as well as other points of contact during everyday life,[18] are exploited and reinforced in a scene with an unpleasant gate-keeper at the edge of the world of America's elite class. Ferris, a high school student, accompanied by his best friend and girlfriend skip school and enjoy a day on the town—downtown Chicago. For lunch Ferris chooses an exclusive French restaurant, "Chez Quis," and, after scanning the reservations list for a party of three, claims to be Abe Froman, the "sausage king of Chicago." The maître d', the embodiment of snobbery, scans the three "kids" and is suspicious. Everything in this scene sets Ferris and his companions apart from the world of Chez Quis: their age and their clothes define them as imposters, invading a space that is not theirs. This world of America's elite class is marked by luxurious surroundings, snobby people, haute cuisine, and eighteenth-century comic-style instrumental music. In an accurate reflection of the "real" sounds of fine dining, the minuet of Boccherini's String Quintet in E Major plays as if on the restaurant's sound system during the conflict with the snooty maître d'; the slow movement of Mozart's String Quartet in D Major K. 499, sounds when Ferris and his companions are seated, victorious. Ferris infiltrates this world of unlikable snobs while maintaining his middle-class image (reinforced subsequently by a lip-synched performance of "his" music, The Beatles' cover of "Twist and Shout") as viewers cheer him on.

That the film's viewer might experience a distinct pleasure in hearing classical music in a soundtrack—that is, actively align its meanings to suit her own interests—is suggested by its frequent and prominent use in one of the longest-running sitcoms in television history, NBC's hit series *Frasier* (1993–2004). Classical music plays a crucial role in the characterization of the wealthy and elitist brothers Frasier and Niles Crane. In addition to their gourmet tastes, apartments full of fine art, and memberships in wine clubs, they are always off to the symphony or the opera. They have impeccable taste in everything from food to clothing to music. Along with wealth, they possess much cultural capital. But, unlike its negative regard for the maître d' in *Ferris Bueller's Day Off*, the American public seems to like these snobs. Perhaps viewers sense a certain genuineness in the Cranes' tastes and choice of lifestyle and would hesitate to brand them "phonies," no matter how affected their mannerisms seem or, alternatively, how natural the discourse of culture makes their preference for opera over football appear. Their behavior, genuine or not, unfailingly entertained the millions of loyal viewers among *Frasier*'s mainstream American audience for over a decade.[19] But beyond mere entertainment, the Cranes' condescending behavior and contempt for anything but the highest forms of culture ultimately offer the American public an overt text of resistance: their arrogance, status, and utter inability to communicate in the cultural vernacular lands them in nothing but trouble.

At the beginning of the episode "Three Valentines," for example, which first aired in the United States on 11 February 1999, Dr. Niles Crane, expecting a date with discriminating taste, calls "François" to complain that the champagne he sent over is the '88 instead of the '85. He then turns on the stereo, and the finale of Mozart's "Great G Minor" Symphony fills his brother's Seattle high-rise apartment, borrowed for the evening. Upon sitting on the sofa to wait for his date and champagne delivery, Niles notices that the crease in his trousers is not quite as crisp as he would prefer it to be. After fussing quite a bit (all wonderfully synchronized to the rhythms of the music) he gives into temptation: he takes off the trousers, retrieves the ironing board, and proceeds to sharpen the crease. As the action becomes increasingly humorous—involving such antics as bleeding fingers, fainting spells, spilled flammables, burning furniture, out-of-control fire extinguishers, and parading around in underwear—the fire and intensity of the G-minor finale gives way to the comic style of the overture to Mozart's *Le nozze di Figaro*. Eddie, the dog, enjoys a pile of pasta that has ended up on the sofa just as the overture's final cadence sounds and the episode cuts to commercial.

Mozart's music plays a crucial role in the class conflict that drives *Frasier*'s humor. Mozart is Dr. Frasier Crane's music, but not down-to-earth retired cop Martin's (the brothers' father) music, not the charmingly odd housekeeper and physical therapist Daphne's music, or the single mom and radio station producer Roz's music. And neither, most significantly, is it "ours." For *Frasier* to offer the American middle class the pleasure of resistance, the viewer must maintain active control over its meanings. Nowhere is this control more apparent than in the resignification of the *Figaro* overture in the scene just described. The humor of this scene is largely dependent on the incongruity between what viewers hear and what viewers see. We hear something serious—Mozart's music—while we see something comic—Niles's antics. But Mozart's opera *Le nozze di Figaro* is a comedy, and the music of the opera is in a distinctly comic style. The comic pacing of this music—the phrase structure, the melodic lines, the rhythms—supports the brilliant physical comedy of David Hyde Pierce's performance as Niles Crane. Yet many today, and certainly most of the American viewers that make up *Frasier*'s audience, do not hear Mozart's music as comic. Once "Mozart" is aligned with elitism in contemporary American culture, this music remains serious, inaccessible, even alienating, despite the comic elements of its musical code.

On the surface, the use of the overture to *Le nozze de Figaro* as the main title of

John Landis's 1983 comedy *Trading Places* would also seem to offer an example of this fundamental resignification. But here, as we shall see, Mozart's music is ironic—in fact, doubly so. During the first few minutes of the film there is an incongruity between music and visuals parallel to that in the *Frasier* episode. Although the film's very first image—crew teams training on the Schuylkill River, the University of Pennsylvania boathouses in the background—reinforces the cultural associations middle America largely maintains for Mozart's music, following this opening shot the scenery immediately changes to images of working-class Philadelphia: vendors work in open-air markets, workers ride public transportation, and kids play basketball on a street court, all tracked by the overture to *Le nozze di Figaro*. Close to the end of the opening credits, the editing cuts back and forth between images of wealth and images of poverty. A shot of a butler preparing breakfast on a silver tray, for instance, is immediately followed by a shot of people standing in the unemployment line; after the same butler removes freshly baked croissants from an oven, we see a homeless person sleeping on the street. The purpose of this editing is undoubtedly to show the extremes, to place the elite and lower classes in direct contact. By the end of the credits (and the overture), however, the scene returns to the world of the elite, and viewers meet one of the film's central characters, a futures broker named Winthorpe. Elmer Bernstein's soundtrack music, composed in the same musical idiom as the opera overture, tracks this introduction. The music is not Mozart, but Bernstein has supplied music in the style of Mozart, so there is a certain continuity between the main title and the music of the film's first scene.

This musical characterization of Winthorpe is not only fitting but direct: it complements his Philadelphia brownstone, its contents, his butler, even his breakfast—freshly squeezed orange juice and freshly baked croissants served on a silver tray. Mozart (actually *faux* Mozart at this point), the music of "snobs," completes the picture. But in the music of the opening montage, we can only assume Landis is being quite clever, if not a bit cheeky. The irony of hearing Mozart while seeing working-class Philadelphia *isn't* ironic if the viewer recognizes the overture and knows the opera from which this main-title music comes. *Le nozze di Figaro*, like Beaumarchais's play *Le mariage de Figaro* on which the opera is based, is, like *Trading Places*, a comedy that engages in the serious political business of class warfare. Perhaps, through his choice of music, Landis is acknowledging the opera's resonance in the film, for both stories reveal the potential power of the powerless. In this case, there is no irony, which is, of course, only more ironic.

The Entertainments of "Mozart" in American Media and Culture

Beyond irony, though, the use of Mozart's music in *Trading Places* may also suggest the film not as a text of resistance for its mainstream American audience but rather one of subordination. Most of this film's viewers (and we must remember that this film is a comedy starring Dan Aykroyd and Eddie Murphy, not an art house film) simply hear classical music and either align it with Winthorpe's world or perhaps notice its incongruity with the rest of the film's world. The only people who are likely to recognize the piece and understand the reference are themselves elite. To be sure, it is impossible to know if such a cynical meaning was intended by the filmmakers, but a subsequent musical reference to *Figaro* virtually eliminates the possibility that Landis or Bernstein (or whoever else was responsible for the choice of music in *Trading Places*) stumbled unknowingly onto one of the most explicit engagements with the politics of class warfare in the classical repertory. A few scenes later, after earning his employers, the wealthy Duke brothers, an extra $347,000, Winthorpe innocently whistles Figaro's cavatina "Se vuol ballare." He doesn't know it yet, of course, but he, like Figaro, is an entirely discardable servant who will, in the end, teach his malicious employers "the art of stinging, the art of conniving."[20] The film's story may depict an upending of the social order, but its soundtrack, at least momentarily, can be read as reinforcing the status quo. Like the use of the *Figaro* overture as the main title, Winthorpe's whistled tune is ultimately an inside joke—one made by the elite for the elite. The situation of this "cultured" reference within an obvious vehicle of popular entertainment only heightens its effective exclusivity.

Indeed, this seemingly harmless inside joke is, in the end, made at the expense of the film's primary audience—the mainstream and largely middle-class American public. The *Trading Places* viewer, may, like *Frasier's* viewer, experience real pleasure in *not* knowing this music and thereby actively adopt the film's subversive position relative to the signified of the Mozart signifier, the elite class. But to do so the viewer must also acknowledge the musical meaning she has, through years of exposure to media texts, been conditioned to construct—that these are cultural values she should *want* to adopt. If part of the American Dream is the pursuit of wealth along with happiness, late-eighteenth-century instrumental music, according to what we learn on television and at the movies, will accompany us all the way to the bank.

But beyond the musical representations of wealth, privilege, intelligence, and elite culture in American media texts, classical music has been promoted in the United States, for at least the past decade, as an active and even essential ingredient in the production of a successful, educated, and industrious citizen. A palpable result of the Mozart Effect, eighteenth-century "instrumental" music (any vocal selection is almost always presented as an orchestral rendition) is routinely promoted to expectant and new mothers on the claims that this music will produce a superior child. Toward this end, for example, in 1998 Georgia governor Zell Miller added a $105,000 line item to the state budget to provide every baby born in the state with a copy of *Build Your Baby's Brain through the Power of Music*, a compact disc compilation of greatest classical hits, all of which were composed during the eighteenth or early nineteenth century.[21] (Incidentally, the first track on the compact disc is the first movement of Mozart's *Eine kleine Nachtmusik*.)[22]

Behind the now largely discredited claims that Mozart's music (or classical music in general) will turn your child into a genius lurks the broader cultural alignment of the appreciation of high art with superior social status, a situation that bears striking resemblance to the cultivation of taste as a means to social promotion in the eighteenth century. Moreover, just as Anna Larpent seems to have found the fine arts more edifying than enjoyable, so too, apparently, do those Americans attempting to develop an appreciation of classical music as either a means to, or a product of, social advancement—a situation ripe for generating real resentment toward high art and all it has come to represent. As Small observes, the real and distinctive permeability in the American class system "is reflected in the greater hostility shown in the United States by those outside the classical-music culture toward those on the inside. . . . American culture teems with images of that resentment, from 'Roll over Beethoven and tell Tchaikovsky the news' to the Marx brothers' hilarious destruction of a performance of *Trovatore*." Small's conclusion: "There's real malice there" (2001, 351).

Further, social promotion in America also appears to require the adoption of high cultural values, at least to a point, even when these values are obviously not genuine, a likely source for most Americans' deep suspicion that the behavior of the elite class is somehow phony. Like Dusty in Woody Allen's 1986 film *Hannah and Her Sisters*, a philistine rock star who suddenly feels compelled to buy fine art because his new house in the Hamptons has "a lot of wall space," the acquisition of material wealth seems to demand the subsequent acquisition of cultural capital. But acquiescing to this requirement, whether on the part of the arrived or the merely aspirational, engenders a real act of subordination, for in so doing we not only sacrifice part of our identity but conform it to what those in positions of power—however much of a media construction such positions of power have now become—determine it should be.

While this alignment between social status and cultural consumption is, of course, neither new nor unique to either the eighteenth century or the twenty-first, what connects the enlightened listener of two hundred years ago to today's postmodern listener is the dialectical relationship between pleasure and entertainment that plays itself out while she experiences the same music—the public instrumental music of the late eighteenth century—in entertainment contexts. On the one hand, the listener may experience real pleasure in her control over the meanings of this music, particularly when the meanings she constructs enable her to imagine resistance to some established authority, as a late-eighteenth-century listener might hear at various points in Haydn's Symphony No. 93 or the late-twentieth-century viewer might hear in the use of Mozart's music in an episode of *Frasier* or *The Simpsons*. But on the other hand, this imagined resistance is also a means to listener subordination. Through wildly different and often opposite cultural associations and social meanings—the music of democratic enthusiasm Haydn's eighteenth-century listener may have heard in the boisterous dance movement of the composer's Symphony No. 104, for example, suggests privilege in Barbra Streisand's 1991 film *The Prince of Tides*[23]—the meanings both listeners construct may ultimately be carnivalesque. Subversive energy is spent in the concert hall or the movie theater, thereby effectively diminishing its power in other settings and situations.

Even when the listener experiences the meanings of this music as self-generated, they do not, in the end, necessarily reflect her own interests. In either case, late-eighteenth-century public instrumental music remains "merely" entertaining.

The Pleasures of the Classical Symphony in the Contemporary American Concert Hall

As readers of this book are surely aware, there has been much anxiety recently about the ostensible decline, if not impending "death," of classical music in America. In both journalistic and scholarly writing, theories for the causes of this decline abound, as do targets for the blame: cutbacks in arts education in public schools; modernism's alienation of the audience; the lack of publicly celebrated living American composers; classical music's status as a cultural import; the homogenizing effects of Ford Foundation grants, the Public Broadcasting Service's *Great Performances at Lincoln Center,* and other such institutions; downturns in the American economy, especially since September 11th, 2001; and the misguided marketing strategies of the classical music industries themselves. Undoubtedly, all of these things have contributed to the waning health of classical music in America. Others, however, particularly those variously invested in classical music as a business, argue that classical music is alive and quite well in this country. The American Symphony Orchestra League, for example, points to the more than 1,800 adult and youth orchestras across America. In the 2003–2004 concert season, these orchestras reportedly engaged more than 635,000 people (more than 75 percent of whom are volunteers), offered 36,000 concerts, attracted nearly 28 million listeners, reached 15 to 20 percent of American households, and generated $1.47 billion in revenue. And presumably to counter the widely held "blue-haired" image of the classical music audience, the ASOL cites statistics revealing a rather youthful audience: half of the audience at subscription concerts is fifty-five or under; an even younger audience attends family, summer, and educational concerts (American Symphony Orchestra League 2005, 3–4). But while such quantifiable evidence may reveal an economic "pulse," is this really enough to declare classical music "alive" in America? Alternatively, would the lack of such economic viability effectively pronounce classical music "dead" in America?

There is no denying that classical music has, at the very least, something of a communication problem within mainstream American culture. The great majority of Americans are largely uninterested in classical music (as even those seemingly positive ASOL statistics reveal), whether experienced live or on recordings. In the terms of this study, such widespread indifference would suggest a tangible lack of listening pleasure, the cause of which, as I have theorized, is the listener's inability to determine and control the meanings of this music. To the above list of causes for classical music's decline, then, I would add the overdetermination of the meanings of classical music in contemporary American culture, particularly its signification within popular visual media.

On the one hand, various styles or "categories" of classical music, because of their repeated use in soundtracking specific types of visual characters and events, have effectively been assigned singular and quite specific meanings. For example, as we have seen in this chapter, late-eighteenth-century comic-style instrumental music suggests superior intelligence or a high social standing; similarly, gothic choral music (e.g., Orff's *Carmina Burana,* Mozart's *Requiem*) threatens supernaturally; "bombastic" nineteenth-century instrumental music (e.g., Wagner's *Ride of the Valkyries,* the scherzo of Beethoven's Symphony No. 9) threatens terrestrially; and ruminating "morning" themes (e.g., the opening of Beethoven's Symphony No. 6, the opening of Grieg's *Peer Gynt* Suite No. 1) evoke a sense of tranquility soon to be disrupted comically. And yet, once divorced from visual contextualization, classical music of *any* kind—any style, any period, any genre—seems incapable of shedding a certain elevated class coding within the American imagination. With listeners perhaps taking their cue from the uses of late-eighteenth-century music in mainstream American media, classical music is now widely heard as elite music. Unable to inspire any *new* and therefore individually consequential meanings in the minds of the majority of potential listeners, classical music—subject to such prescription—affords most Americans little opportunity to experience the pleasure of listening.

In a reverse feedback cycle of the signification explored above, the ubiquitous use of "Mozart" as a musical sign for elite characters, behaviors, and situations in film and televisual contexts inescapably affects the listener's construction of meaning for the Classical symphony in the contemporary American concert hall. To be sure, extensive ethnographic research would be needed to explore the many implications of this interpretive path, not only for the meanings of classical music in America but also for the future health of its institutions. But, as a first step in tracing the interpretive consequences of this reverse feedback for our own engagements with late-eighteenth-century public instrumental music, we should consider how these ostensibly predetermined musical meanings shape the interpretive processes of a contemporary concert-goer.

The makeup of today's classical concert audience is a mixture of music enthusiasts, socialites, students, and tourists, the overwhelming majority of whom are undeniably educated and at least reasonably prosperous. Concert programs for America's top national and regional symphony orchestras typically offer two or three large orchestral works, one of which is often a concerto or other composition featuring a headlining soloist. Such uniformity, Joseph Horowitz suggests, is a result of the contemporary classical music marketplace: the need to sell tickets, to raise funds, and to sustain a healthy relationship with the public while "seducing but not challenging the laissez-faire listener" (2005, 517). Certainly all successful businesses require adequate and sustainable sales, varied sources of revenue and capital, and good public relations. But does attracting and keeping the largely elite classical concert audience require seduction and pandering, especially if this is "great" music? Within the current consumer culture of the early twenty-first century, it would seem so—for the meanings listeners may construct while hearing these concert warhorses are continuously reinforced (if not largely generated) by the meanings suggested for this music by its visually mediated contexts.

By regularly programming the well-known symphonic masterpieces from the late eighteenth and early nineteenth centuries—and here we must note that, according to the ASOL, the top two performed composers for the 2003–2004 concert season were Beethoven and Mozart—the "tastemakers" (Horowitz's label for "the people who run orchestras and opera companies, write about then, broadcast and record them" [2005, 538]) provide a sizable and secure step toward sustaining the economic health of classical concert life in America. Because listeners tend to go to concerts today less to experience new music than to hear favorite recorded music performed live,[24] to program works from the Classical symphonic repertory—the heart of the canon—is to offer many in the audience just what they want: the comfort and predictability of a known entity performed flawlessly (if not necessarily interestingly) by a premiere ensemble. Obviously good for ticket sales, this programming strategy nearly ensures that the prospective listener will be entertained, at least during the "canonical" portion of the program (and for many concerts, that would mean the whole evening). A satisfied customer is, of course, also good for public relations. But the question most relevant to my purpose here is *why* the concert-going public is so predictably satisfied by hearing these canonical works over and over again.

Familiarity, repeatability, and an unchallenging aesthetic are certainly part of the answer, as Douglas Dempster, in a private correspondence with Horowitz, clearly implies in his apt comparison of the contemporary American symphony orchestra to a McDonald's hamburger: "its very success . . . is built on uniformity (all look exactly alike) [and] reliability (the bathrooms are always clean and the fries always salty)." But, to explain the "perceived value" today's concert audience maintains for classical music, Dempster also points to "the marketed perception that this is an acceptable and even wholesome pastime" (quoted in Horowitz 2005, 515). While I do not doubt that most in an audience genuinely enjoy the music programmed on a symphony orchestra concert, I suspect that at least some part of the aesthetic satisfaction for many listeners stems from the belief that classical music is culturally, socially, and intellectually "good for them." At the top of the ASOL's guide to answering Frequently Asked Questions is a quotation from a concert-goer who notes an "exuberance" stemming from "having others all experiencing something good, positive, and wonderful" (American Symphony Orchestra League 2005, 2). To my ears, "positive" is the marked word here, and its use implies that other forms of entertainment are, if not "negative," "less positive." Such a belief taps directly into the late-twentieth-century class coding of late-eighteenth-century instrumental music, the resignification of which seems to extend to nearly all classical music once it is divorced from the visually mediated contexts in which it is most frequently encountered.

While such undoubtedly satisfied listeners may regard concerts as truly enjoyable experiences, today's classical concert culture rewards aesthetically those who acquiesce to its arguably classist demands. The position of the listener is strikingly parallel to Mulvey's Hollywood film viewer in whom, whatever his or her actual gender, a masculine subjectivity is produced. To be sure, I am granting the musical text tremendous social and political power here—in particular, the power to determine listener subjectivity. But in this case, the reverse feedback allows the mediated meanings and the perceived cultural value of classical music mutually to reinforce one another. A stagnation in signification results, effectively eliminating the possibility of newly constructed meanings and, along with it, the listener's control over meaning. With the listening pleasure of its primary audience so forfeited, classical concert culture may indeed suffer a "death" of personal vitality.

But if, on the other hand, we embrace wholeheartedly the many points of contact between classical music as we enjoy it in live or recorded performances and as we experience it in various mediated contexts, the interpretive process would involve our negotiation through a complex web of intertextual meanings. To arrive at musical meanings that are the most personally satisfying, if not also socially and culturally rewarding, would require the listener's active participation in and control over the construction of meaning. For example, when the reverse feedback cycle inspires meanings for classical music that are not necessarily reinforced by its "perceived value" and high social status, pleasure may be reinvested in the listener's experience as she negotiates between these mediated meanings and her own sense of this music's cultural value. Such may be the case when listeners hear exceptionally mediated works like Beethoven's Fifth Symphony or Wagner's *Ride of the Valkyries* in the concert hall or opera house.[25] Alternatively, for listeners with more intellectual and musical than social investments in classical music, the "perceived value" of classical music may be less of a force in the interpretive process. Rather than constraining meaning, the ubiquitous class coding of classical music in American media may trigger interesting moments of antagonistic signification, a realigning of musical and personal identities, willful indifference or even ignorance, collisions of cultural spaces, and myriad other interpretive routes. Whatever the case, the listener's dynamic engagement in the musical experience may yield fresh and individually rewarding meanings.

By hearing late-eighteenth-century music within an inclusive echo chamber of our own twenty-first-century culture, we also, paradoxically, regain something of this music's *historical* means of communication. Our interpretations may be wildly different from those of Haydn's and Mozart's first listeners, but the interpretive process is strikingly similar: the listener hears expressive echoes of her own world in the real time of a musical performance, renders the music intelligible by associating those echoes with her own experiences, musical and otherwise, and charts a course of signification according to her personal needs, individual situation, and unique listening subjectivity. Part of a listener's experience may be a musical education that informs the meanings she constructs, and her listening pleasure may rest, at least partially, on using her understanding of late-eighteenth-century music to construct historically appropriate meanings. But just as in the late eighteenth century, neither a musical education nor an elite social status need be a prerequisite for finding meaning in a Classical symphony. The pleasure of listening lives in the process, not the product, of our interpretive activities.

Notes

Introduction

1. According to Mozart, "the audience were quite carried away" by the performance of his Symphony in D major K. 297 at the *concert spirituel* in Paris on 18 June 1778. "There was a tremendous burst of applause" in the middle of the first Allegro, "shouts of 'Da capo'" at the movement's close, calls to "'hush' at the soft beginning" of the last Allegro, and more applause during the following forte passage (Anderson 1966, 2: 558). At Mozart's academy in the Hofburgtheater in Vienna on 23 March 1783, "the entire audience accorded him such unanimous applause as has never been heard of here," so reports the *Magazin der Musik* (quoted and trans. in Zaslaw 1989, 380). Glowing reviews of Haydn's symphonies, the featured works of Salomon's concert series in London in the early 1790s, note time and again "the most marked," "fervid," and "abundant" applause. The 8 June 1792 *Morning Herald* proclaims that "the instrumental pieces of Haydn were received with an extacy [*sic*] of admiration" (Landon 1976, 136–73).

2. Dozens of reviews of late-eighteenth-century public concerts use the same handful of words to capture the social makeup of the audience. Quoted here are *The Oracle*'s review of Salomon's concert on 24 February 1792 (Landon 1976, 137) and Frédéric-Melchior Grimm's description of the audience of the Concert des Amateurs (J. Johnson 1995, 74).

3. *The Oracle*, 6 January 1792, and *The Morning Chronicle*, 30 May 1786, respectively, both quoted in McVeigh (1993, 33–41). The *Morning Chronicle* reviewer even suggests an egalitarian atmosphere at the Vauxhall Jubilee of 1786 in which "the cit and the courtier jostled each other with the usual familiarity" (McVeigh 1993, 41).

4. Police report, 17 frimaire, an IV (8 December 1795), quoted in J. Johnson (1995, 156).

5. The Germania Society was a European orchestra founded in Berlin by twenty-five young men. The founders had a democratic spirit unique to such societies at the time and drew up a constitution to ensure equal earnings and equal rights among the members. Their ambition was to bring the music of the great German composers to the "politically free people" of the United States. The society performed in the United States from 1848 to 1854. See H. Johnson (1953).

6. Lawrence Levine (1998) and Alan Trachtenberg (1982) locate the "sacralization" of culture in the Gilded Age; Joseph Horowitz (2005), alternatively, argues for the decades between the two world wars.

7. The often noted distinction between two stylistic poles in late-eighteenth-century music, most commonly delineated as public music and private music in present-day musicological writing, rests on both eighteenth-century theoretical

explications of style and our own analytical observations. Johann Georg Sulzer (1771–74), Heinrich Christoph Koch (1782–93), and Augustus Friedrich Kollmann (1799), among others, define symphony style and sonata style primarily in terms of expressive character: the symphony style is grand, exalted, festive, and sublime; the sonata style is intimate, personal, and flexible. Noting our discomfort with the elusive and subjective nature of musical expression in eighteenth-century theoretical and aesthetic writings, Michael Broyles fleshes out eighteenth-century descriptions of the melodic features of the two styles and offers his own analytical observations regarding differences in rhythmic propulsion and cadential manipulation (1983). Charles Rosen locates the distinction between public and private music in aspects of performance as well as musical style: the structural features of symphonic music require a steady tempo whereas those of solo music invite flexibility in tempo; public music speaks primarily to the listeners, private music also to the players (1997, 143–45). In scrutinizing Sulzer's analogy of the symphony to the Pindaric ode, Mark Evan Bonds points to compositional artifice, the musical texture of interweaving voices, and the expression of communal sentiments as features that distinguish the public, symphonic style of the late eighteenth century from the private, sonata style (1997).

8. Lawrence Kramer makes a similar point about "internal" and "external" meanings in his essay on representation in Haydn's *Creation* (1995, 67).

1. On Meanings of Musical Meaning

1. While Hanslick's (in)famous line—"the content of music is tonally moving forms"—summoned forth a new, purely musical ideal, the polarization of idealism and formalism is a product of the reception and subsequent revisions of Hanslick's treatise more than his original ideas themselves. See Bonds (1997a) on significant deletions from Hanslick's treatise in later editions, as well as for an argument for the compatibility of idealism and formalism.

2. An "abstract interiority of pure sound" is Hegel's idea. See Goehr (1992, 155n11).

3. For a list of scholars who make this claim, see Bonds (1997a, 389n6).

4. Bonds (1997a, 420n102) notes Walter Wiora's point that "if music were detached from the realm of extramusical ideas, it would not have attained such importance in the minds of so many writers from this period." But then Bonds (390–91) also sets idealism in direct opposition to the naturalism of eighteenth-century aesthetics, the philosophical basis for mimesis.

5. For example, "It is not merely and absolutely through its own intrinsic beauty that music affects the listener, but rather at the same time as a sounding image of the great motions of the universe. Through profound and secret connections to nature, the meaning of tones is elevated high above the tones themselves, allowing us to perceive at the same time the infinite in works of human talent. Because the elements of music—sound, tone, rhythm, loudness, softness—are to be found throughout the entire universe, so does one find anew in music the entire universe." Eduard Hanslick, *Eduard Hanslick: Vom Musikalisch-Schönen*, ed. Dietmar Strauß, 2 vols. (Mainz: Schott, 1990), 1:171; quoted and trans. in Bonds (1997a, 414–15). Bonds argues that the polarization of idealism and formalism is a product

of the reception and subsequent revisions of Hanslick's treatise more than his original ideas themselves.

6.　For further discussion of idealism and absolute music, see Dahlhaus (1989).

7.　Many writers make this point. See Scruton (1980, 1:26): "The best way to speak of a thing that claims to be 'absolute' is to say what it is not"; Dahlhaus (1989, 7): "The idea of 'absolute music' . . . consists of the conviction that instrumental music purely and clearly expresses the true nature of music by its very lack of concept, object, and purpose"; and Bonds (1997a, 419): "Hanslick's deletion of the final sentences for the second edition reflects the emerging dichotomy between absolute and program music and thus the emergence of absolute music in the sense in which it is generally understood today—that is, in terms of what it is not."

8.　This assessment echoes Harold Powers's criticism of Agawu's theory: "The specificity of the topics and the generality of the reductions are too far apart—they are chalk and cheese, they don't 'play' nicely" (1995, 31).

9.　A fascinating demonstration of dialogue among musical, cultural, and physical entities, Hatten's theory of musical gesture and the richly textured interpretations that result from its application argue compellingly for a synthetic approach to musical meaning (Hatten 2004).

10.　For an article-length introduction to intertextuality in music studies, see Hatten (1985); for a book-length reconsideration of intertextuality in music, see Klein (2005).

11.　Batteux observes, for example, that "sound is the essential expression of music, as color is of painting and movement of the body of dance" (1746, quoted and trans. in Neubauer 1986, 63).

12.　Types and styles are Ratner's two broad categories of musical topics. Many analysts have embraced his simple bipartite division of the topical universe while adding varying degrees of specificity. Sisman, for example, proposes two additional categories: rhythms, sometimes connected with dance but which also include unrelated categories like *alla zoppa,* and genres, for topics like the French overture and aria. Hatten broadens Ratner's classification scheme to include codes of feelings and passions alongside topics in a cosmos of expressive subjects. Agawu, on the other hand, simply offers an alphabetical listing. See Ratner (1980, 9), Agawu (1991, 30), Sisman (1993b, 46), and Hatten (1994, 74–75). For a call for the full cultural study of each topic, a rich historical, cultural, and musical exploration of the military topic, and a history and criticism of Ratner's topical theory, especially his varying relationships to eighteenth-century sources, see Monelle (2000, 14–40).

13.　Ratner offers three examples from Mozart's *Don Giovanni:* the introduction to the overture, the duel in Act I, and the "supper" scene in Act II (1980, 24).

14.　Although the difference between representation and expression was first addressed explicitly in aesthetic discourse in 1902 by Benedetto Croce (1992), Scruton notes that a categorical distinction has been implicit in aesthetic theories since Kant (1997, 119).

15.　Scruton's concept of expression is quite complex (too complex to summarize here), but two key components are (1) its link to his theory of musical understanding: "if a piece of music is expressive, then this must be understood by the one who hears with understanding" and (2) its dependence on structure: "expression is *developed* through a musical argument [and] for a work to be expressive, it must provide a musical articulation of its content" (1997, 170).

16. For Goodman, expression is the metaphoric possession of a property (e.g., an emotion) by a work of art (1968, 50–52).

17. For a groundbreaking theory of musical gesture, one that combines traditional music theory with biological and psychological foundations of meaningful human movement, see Hatten (2004), especially part 2.

18. A trope in Hatten's theory is a figurative meaning that occurs "when two different, formally unrelated types are brought together in the same functional location so as to spark an interpretation based on their interaction" (1994, 295).

19. See Hatten (2004, 9–11) for further discussion of the opposition of structure and expression.

20. Agawu explicitly acknowledges his evasion of "the 'what' question": "The recurring question for me throughout these pages concerns *meaning* in Classic music—not 'what does this piece mean?' but, rather, '*how* does this piece mean?' In other words, it seems more useful, in the face of the multiplicity of potential meanings of any single work, to frame the analytical question in terms of the dimensions that make meaning possible; only then can we hope to reduce away the fanciful meanings that are likely to crop up in an unbridled discussion of the phenomenon, and to approach the preferred meanings dictated by both historical and theoretical limitations. This is one reason why I have borrowed certain concepts from semiotics, even if it ultimately evades—or declares irrelevant—the 'what' question" (1991, 5).

21. Theorized first by American philosopher Charles Sanders Peirce in 1867 (see Peirce 1984, 2:49–59) and now taken up by many, an interpretant is that which is brought into being in the mind of the producer, the receiver, or both by the relationship of the signifier and the signified. The interpretant subsequently becomes another sign, generating another interpretant, and so on ad infinitum. In other words, an "interpretant" is simply an idea that generates an infinity of further ideas. See Almeder (1980, esp. 27–32) for more on Peirce's concept of the interpretant.

22. In his analyses Nattiez concentrates his energies on the "neutral level," rather than the "poietic level" (composition) or the "esthetic level" (reception), thereby implying, if tacitly, that musical meaning resides in the score, fixed and absolute. See Nattiez (1990), especially part 2, "The Semiology of Discourse on Music."

23. Pieter van den Toorn, for example, famously takes to task feminist criticism, postmodern criticism, and the application to music of psychoanalytic, sociopolitical, and critical theories, accusing them (in a response to the work and ideas of Joseph Kerman, Susan McClary, Lawrence Kramer, and especially Leo Treitler) of forcing a subject-object polarity and assigning all virtue to the subjective (1995, 67).

24. In philosophical explorations of musical meaning, intentionality seems not so easily dismissed, for a work of art originates in human actions and must therefore be understood analytically as an intended object. For example, many music

philosophers, on the grounds that representation is an intentional category, maintain that a composer must intend a work to represent something for musical representation to exist. Kivy, however, argues the converse: should we discover documentary evidence "proving" that a composer did not intend for a given passage to represent anything, any claim to representation is defeated. But, of course, rarely do we have concrete evidence of a composer's intentions. For this reason he stipulates that representation is also a "success" concept: there must be some "modicum of success . . . to make the intended representation a representation in fact." Intention, then, is for Kivy a necessary but not sufficient condition for representation. Scruton also maintains that intention is necessary for representation in art, but, as noted above, denies music any representational capabilities, thereby rendering the question moot in considerations of musical meaning. He also categorically dismisses the "intentional fallacy," arguing, after Stanley Cavell (1969), that "there is no real distinction between studying an artist's intentions and studying his work"; or, put more forcefully, "an artistic intention is revealed in the work that expresses it," a stance that, like Kivy's, locates meaning entirely within the work itself. See Kivy (1984, 213–15) and Scruton (1997, 145 and 409).

25. In his observations that (1) the ideas music raises are dependent on the "temporary disposition" of the listener and (2) the listener may choose the ideas he finds most agreeable to him at a given moment, Thomas Twining anticipates these foundations of postmodern criticism. See Twining (1789, 49 note *s*) and chapter 3 of this book.

2. The Immediacy of Structural Understanding

1. "Alle diese angeführten Stücke zu beurtheilen, ist, nach erstem und einmaligem Anhören, besonders da die Rede von Beethovenschen Werken ist, deren hier so viele nach einander gegeben wurden, und die meistens so gross und lang sind— geradezu unmöglich."

2. A rare exception is Mozart's "Great G Minor" symphony K. 550, which Ernst Gerber found "difficult to follow" (see chapter 4). By the middle of the first decade of the nineteenth century, however, more critics found that Mozart's music, like Beethoven's, required more than one hearing. Zaslaw conflates two notices from the *Allgemeine musikalische Zeitung* (1804–1805, vii, col. 579; 1806–1807, ix, col. 94) to make this point: "One must hear . . . Mozart's deep, artful and emotion-filled Symphony in G minor [K. 550] . . . several times to be able completely to understand and enjoy it" (Zaslaw 1989, 530). It is important to note, however, that these reviews were written (1) over fifteen years after Mozart composed this symphony and (2) strikingly close in time to similar comments made about Beethoven's music. In addition to reacting to the undeniable difficulty of Mozart's music, such reviewers likely bear witness to the changes in listening behavior and musical expectations that accompanied early Romanticism.

3. There are, of course, exceptions. Listeners sometimes found Mozart's music "difficult," prompting Sisman to propose a "topic of difficulty" in late-eighteenth-century music. See Sisman (1997, 53) and chapter 4.

4. On critical problems with the text/context binary, see chapter 3.

5. Figures are part of *elocutio*, the third stage of the rhetorical process in which the

argument is shaped, whereas topics are part of *inventio,* the first stage of the rhetorical process, in which the subject is discovered. See Sisman (1993b, 69–71; 1997, 52–53).

6. Hatten suggests the slower style growth of the sacred style relative to the chamber and theater styles as an agent in this correlation, the result of which is a "historical style" that adheres to an "older compositional creed" (1994, 75–76).

7. To be fair, nor does Allanbrook assert these particular "extra-musical" meanings for the *Sturm und Drang* in modulatory passages; in fact, she does not seem to allow any meaning beyond the "purely musical" for topical references in instrumental music.

8. Allanbrook's deeply rewarding analyses of the first movements of Mozart's Piano Sonatas K. 332 and K. 333 show how these two movements, despite their exceptionally similar formal procedures, "unfold in strikingly different fashions due to the nature of the expressive gestures that characterize them" (1992, 130).

9. "Presentational" is Janet Levy's term for stable passages that promote coherence (1982, 482–97).

10. Allanbrook makes a similar point about the second group's minuet topic in the first movement of Mozart's Piano Sonata K. 332 (1992, 137).

11. See chapter 4 for a discussion of this review.

12. See chapter 4 on Busby's opinion of this piece.

13. These phrases all come from a review of a set of Haydn minuets published 6 October 1787 in the *Neue Leipziger gelehrte Zeitungen,* quoted and trans. in Morrow (1997, 113–14).

14. I would like to thank the anonymous reader who pointed to the compatibility of listener-oriented and composer-oriented approaches in my work.

15. Specifically, Agawu (1991), Allanbrook (1992, 1996), Hatten (1994), Levy (1982), and Sisman (1993b, 1997).

16. Agawu also limits parts of his semiotic interpretation to the three rhetorical functions of beginning, middle, and ending, and likewise evaluates certain topics for their rhetorical implications. But in his pursuit of structural meaning he employs primarily paradigmatic and structural-tonal voice-leading analysis.

17. Much of the renewed interest in Classical formal theory centers on form-functional constituents at various levels of musical discourse. William Caplin's theory of formal functions, for example, identifies presentation, continuation, and cadential functions at the level of the sentence; antecedent and consequent functions at the level of the period; exposition, contrasting middle, and recapitulation functions at the level of the small ternary theme; the interthematic functions of main theme, transition, and subordinate theme at the level of the sonata-form exposition; exposition, development, and recapitulation functions at the level of the sonata-form movement; and introduction and postcadential functions, among others. Caplin's functions are distinguished primarily by harmonic progression, tonal design, motivic development, and phrase-structural organization. Taking a somewhat different approach, Hatten defines the musical materials that determine thematic, developmental/transitional, and cadential/closural formal functions in the Classical style in terms of specific stylistic oppositions:

periodic/aperiodic, tonally stable/tonally unstable, and conventional material/ distinctive material. For example, thematic material is periodic, tonally stable, and distinctive whereas developmental/transitional material is aperiodic, tonally unstable, but still distinctive. The rewards of this strategy are rich and immediate. Six new categories are revealed by cross-referencing material and location (e.g., an unstable theme or a developmental coda), demonstrating a logical process of growth "motivated by an interest in enhanced expressivity and achieved by strategic markedness." See Caplin (1998) and Hatten (1994, 112–32).

18. Although this symphony was intended for the celebration of Haffner's ennoblement on 29 July 1782, the symphony may not have arrived in time for the parties. A revised version was performed at Mozart's academy in the Hofburgtheater in March of the following year, a concert at which Joseph II was present. For more details, see Zaslaw (1989, 376–82).

19. This term comes from László Somfai's description of opening gestures in Haydn's Opp. 71–74 string quartets (1973–74, 159–74).

20. See, for example, Ratner (1980, 315) and Waterman (1980, 6: 822). Marianne Danckwardt, however, proposes the fanfare as the main forerunner for the slow introduction (1977, 219–34).

21. Sisman suggests that the "Prague" Symphony's opening unison passage is particularly striking because it is *not* a French overture topic. She also notes Mozart's use of the same ascending flourish in the two opera overtures and the "Jupiter" Symphony (1997, 35–36).

22. Allanbrook makes the same point about the "simple 'tune,'" labeling it the "most stabilizing of *galant* topoi" (1996, 135).

23. Levy also notes that such textures occur frequently at the beginning of the second key area (1982, 491).

24. Many writers have noted the conventional material of cadential passages and closing groups. Among them, see Caplin (1998, 11) and Hatten (1994, 115–17). See also note 17 above.

25. The use of tremolos in the bridge passages of symphonic sonata forms is common in even the earliest independent symphonies. For two widely known examples, see the first movements of Sammartini's Symphony in F Major, No. 32, and Stamitz's Sinfonia a 8 in E-flat Major (*La melodia germanica*, No. 3), both included in the *Norton Anthology of Western Music*, 5th ed., vol. 2.

26. Sisman argues that much of Haydn's so-called *Sturm und Drang* music was either composed for immediate use in the theater or composed in such a way as to accommodate later use as overtures and entr'actes (1990).

27. In addition to the stylistic parallels, Sisman notes that Mozart copied the incipit of this symphony along with two others, perhaps considering using them in his benefit concerts; that the variation movement in Mozart's Piano Concerto in B-flat Major K. 450 was modeled on the slow movement of this work; and that Bonds has argued that when modeling a work on someone else's, Mozart was inclined to "outdo" that work (Sisman 1993a, 202–209; 1997, 45; Bonds 1997a, 365–409).

28. In eighteenth-century usage the term "symphony" referred to three categories of orchestral music: chamber symphonies—multimovement orchestral works; thea-

ter symphonies—overtures to operas and plays, as well as entr'actes; and church symphonies—overtures to oratorios and cantatas, as well as orchestral music played during the liturgy. Unless used in quotation, I use the term "symphony" to refer only to pieces in the first category. The term "overture" will be used to refer to pieces in the last two categories—overtures to operas, plays, oratorios, and cantatas, as well as concert overtures (i.e., overtures to theater pieces that have been revised for concert use).

29. As early as the last two decades of the seventeenth century, overtures—or *sinfonie*, as they were called—were performed independently as concert works, giving rise to what later became the concert symphony. Although Alessandro Scarlatti instituted the three-movement structure for Italian *sinfonie* as early as the 1680s, the style we now associate with Classical symphonies—homophonic texture with clearly articulated themes over a relatively slow harmonic rhythm, and contrasting key areas presented within the first part of a binary form (in other words, the characteristics of the Classical style and the Classical sonata form)—emerged only in Neapolitan opera overtures of the 1740s, in the works of Leonardo Vinci, Giovanni Battista Pergolesi, Niccolò Jomelli, Baldassare Galuppi, and Leonardo Leo. These Neapolitan opera *sinfonie* provided the most important model for the influential composers at the German court of Mannheim, who adopted the *sinfonie*'s style in their symphonies. See Wolf (1980, 200).

30. See, for example, the Hanover-Square concert program for 26 March 1783, quoted in Ratner (1980, 144), in which the opening Haydn symphony is listed as "Overture."

31. Traeg's catalog does, however, note this combination. See Zaslaw (1989, 515).

32. "Seitdem die Opern in Italien ihren völligen Klang erreichet haben: so hat man auch darauf gesehen, ihnen eine Gattung von Instrumentalstücken vorzusetzen, die, bevor der Vorhang der Schaubühne aufgezogen wird, die Zuhörer zu der ganzen Oper auf eine bequeme und sinnereiche Art vorgereitet. Diese Stücke nennt man Symphonien."

33. When recycling an overture as a symphonic first movement, for example, Haydn generally added repeat signs at the end of the exposition and recapitulation. See Fisher (1985) and Lowe (1998, 58–75).

34. Fisher notes that the main difference between Haydn's overtures and symphonic first movements is structural: formal sections may be shorter in overtures but proportions remain the same (1985, esp. ch. 6).

35. There is some debate about whether the rest of a concert would have been "inserted," as it were, between the third and final movements of the opening symphony or whether the finale of the opening symphony would have been reprised as a closing number. For more on the issue, along with selected sample concert programs, see Morrow (1989, ch. 5 and app. 1) and Zaslaw (1989, esp. 380–81).

36. Webster's work confirms that tonal, structural, motivic, and gestural links among movements integrate Haydn's instrumental cycles (1991a).

37. "Diese muß insonderheit sinnreich, angenehm und fließend sein. Sie muß die Zuhörer mehr ergetzen [ergözen?] und vergnügen, als sie in eine allzuheftige Bewegung bringen, oder in einem allzutiefen Nachdenken hinterlassen."

38. "Das Schöne und Natürliche dieser Schreibart aber besteht eigentlich darinnen, wenn die Melodie überaus deutlich, lebhaft, fließend, und doch scharffinnig ist, wenn sie sich auf ungezwungene Art mancherlei wohl ausgesonnener Zierrathen bedienet, wenn sie frei, ungezwungen und allemal neu ist. Die Harmonie muß die Melodie nur allein deutlicher und vernehmlicher machen; sie muß aber keineswegs hervorragen: denn das kommt allein der Melodie zu."

39. Sisman also notes this expressive descent in eighteenth-century symphonies (1993b, 8; 1997, 83).

40. On Mozart's "difficulty," see chapter 4 of this book and Sisman (1997, 47–56).

41. As Hatten sensibly suggests, "because of the narrowed range of the tragic (predictable from the markedness of minor mode) and the variety of genres possible in the comic arena (*buffa,* pastoral, high comic), the unmarked comic is more appropriately labeled 'nontragic.'" Hatten supports his use of this term by noting Ratner's citation of an article by Daniel Weber which labels "nontragic" such musical types as "mimicry, wit, parody, and artful imitation of musical bungling." See Hatten (1994, 77 and 305n10), Ratner (1980, 387), and Weber (1800, 137–43, 157–62).

42. See chapter 3n1.

3. Enlightening the Listening Subject

1. See, for example, Bauman (1995), Geiringer (2002), Hatting (1981), Keefe (2001), Knepler (1989), Lutteken (1999), McClary (1986), Schroeder (1990), Splitt (1998), Subotnik (1991), Till (1993), Waldoff (1998), Webster (1997), and Zeman (1982).

2. Recent explorations of gender, exoticism, and identity in late-eighteenth-century music include DeNora (1997), Head (2000), Hunter (1997), Perl (2000), Rabin (1997), and Wallace (1999).

3. Both an adaptation and critique of Foucauldian tenets, Jairo Moreno's recent book on musical representations, subjects, and objects takes a very different tack. Moreno locates the emergence of the "early modern subject" in musical-theoretical writings in Descartes's *Compendium musicae,* reads a "participatory subject" capable of manipulating reality in Rameau, and interprets Weber's *das Gehör* as an "interpreting subject." This last subjectivity, Moreno argues, establishes a new modality for the efforts of music theory, one in which temporality of listening experience and interiority of listening subject become "empirical addressees of musical thought" (2004, 19).

4. Other writers delineate this hierarchical relationship more precisely. See, for example, Johann Elias Schlegel's commentary to the German translation of Batteux's treatise by his brother Johann Adolf Schlegel.

5. See, for example, Yves Marie André (1741), Jean le Rond D'Alembert (1751), Johann Mattheson (1739), Christian Gottfried Krause (1752), Johann Adam Hiller (1754), Friedrich Wilhelm Marpurg (1754–62), James Harris (1783), and Daniel Webb (1769).

6. It is important to note that, despite his intention to distinguish between the two

aesthetic categories, Batteux uses imitation and expression practically inter-changeably. See Le Huray and Day (1981, 40–41), Lippman (1992, 88–89), and Neubauer (1986, 62–64).

7. "Les expressions, en général, ne sont d'elles-même, ni naturelles, ni artificielles: elles ne sont que des signes."

8. Batteux is by no means consistent in this claim, however, or in the apparent im-portance he assigns the mind over the body. Later in the same chapter his celebra-tion of feeling echoes Du Bos: "It is true, you may say, that a melodic line can express certain passions: love, for instance, or joy, or sadness. But for every pas-sion that can be identified there are a thousand others that cannot be put into words. That is indeed so, but does it follow that these are pointless? It is enough that they are felt; they do not have to be named. The heart has its own under-standing that is independent of words. When it is touched it has understood everything. Moreover, just as there are great things that words cannot reach, so there are subtle things that words cannot capture, above all things that concern the feelings" (1746, trans. in Le Huray and Day 1981, 50).

9. Some earlier remarks in Section 51 of the Third Critique shed light on Kant's dilemma. On the one hand, because he cannot determine whether the emotional response to the physical stimuli of sound and color is based on perception or on reflection, Kant must concede that "we cannot confidently assert whether a col-our or a tone (sound) is merely an agreeable sensation, or whether they are in themselves a beautiful play of sensations, and in being estimated aesthetically, convey, as such, a delight in their form." Because we cannot perceive the time in-tervals of the vibrations, we cannot judge them, and Kant first concludes that painting and music must be merely pleasant arts. But he immediately follows with two counterarguments: (1) the vibrations are mathematical and thus judged and (2) colorblind and tone-deaf people are still capable of judging changes in the quality of color or sound (1790, trans. in Le Huray and Day 1981, 220–21).

10. Kant famously complained that the noisy hymn-singing by the inmates in the city jail adjacent to his apartment disturbed his concentration.

11. For more on this particular dilemma, see Hatten (1985, 69) and Monelle (2000, 150).

12. Incidentally, eighteenth-century literary precursors of Eco's theoretical open work may be found in Lawrence Sterne's *Tristram Shandy* and Diderot's *Jacques le fataliste,* two novels that, by requiring the reader to draw upon his own experi-ence and fantasy to fill in the gaps in their narratives (Jauss 1989, 30), provide an-other example of the Enlightenment's anticipation of postmodernism.

13. For more on text/context duality see Korsyn (1999, esp. 32–46).

14. This is Hatten's strategy (1985).

15. To be sure, I am spinning the personification of "context" somewhat, but Eco's assertion that "a text is a place where the irreducible polysemy of symbols is in fact reduced because in a text symbols are anchored to their context" (1994, 21) grants the context—however and by whomever delimited—the greater control over meaning.

16. Peirce defines the final interpretant as "that which *would finally* be decided to be the true interpretation if consideration of the matter were carried so far that an

ultimate opinion were reached" (1958, 8:139, italics in original). See also Almeder (1980, 28–29).

17. It is important to note, however, that Eco does not endorse "the 'repressive' idea that a text has a unique meaning, guaranteed by some interpretive authority." He writes: "Thus many modern theories are unable to recognize that symbols are paradigmatically open to infinite meanings but syntagmatically, that is, textually, open only to the indefinite, but by no means infinite, interpretations allowed by the context. To recognize this principle does not mean to support the 'repressive' idea that a text has a unique meaning, guaranteed by some interpretive authority. It means, on the contrary, that any act of interpretation is a dialectic between openness and form, initiative on the part of the interpreter and contextual pressure" (1994, 21).

18. For a more detailed discussion of this connection, see Eagleton (1990) and Korsyn (2003, esp. 42–46).

19. Echoing Jauss (1989, 200–201), Klein makes nearly the same point, though without my Benjaminian allusion (2005, 74).

20. I borrow the specific terms "canonic horizon" and "historical horizon" directly from Klein (2005, 74–76), but the concept of the horizon within literary hermeneutics receives extensive analysis in Jauss (1989, 197–231).

21. Incidentally, "probability" was precisely how Samuel Johnson, in his *Dictionary of the English Language*, defined "Verisimilitude" in 1755. See also Bender (1997).

22. Diderot wrote letters from a fictional nun "Suzanne" to the Marquis de Croismare to entice him to return to Paris. These letters became the basis for *La Religieuse*, published in 1796.

23. Particularly useful for this brief character sketch were Beals (1996), Morrow (1989), Pezzl ([1786–90] 1991), Robertson and Timms (1991), and Wangermann (1973).

24. Excerpts from Zinzendorf's diaries are translated in Morrow (1989, 229–331).

25. My thanks to Dorothea Link for sharing her impressions of Zinzendorf, gleaned from countless hours spent working with his diaries.

26. For further description of the Burgtheater, see Morrow (1989, 71–78).

27. For a calendar of public concerts in Vienna in 1761–1810, see Morrow (1989, 237–364).

28. For further commentary on the significance of the combination of sentimental and martial elements in "Porgi amor," see Allanbrook (1983, 101–102) and Webster (1991b, esp. 152).

29. See Pezzl ([1786–90] 1991, 140–41) for more on Carnival in late-eighteenth-century Vienna.

30. See Pezzl ([1786–90] 1991, 149–50), "Redoutensaal Activities" for more on the activities and atmosphere of the Imperial ballrooms, and "The Nobility of the First Rank" for more on the particular anxieties of the nobility in Joseph II's Vienna.

31. See J. Johnson's cultural history of listening in Paris for rich descriptions of Parisian concert audiences, a rewarding investigation as to why French audiences be-

came silent, and sources for the quotes offered above (1995, 156, 197–205, and 320n5).

32.   See also Lyons (1975, 143–44).

33.   J. Johnson notes that "for one staunch republican the evening [at a concert that featured vocal and instrumental works] was a mockery of everything he had learned about music during the Revolution. First, the songs were in Italian, which deprived them of any practical value to French audiences. Worse, the featured selection was a symphony. 'Tell me what the author wanted to paint in the symphony that starts with the kettledrums making a horrible racket and continues with tender, languorous phrases only to be interrupted by more beating and meaningless chords'" (Johnson 1995, 140).

34.   George Rudé draws this conclusion from documents detailing eyewitness accounts of the composition of the crowd of rioters at various uprisings (1971, 100–101).

35.   Jeremy Black argues that the increasing importance of middle-class patronage "does not imply that their tastes were necessarily very different from those of the nobility. In numerous spheres the bourgeoisie shared noble tastes, which was not surprising, as the permanent or seasonal urban sojourns of, in particular, the wealthy nobility helped to provide a model for behaviour" (1990, 234).

36.   Colquhoun's data are listed in an appendix in George (1953, 152–53).

37.   For more on private concerts in London, see McVeigh (1993, esp. 47–48).

38.   For more on coffeehouse culture in London, see Lilliwhite (1963) and Rudé (1971, 46).

39.   McVeigh, however, argues that while this review "suggests a belligerent independence on the part of the middling ranks, one of the main objects of visiting the gardens was in fact to relish social distinctions, emphasizing the ambiguous British attitude towards class." See McVeigh (1993, 41–43) for the full reference and further comment.

4. Entertaining Pleasure

1.   While Webster argues compellingly that "there is no reason why an approach to composition as entertainment should be considered . . . inherently incompatible with the production of great art," his defense of these works ultimately rests on the complexity and sophistication he finds lurking beneath their accessible surfaces. In its implication that complexity is integral to great art, Webster's argument ironically aligns with much of the criticism he is criticizing. Webster is, of course, aware of this contradiction, as he acknowledges his attempt "to have his cake and eat it too" (1998, 218–45).

2.   On aesthetic pleasure in eighteenth-century English culture, see Brewer (1997), especially chapter 2.

3.   See, for example, Schopenhauer ([1818] 1958, Book 3), in which, like Kant, he maintains aesthetic pleasure as disinterested pleasure. For Schopenhauer, though, it is the metaphysical Idea of an object, not its pure form, that attracts the attention of the subject and, for the moment of aesthetic beholding, alleviates the interminable striving of the will.

4.   According to Freud, unconscious mental processes are "the residue of a phase of

development in which they were the only kind of mental process. The governing purpose obeyed by these primary processes is easy to recognize; it is described as the pleasure-unpleasure *[Lust-Unlust]* principle, or more shortly the pleasure principle. These processes strive towards gaining pleasure; psychical activity draws back from any event which might arouse unpleasure" ([1911] 1989, 301).

5. These adjectives and terms come from contemporary literature on taste and politeness. See, for example, *The Spectator* (Addison et al. 1965); Bermingham and Brewer (1995, esp. 1–2).

6. See, for example, Voltaire ([1732] 1959), Burke ([1756] 1958), Gerard ([1764] 1970), and Alison (1790).

7. This phrase comes from Alison (1790), but nearly identical terminology can be found in numerous writings on taste of the time, for example, Hume ([1752] 1965) and Gerard ([1764] 1965).

8. Anna Larpent's diary is housed in the Huntington Library, San Marino, California, catalogued as Huntington Manuscripts 31201.

9. I borrow this terminology from Agawu, although he seemingly asserts the opposite in writing "When a movement is labeled 'Minuet,' we cannot assume a fixed generic identity; only an inspection of the actual music will reveal whether title and contents are congruent" (1991, 40). In the end, we both argue the same point—that a minuet's title and expressive content do not necessarily agree. I am, however, suggesting that there is an additional layer in the interpretive process: the implications of the title "Minuet" for an eighteenth-century audience in fact provide the potential for expressive troping and topical dissonance.

10. Kirnberger, for example, used the minuet as a basic composition exercise, while Koch employed it as an example to demonstrate compositional techniques for melodic expansion (Kirnberger 1757; Koch [1793] 1983, 110–48). See also Sisman (1982).

11. The musical material of the late-eighteenth-century minuet is in essence a "classicized" rendition of the Baroque dance, but the Baroque and Classical minuet differ markedly in affect and tempo. Betty Bang Mather offers much evidence from a variety of sources to support a fast tempo for the Baroque minuet. Among them are a medical treatise and instructions for pricking an organ barrel. Based on her study of dancing manuals, choreographies, and eighteenth-century treatises, Wendy Hilton also argues for a relatively fast interpretation. Further, contemporary pendulum markings not only corroborate a brisk tempo for the Baroque minuet but indicate increasingly slower tempos as the century progresses. See Mather (1987) and Hilton (1981).

12. Allanbrook suggests that "the motto seems to be a deliberate attempt to signal 'minuet.' Its percussive repeated notes in thick chordal texture intensify the dance's traditional even movement and restraint, in addition to protecting the dance against the distortion of a rapid and light execution" (Allanbrook 1983, 34).

13. "Mais au contraire le caractère du menuet est une élégante & noble simplicité."

14. "Der Ausdruck muß edel sein und reizenden Anstand, aber mit Einfalt verbunden, empfinden lassen."

15. "Der Tanz selbst ist durchgebends wol bekannt und verdienet in Ansehung seines edlen und reizenden Wesens den Vorzug vor den andern gesellschaftlichen Tän-

zen. . . . Er scheinet von den Grazien selbst erfunden zu sehn, und schiket sich
mehr, als jeder andere Tanz für Gesellshaften von Personen, die sich durch seine
Lebensart auszeichnen."

16. "Die [Einfalt] aber nicht als etwas dummes, albernes oder gemeines; sondern vielmehr als etwas edles, ungeschmücktes und recht sonderbares zu verstehen ist."

17. "Will man Muster und Vorbilder haben, so darff nur die alte Mahleren, Bild-
hauer und Münz Arbeit angesehen werden. Welche starcke Züge, majestätische
Gesichter und nachdrückliche Stellungen trifft man da nicht an?"
"If one seeks models and ideals, one need only examine ancient painting, sculpture, and engraving. Which strong features, majestic faces, and emphatic postures
will one not encounter there?"

18. "Man hat in der Musik insgemein einen falschen Begriff von der hohen
Schreibart. Man nennet nur dasjenige hoch, was außerordentlich künstlich und
durch einander geflochten ist, oder was überhaupt ein wunderliches, un-
vernehmliches, oder schwärmendes Geräusche verursachet."

19. "Wenn wir aber auf das Natürliche und Deutliche, als das eigentlich Kenn-
zeichen einer guten Schreibart, sehen, so werden wir dadurch auf eine ganz
andere Höhe gebracht, indem jene [was überhaupt ein wunderliches, un-
vernehmliches, oder schwärmendes Geräusche verursachet] vielmehr hochtra-
bend, schwülstig oder gezwungen, und also unnatürlich und undeutlich ist."
"If, however, we consider the Natural and the Clear as the true sign of good style,
then we are brought to an entirely different level, in which the former [that
which produces altogether eccentric, incomprehensible, or stirring sounds] are,
on the contrary, pompous, bombastic, and forced, and therefore unnatural and
unclear."

20. "Man soll sich aller Fugenarbeit enthalten, und folglich nicht durch ein
beständiges, arbeitsames und harmonisches Gewebe der Instrumenten und der
Singestimmen den Gesang schmülstig und undeutlich machen. Es können auf
dem Theater nicht so, wie in der Kirche, Bindungen, concertirende Sätze, Contra-
puncte und andere künstliche, ernsthafte und eingeschränkte Gänge statt finden;
weil solche der Freiheit und der natürlichen und lebhaften Melodie, die auf die
Schaubühne eigentlich gehöret, widersprechen."
"One should refrain from all fugal work, and consequently not make the singing
overbearing and unclear though an unchanging, active, and harmonious texture
of the instruments and the vocal parts. In the Theater, unlike in Church, transitions, [Bindungen], instrumental movements, counterpoint, and other artificial,
earnest, and restricted passages would not take place, since such contradict the
freedom and the natural and lively melody that truly belong to the stage."

21. "Eine wahre hohe Schreibart muß . . . prächtig und nachdrücklich sehn, sie muß
den Personen, mit den Sachen und Verrichtungen, dazu sie gebrauch wird, aufs
genaueste übereinstimmen. . . . Dieses Prächtige und Nachdrückliche wird nun
erlanget, wenn die Harmonie voll ist, wenn alles überaus durchdringend gesetzet
wird, wenn alle Stimmen nach gewissen Stufen, oder auch zugleich, in einer
feurigen Beschäfftigung fortarbeiten. Die Melodie muß reich an Gedanken, neu,
lebhaft und erhaben sehn." See also Scheibe (1745, 275–76).

22. "Man scheinet aber darin durchgehends übereinzustimmen, daß der Menuet der
Vorzug über alle Tänze dieser Art einzuräumen sein. Es ist auch in der That

schwerlich ein andrer Tanz erfunden worden, worin so viel Zierlichkeit, edler Anstand und höchst gefälliges Wesen anzutreffen wäre."

23. "Die vierte Classe begreift die Tänze von ernsthaftem hohen Charaktern, wie die tragische Schaubühne ihn erfodert. Sie bestehen entweder in Solotänzen, die blos große und ernsthafte Charaktere schildern, oder in ganzen Handlungen von bestimmtem Inhalt. Hier muß schon alles, was die Kunst an Stellung und Bewegung zum Ausdruck großer Empfindungen darzustellen vermag, zusammen kommen."
     Allanbrook also interprets this class as including "the noblest triple and duple gestures—the minuet, sarabande, and exalted march" (1983, 69).

24. "Sie muß also nur bei Helden, Königen, und andern großen Männern und erhabenen Geistern . . . angebracht werden."

25. James Webster offers a detailed description of the conventions of the Austrian-Bohemian symphony in the second half of the eighteenth century, noting that even in Haydn's earlier years, the most common pattern of movements in his symphonies was the four-movement Fast-Slow-Minuet-Fast design (Webster 1991a, 176–78).

26. For explication and exploration of musical troping, see Hatten (1994, esp. 161–202; 2004, esp. 68–89, 217–32).

27. Although clearly based on Hatten's delineation, the succinct definition of topical troping offered here emphasizes the listener's agency in the creation of new musical meanings.

28. Johann Friedrich Daube, for one, complains in 1797 that "in former times . . . so many menuets came to be written, of which the fewest could be used for dancing" (1797–98, 12 and 38; quoted and trans. in Kirkendale 1979, 174).

29. Wheelock too notes how the immediate repetition of a phrase accommodates the structural requirements of the dance in Haydn's canonic minuets: "In open-ended canons such reiterations would seem gratuitous delays, but in minuets they effect prolongation and emphasis of formal procedures and harmonic goals, affirming stability, sustaining tension, and reinforcing resolution" (1992, 64).

30. See chapter 2n41.

31. For explication and exploration of markedness in musical expression, see Hatten (1994, esp. 29–66, 133–60).

32. Ernst Gerber, among others, clearly aligns the aesthetic category of parody with the low style (1799, 296).

33. The "Tempo di Menuet" finale of the Piano Sonata in E-flat Major, Hob. XVI: 25 and the minuet of Haydn's String Quartet in D Minor, Op. 76, No. 2, are also conspicuously canonic; audible but less salient is the canon in the minuet of Haydn's Baryton Trio in A Major, Hob. XI:94.

34. As David Schroeder notes, enlightened thought arrived in Austria much later than in other parts of Europe. Regarding Haydn in particular, Schroeder argues that the composer was deeply concerned with combating ignorance, prejudice, and superstition, and "that it was his Paris and subsequent symphonies which argue most eloquently for tolerance, intelligence, and morality" (1990, 35). See also Schroeder (1990, 91–122) on "reflective listening."

35. Although we celebrate Haydn's compositional trickery more than that of other composers of his time, he was not the only one playing such musical games. As Kirkendale reminds us, canonic experimentation in minuets was not unusual, at least in chamber music. In eighteenth-century orchestral works, however, one encounters the learned style less frequently, I suspect, because of the public nature of the genre, the correspondence of instrumental forces required for a dance orchestra and the performance of a symphony, the resulting similarities in overall sound between the dance minuet and the symphonic art minuet, and indeed the expectation that an artful presentation of the minuet echo the minuet as danced. Kirkendale too notes that "no sizable repertoire of orchestral fugues . . . exists in this period." See Kirkendale (1979, 148–49) for a list of eighteenth-century chamber works with canonic minuets and Appendix I (275–318) for a list of eighteenth-century works, orchestral as well as chamber, containing fugue, fugato, and other learned presentations.

36. Morrow (1989, 278) suggests and Solomon (1995, 474) reports that Mozart's G Minor Symphony K. 550, was performed on the Tonkünstler-Societät concerts on 16 and 17 April 1791.

37. Pointing to "several documented instances suggest[ing] that he seldom began a large-scale work without a clear use for it in mind," Zaslaw argues that Mozart would hardly have composed three symphonies with no planned performance opportunity. He also notes that (1) Mozart would often abandon composition on a work if its performance or publication opportunity did not pan out; (2) Mozart would not have revised the symphony unless for a performance; and (3) the works were likely performed at least in Dresden (1989, 422–31).

38. For speculation about the reasons Mozart has been perceived as apolitical, see Zaslaw (1989, 528).

39. Michael Kelly and Lorenzo Da Ponte acknowledge that the choice of Beaumarchais's *Le Mariage de Figaro* was entirely Mozart's (Deutsch 1932).

40. Just how sincere Mozart was in his commitment to Freemasonry has been the subject of some debate. See Deutsch (1932), Nettl (1957), Landon (1982), Autexier (1984), Schuler (1987), and Solomon (1995).

41. Solomon offers this letter as evidence of Mozart's revenge fantasies as well as his deep empathy for a wrongly accused man (1995, 353–55).

42. In a 20 June 1781 letter to his father Mozart remarks that "it is the heart that ennobles a man; and though I am no count, yet I have probably more honour in me than many a count" (Anderson 1966, 2:747), a striking echo of Figaro's lines near the beginning of Act V in Beaumarchais's play: "Because you are a great lord, you think you are a great genius. Nobility, wealth, honors, emoluments—it all makes a man so proud! What have you done to earn so many advantages? You took the trouble to be born, nothing more. Apart from that, you're a rather common type. Whereas I—by God!—lost in the nameless herd, I had to exert more strategy and skill merely to survive than has been spent for a hundred years in governing the Spanish Empire" ([1784] 1961, 193).

43. Two notable tonic-minor minuets are in Mozart's "Little G Minor" Symphony K. 183 (1773), and Haydn's Symphony in C Minor, No. 95 (1991). There is reason to suspect, however, that the minor-mode minuet of Mozart's "Great G Minor" in-

fluenced the minor-mode minuet of Haydn's Symphony No. 95, for the finale of the latter is modeled on the finale of the former.

44. The minor-mode minuets in general inhabit the expressive category of the tragic. But the addition of a learned presentation in the minuet movements of several of Haydn's so-called *Sturm und Drang* symphonies—the minuet of the Symphony in E Minor, No. 44, "*Trauersinfonie*" (by 1772), is a two-part canon; the minuets of the Symphony in F Minor, No. 49, "*La passione*" (1768), and Symphony in C Minor, No. 52 (1774), are constructed of two-part counterpoint—leads to the marked expressive domain of Passion (Lowe 2002b, 201–202).

45. On the expressive stagnation of the minuet in the third quarter of the eighteenth century, see Lowe (2002b).

46. "Ihr vornehmster Charakter, mit dem sie [die niedrige Schreibart] zu thun hat, ist unstreitig der Schäfer; und also wird man leicht urtheilen können, daß auch die Schäferspiele und Schäfergedichte darinnen abzufassen sind. Ferner ist auch ein Bettler, ein Sklave, ein armer Gefangener, ein Feiger, ein Verzagter, ein Trostloser, ein Niederträchtiger, ein Bauer, ein Dummer, ein Grober, u. d. gl. nur in der niedrigen Schreibart auszubrucken. So wird auch die Einfalt, die Dummheit, die Niederträchtigkeit, die Grobheit, die Ungeschicklichkeit, der Scherz, wenn er einfältig ist, die Unachtsamkeit, die Faulheit u. d. gl. am besten in dieser Schreibart nachgeahmet. Endlicht gehören noch darzu alle Verrichtungen, Handlungen und Wirkungen, die von angeführten Personen und Sachen geschehen, oder verursachet werden. Hierzu sind noch die meisten Arten der Tänzen zu rechnen." Scheibe (1745, 129–30).
"The most distinguished character with which [the low style] has to do is indisputably the shepherd; and thus one easily determines that pastoral plays and pastorals will be composed in this style. Further, the beggar, the slave, the indignant prisoner, the coward, the despondent, the wretched, the vile, the peasant, the fool, the crude, and the like are also only composed in the low style. So too would simplicity, stupidity, vileness, crudeness, clumsiness, joking, if it is simpleminded, carelessness, laziness, and the like, be best imitated in this style. Finally, all performances, plots, and actions in which the mentioned persons and qualities occur, would also belong to it, or produce it. Yet most types of dances are still to be counted here."

47. "Und zu niedern, was mehr populär und faßlich als edel, mehr lustig und tändelnd als geistreich, und überhaupt salles was zum Komischen und zur Karrikatur gehört."

48. On Haydn's concern to win the approval of his public audience, see Schroeder (1990, esp. 91–122). On the composition of the London concert audience, see Hughes (1971, esp. 154–88), Schroeder (1990, esp. 91–122), and McVeigh (1993).

5. Pleasure and Meaning in Haydn's Symphony in D Major, No. 93

1. Thomas Tolley, in an engaging study of late-eighteenth-century music within the context of popular visual culture, considers Haydn's aim to communicate with a "universal audience" (2001, esp. ch. 2). Sisman, alternatively, explores Haydn's career and the idea of the "multiple audience" (2005).

2. The concert was reviewed by three newspapers: *Morning Herald* on 18 February

1792; *Diary; or Woodfall's Register* on 18 February 1792; and *The Times* on 20 February 1792 (Landon 1976, 3:134–35).

3. McVeigh also points out that "the social make-up of audiences as a whole remains a matter of speculation" (1993, 20–21).

4. Landon suggests that this five-note subject "is in fact pasted together from two fragments, one from the first and one from the second subject." He continues rightly to point out, however, that "the average listener could hardly make this kind of analysis aurally" (1976, 519).

5. Webster uses "cyclic integration" or "organization" to refer to "commonalities of material, tonal relations, and the like" (1991a).

6. As Peter Gay argues, the *philosophes* "undertook to devise forms—a social, ethical, political, and aesthetic program—for the sake of freedom, rather than as a curb on anarchy" (1969, 3).

7. See, for example, Susan McClary's interpretation of the second movement of Mozart's Piano Concerto in G Major K. 453 (1986, 129–69).

8. For more on the Concert of Ancient Music and the Academy of Ancient Music, see McVeigh (1993, esp. chs. 2 and 3).

9. By the fourth quarter of the eighteenth century the tempo of the dance minuet had slowed from its earlier brisk pace to a stately—stodgy even—tempo. The symphonic minuets for which Haydn specifically indicates a faster tempo embrace a more popular or countrified affect (Lowe 2002b, esp. n65).

10. This tradition goes back at least to the sixteenth century (Blom 1941, 177).

11. Webster observes that the "quiet answering phrases ignore the tonic: each one interprets the loud D as a consonant common-tone in a different key—until the third time, when the strings leap in 'prematurely' and transform D into a *dissonance,* V_5^6/V, whose resolution forces the music into the dominant" (1991a, 158–59).

12. Webster's translation in *Haydn's "Farewell" Symphony* is quoted here instead of the more commonly cited translation by Landon in *The Collected Correspondence and London Notebooks of Joseph Haydn.* Landon's translation implies that Haydn found the finale weak in comparison to the first movement only, whereas Webster (rightly) suggests that Haydn found it weak in comparison to the rest of the symphony. The phrase in question reads: "weil ich willens bin, das lezte Stück von derselben abzuändern, und zu verschönern, da solches in rücksicht der Ersteren Stücke zu Schwach ist." See Haydn (1959, 131; 1965, 279–80) and Webster (1991a, 183).

13. These are the terms used most frequently in contemporary writings to describe the symphony's style. For example, J. A. P. Schulz's entry for Sulzer's *Allgemeine Theorie der Schönen Künste* opens as follows: "The symphony is excellently suited for the expression of the grand, the festive, and the noble" (Churgin 1980). See also Sisman's summary of the public expectations of the symphony (1993b, 7–8).

6. Old Entertainments, New Pleasures

1. Statistics vary, but assuming four hours of television a day, each hour with six breaks of four thirty-second commercials, the total number of television commercials consumed in one year is 35,040.

2.　Since Winkler's autobiography reads largely as self-promotion, I offer the "confession" in its entirety: "In desperation we turned to crime. We began to dismember the great masters. We began to murder ruthlessly the works of Beethoven, Mozart, Grieg, J. S. Bach, Verdi, Bizet, Tschaikowsky and Wagner—everything that wasn't protected from our pilfering by copyright. The immortal chorales of J. S. Bach became an 'Adagio Lamentoso' ('for sad scenes'). Extracts from great symphonies and operas were hacked down to emerge again as 'Sinister Mysterioso' by Beethoven or 'Weird Moderato' by Tschaikowsky. Wagner's and Mendelssohn's Wedding Marches were used to portray mock marriages, fights between husbands and wives, and divorce scenes: we just had them played out of tune—a treatment known in the profession as 'souring up the aisle.' If they were to be used for happy endings we jazzed them up mercilessly. . . . Any piece using a trombone prominently would infallibly be dedicated to the home-coming of a drunk: no other instrument could hiccup with such virtuosity. Today I look in shame and awe at the printed copies of these mutilated masterpieces and I hope that this belated confession will grant me forgiveness for what I have done" (1951, 237–38).

3.　The now widely quoted review in the 18 July 1915 *Chicago Examiner* attests to the public's recognition of Wagner's music as well as the strong connection forged between image and accompanying music: "One leaves the play with strange, weird, melodic calls of Wagner's 'Ride of the Valkyries' and 'Flying Dutchman' ringing in the ears. This is because the call sounded in reeds and trumpets in the rush of the Ku Klux Klan are modifications of these themes. This call is sounded most impressively, and more than any stage mechanism brings right to mind the rush of legions of men. It brings convincingly the idea that these men of the play had an absolute consecration to a cause that they believed to be a holy one." For more reviews and discussion, see the special issue of *Film Culture* devoted to *The Birth of a Nation* (*Film Culture* 36).

4.　Such a heavy meaning is disconcertingly challenged in Sam Mendes's film *Jarhead* (2005), when Marine recruits preparing for the first Gulf War hoot and howl while viewing the Wagner-tracked helicopter attack in *Apocalypse Now*.

5.　Instructors of Music Appreciation classes across America experience this phenomenon all the time. My students recognize *Also Sprach Zarathustra* as the "theme" from "that old space movie."

6.　See chapter 4.

7.　See Goldmark (2005) for more on the use of classical music in cartoon scores.

8.　This is not to suggest, however, that the cultural and social situation of classical music was the same in all performance contexts. An opera favorite heard on the minstrel stage or in the dance hall performed cultural work quite distinct from that of its original theatrical presentation.

9.　Russell Lack, on the other hand, hears a reference to Griffith and therefore a different irony: "Francis Ford Coppola reprised Griffith's use of Wagner in *Apocalypse Now*, lending on [*sic*] ironic undertone as the same piece of music blares from American helicopters strafing Vietnamese villagers all in the cause of locating the perfect surfing beach" (1997, 35n10).

10.　I first came into contact with *Ride of the Valkyries* in the context of a video game—it was the victory music for the Intelevision game of Checkers. This site for musical first contact is becoming more common as the soundtracks of video games now include much prerecorded music. While viewing *Don Giovanni* in one of my classes, for example, a student exclaimed, "Hey! That's Grand Theft Auto!" Indeed, one of the "radio stations" in Grand Theft Auto: III (2001, for Sony PlayStation 2) plays, among other operatic selections, "Finch'han dal vino," performed by Sesto Bruscantini with Carlo Guilini conducting the Orchesta e Corodi Roma della RAI. My thanks to Martin-Patrick Eady for this reference.

11. Stilwell discusses the intended intertextual connection of preexisting music in John McTiernan's *Die Hard* with Stanley Kubrick's *A Clockwork Orange*. In this case, McTiernan conceived the "Ode to Joy" of Beethoven's Ninth Symphony and Arthur Freed and Nacio Herb Brown's "Singin' in the Rain" as suggesting the villains in *Die Hard* as "lineal descendants of the adolescent gang members in *A Clockwork Orange*." But while it is difficult to discern if viewers make this extra-filmic connection, Stilwell notes that they are at least led to read the "Ode to Joy" socially: viewers "are cued to the music's high-art status by its first intelligible presentation by [a] string quartet" (1997, 568–72).

12. For Roland Barthes, cultural codes are one of the "five major codes under which all the textual signifiers can be grouped: . . . cultural codes are references to a science or a body of knowledge; in drawing attention to them, we merely indicate the type of knowledge (physical, physiological, medical, psychological, literary, historical, etc.) referred to, without going so far as to construct (or reconstruct) the culture they express" (1974, 20).

13. The musical depiction of Native American identity heard so often in film, characterized by open fifths, modal harmonies, pentatonic melodies, harmonic stasis, etc., not only provides a compelling example of this phenomenon but also demonstrates how removed from the subject such depictions may in fact be. As Michael Pisani has shown, the "Indian music" in midcentury film scores, while taking some cues from Native American culture and the "Indian musical realists" of the early twentieth century, is nonetheless rooted in the generic European exoticisms of the nineteenth century (1998, 218–57).

14. My thanks to Stan Link for sharing this interpretation of Mozart's music in *Vertigo*.

15. An extraordinary exception is the Andante from Mozart's Piano Concerto in C Major K. 467, which has all but acquired the title "Elvira Madigan" from its prominent use in Bo Widerberg's film *Elvira Madigan* (1967). Rather than any immediate or subsequent use of this movement in film to track similar scenes of romantic idyll, the use of *Elvira Madigan* to market Mozart's music (e.g., the Sony Essential Classics recording featuring soloist Robert Casadesus and George Szell conducting the Cleveland Orchestra includes the title on the cover) has reinforced this cinematically specific meaning.

16. Stilwell also argues for class implications in the use of classical music in the soundtrack of *Die Hard:* as villain (or antihero) Hans Gruber's theme, Beethoven's "Ode to Joy," asserts his intelligence, "superior sense of style," and class. Bach's Third Brandenburg Concerto, on the other hand, contributes to everyman hero John McClane's feeling "like a fish out of water" at an upscale corporate Christmas party (1997, 571–72).

17. Arising from a neuroscience and music study of Francis Raucher, Gordon L. Shaw, and their colleagues at the University of California at Irvine that concluded that listening to just ten minuets of Mozart's music raised students' abstract reasoning ability in spatial-temporal tasks, the "Mozart Effect" has become an inclusive term referring to the ability of classical music, in particular Mozart's, to raise IQ, assist in concentration, promote health and well-being, and even cure disease. The influence of the "Mozart Effect" on the current situation of classical music in contemporary American culture can hardly be overstated. For one among countless publications, see Campbell (1997).

18. Examples of such contact abound, of course, and undoubtedly we have all experienced them innumerable times. Here is a recent one of mine that stands out as particularly revealing. While waiting in a doctor's office in 2002 for a frustratingly long time, I noted the pieces to which I was treated. Movements from Mozart's piano concertos and Beethoven's symphonies played in random order. There were speakers mounted on two walls, and a receptionist confirmed for me that there was a stereo in the office with a compact-disc changer set to play the tracks of three discs in random order. While inquiring about the music selections, I learned that the same discs stay in the changer for weeks at a time, that they belong to one of the doctors in the practice, and that the staff was instructed not to play any music other than the discs he provided. From the doctor I learned that this music was intended to relax his patients. He also shared with me that a few months earlier a patient had grown agitated when a receptionist switched out one of the classical discs for Enya. When I expressed my (admittedly somewhat exaggerated) surprise that a New Age classic could stir up a listener more than what I had just heard (a Beethoven scherzo), the doctor just shrugged and reiterated the reason for his musical choices: "Classical music is relaxing."

19. The NBC sitcom *Frasier* ran for eleven seasons (16 September 1993–13 May 2004), capturing a record thirty-seven Emmy Awards, including five consecutive wins for Outstanding Comedy Series (another record), four for Outstanding Lead Actor in a Comedy Series (Kelsey Grammer), and three for Outstanding Supporting Actor in a Comedy Series (David Hyde Pierce). *Frasier* has also won the George Foster Peabody Award; three People's Choice Awards for Favorite Television Comedy, Favorite New Television Comedy Series, and Best Actor (Grammer); a Humanitas Prize; Golden Globes for Best Musical or Comedy Series and Best Actor (Grammer); and the TV Guide Award as Favorite Comedy Series. See www.nbc.com/Frasier and www.tvtome.com/Frasier.

20. These lines come from Figaro's cavatina in Act I of Mozart's *Le nozze di Figaro*.

21. Reported in a 16 January 1998 Associated Press story for the *Athens Banner-Herald*.

22. The full contents of *Build Your Baby's Brain through the Power of Music* are as follows (all vocal selections are presented as orchestral renditions):

   1. Mozart, Serenade in G Major K. 525, "Eine kleine Nachtmusik," I: Allegro
   2. Beethoven, Bagatelle for Piano in A Minor, "Für Elise," WoO 59
   3. Handel, *Solomon*, HWV 67, Arrival of the Queen of Sheba
   4. Mozart, Piano Sonata in A Major K. 331, III: Rondo "Alla Turca"
   5. Schubert, Quintet for Piano, Violin, Viola, Cello & Double Bass in A Major, "Trout," D. 667 (Op. posth. 114), III: Scherzo

6. Vivaldi, Concerto, Op. 8, no. 1, "La Primavera," *The Four Seasons,* RV 269, I: Allegro
7. Bach, Cantata No. 147, *Herz und Mund und Tat und Leben,* BWV 147, "Jesu Joy of Man's Desiring"
8. Pachabel, Canon and Gigue for 3 Violins & Continuo in D Major, Canon
9. Schubert, Quintet for Piano, Violin, Viola, Cello & Double Bass in A Major, "Trout," D. 667 (Op. posth. 114), II: Andante
10. Bach, Suite for Orchestra No. 3 in D Major, BWV 1068, "Air on the G String"
11. Bach, Cantata No. 208, *Was mir behagt,* BWV 208, "Sheep May Safely Graze"
12. Handel, Water Music Suite No. 3, HWV 350, Air
13. Mozart, Piano Concerto in C Major K. 467, II: Andante
14. Mozart, Serenade in G Major K. 525, "Eine kleine Nachtmusik," II: Romance
15. Mozart, *Le nozze di Figaro,* "Dove sono"
16. Mozart, *Don Giovanni,* "Là ci darem la mano"
17. Bach, "Bist du bei mir," BWV 508 (spurious)

23.   The minuet proper of Haydn's Symphony No. 104, "London," tracks the first football lessons Tom Wingo, an unemployed schoolteacher and football coach from South Carolina, gives Bernard, a wealthy Phillips Exeter student, New Yorker, violinist, and son of a famous, world-class performing musician. Haydn's music is clearly from Bernard's elite world, but the class coding in this montage is actually more sophisticated. Tracked by Haydn's minuet (incidentally, performed at a stately tempo much slower than Haydn's indicated Allegro), the sound level of which is much higher than the diegetic sounds of the scene, Bernard and Tom appear to "dance" well together, each of them clearly comfortable in the other's company. The soundtrack may therefore also be heard as reflecting Tom's "inner nobility," or at least a refinement greater than his circumstances suggest. That such class coding is likely intentional on the part of the filmmakers is suggested by the dialogue of the immediately preceding scene:

> **Bernard:** So where do you coach, Mr. Wingo, hillbilly country?
> **Tom:** Oh, we're a little class conscious are we? Where do you go to school, Miss Porter's?
> **Bernard:** Phillips Exeter, smartass.

24.   A paradigm shift in the relationship between performances and recordings accompanied the advent of affordable high-fidelity audio systems and long-playing records. As Paul Lansky puts it, "In the maelstrom of popular culture, machines have had an immediate and rather drastic effect. First, the respective roles of concerts and recording have been switched. Recording is the norm and concerts are glorifications of recording" (1990, 104).

25.   The performance of film music on pops concerts (e.g., concert arrangements of John Williams's film scores have been programmed regularly for the past twenty-five years) is another tangible manifestation of this reverse feedback cycle.

Bibliography

Abrams, M. H. 1953. *The Mirror and the Lamp: Romantic Theory and the Critical Tradition.* New York: Oxford University Press.

Addison, Joseph. 1712. "Essay on the Pleasures of the Imagination." In *The Spectator* no. 416, July 2, 1712.

Addison, Joseph, et al. 1965. *The Spectator.* Ed. Donald F. Bond. 5 vols. Oxford: Oxford University Press.

Agawu, V. Kofi. 1991. *Playing with Signs: A Semiotic Interpretation of Classic Music.* Princeton: Princeton University Press.

Alison, Archibald. 1790. *Essays on the Nature and Principles of Taste.* London: J. J. G. and G. Robinson.

Allanbrook, Wye Jamison. 1983. *Rhythmic Gesture in Mozart: Le nozze di Figaro and Don Giovanni.* Chicago: University of Chicago Press.

——. 1992. "Two Threads through the Labyrinth: Topic and Process in the First Movements of K. 332 and K. 333." In *Convention in Eighteenth- and Nineteenth-Century Music: Essays in Honor of Leonard G. Ratner,* ed. Wye Jamison Allanbrook, Janet M. Levy, and William P. Mahrt, 125–71. Stuyvesant, N.Y.: Pendragon Press.

——. 1994. "Mozart's Tunes and the Comedy of Closure." In *On Mozart,* ed. James M. Morris, 169–86. Cambridge: Cambridge University Press.

——. 1996. "'To Serve the Private Pleasure': Expression and Form in the String Quartets." In *Wolfgang Amadè Mozart: Essays on His Life and Music,* ed. Stanley Sadie, 132–60. Oxford: Clarendon Press.

——, ed. 1998. *Strunk's Source Readings in Music History.* Rev. ed. Vol. 5. New York: W. W. Norton.

Allgemeine musikalische Zeitung. Leipzig, 1798–1848.

Almeder, Robert F. 1980. *The Philosophy of Charles S. Peirce: A Critical Introduction.* Totowa, N.J.: Rowman and Littlefield.

American Symphony Orchestra League. 2005. *Music Matters!: The American Symphony Orchestra League's Guide to Answering Frequently Asked Questions.* New York: American Symphony Orchestra League. www.symphony.org/research/pdf/musicmatters.pdf.

Anderson, Emily, trans. and ed. 1966. *The Letters of Mozart and His Family.* 2 vols. New York: St. Martin's Press.

André, Yves Marie. 1741. *L'Essai sur le beau.* Paris.

Autexier, Philippe A. 1984. *Mozart & Liszt sub Rosa.* Poitiers: Autexier.

Barnett, Gregory. 2002. "Topic Theory and the Late-Seicento Sonata." Paper delivered at National Conference of AMS/SMT, Columbus, Ohio.

Barthes, Roland. 1974. *S/Z.* Trans. Richard Miller. New York: Hill and Wang.

——. 1975. *The Pleasure of the Text.* Trans. Richard Miller. New York: Hill and Wang.

Batteux, Charles. 1989. *Les beaux-arts réduit à un même principe.* Ed. Jean-Rémy Mantion. Paris: Aux Amateurs de livres. (Orig. pub. 1746.)

Bauman, Thomas. 1995. *Opera and the Enlightenment.* Cambridge: Cambridge University Press.

Beals, Derek. 1996. "Court, Government, and Society in Vienna." In *Wolfgang Amadè Mozart,* ed. Stanley Sadie, 3–20. Oxford: Oxford University Press.

Beaumarchais, Pierre Augustin Caron de. 1961. "Le marriage de Figaro." Trans. Jacques Barzun. In *Phaedra and Figaro: Racine's Phèdre and Beaumarchais's Figaro's Marriage.* New York: Farrar, Straus and Cudahy. (Orig. pub. 1784.)

Bender, John. 1997. "Enlightenment Fiction and the Scientific Hypothesis." *Representations* 60: 1–23.

Benjamin, Walter. 1992. "The Work of Art in the Age of Mechanical Reproduction." In *Illuminations,* ed. Harry Zohn, trans. Hannah Arendt, 211–55. London: Fontana Press.

Bermingham, Ann, and John Brewer, eds. 1995. *The Consumption of Culture 1600–1800: Image, Object, Text.* New York: Routledge.

Black, Jeremy. 1990. *Eighteenth Century Europe, 1770–1789.* New York: St. Martin's Press.

Blades, James. 1980. "Drum." In *The New Grove Dictionary of Music and Musicians,* ed. Stanley Sadie, vol. 5, 639–49. London: Macmillan.

Blanning, T. C. W. 1994. *Joseph II.* New York: Longman.

Blom, Eric. 1941. "The Minuet-Trio." *Music and Letters* 22: 162–80.

Bonds, Mark Evan. 1997a. "Idealism and the Aesthetics of Instrumental Music at the Turn of the Nineteenth Century." *Journal of the American Musicological Society* 50: 387–420.

———. 1997b. "The Symphony as Pindaric Ode." In *Haydn and His World,* ed. Elaine Sisman, 131–53. Princeton: Princeton University Press.

Bourdieu, Pierre. 1980. "The Aristocracy of Culture" (extract from *La Distinction*). Trans. Richard Nice. *Media, Culture, and Society* 2: 225–54.

———. 1984. *Distinction: A Social Critique of the Judgment of Taste.* Trans. Richard Nice. Cambridge, Mass.: Harvard University Press

Brewer, John. 1997. *The Pleasures of the Imagination: English Culture in the Eighteenth Century.* New York: HarperCollins.

Brown, A. Peter. 2002. *The Symphonic Repertoire Vol. II, The First Golden Age of the Viennese Symphony: Haydn, Mozart, Beethoven, and Schubert.* Bloomington: Indiana University Press.

Broyles, Michael. 1983. "The Two Instrumental Styles of Classicism." *Journal of the American Musicological Society* 36: 210–42.

Bruckmüller, Ernst. 1985. *Sozialgeschichte Österreichs.* Vienna and Munich: Herold.

———. 2003. *The Austrian Nation: Cultural Consciousness and Socio-political Processes.* Trans. Lowell A. Bangerter. Riverside, Calif.: Ariadne Press.

Buelow, George J. 1980. "Scheibe, Johann Adolf." In *The New Grove Dictionary of Music and Musicians,* ed. Stanley Sadie, vol. 16, 599–601. London: Macmillan.

Burke, Edmund. 1958. *A Philosophical Enquiry into the Origin of Our Ideas of the Sublime and Beautiful.* Ed. J. T. Boulton. London: Routledge and Kegan Paul. (Orig. pub. 1756.)

Burnham, Scott. 1995. *Beethoven Hero.* Princeton: Princeton University Press.

———. 1999. "How Music Matters: Poetic Content Revisited." In *Rethinking Music,* ed. Nicolas Cook and Mark Everist, 193–216. Oxford: Oxford University Press.

Busby, Thomas. 1819. *A General History of Music.* 2 vols. London: C. Whittaker.

Campbell, Don. 1997. *The Mozart Effect: Tapping the Power of Music to Heal the Body, Strengthen the Mind, and Unlock the Creative Spirit.* New York: Avon Books.

Caplin, William. 1998. *Classical Form: A Theory of Formal Functions for the Instrumental Music of Haydn, Mozart, and Beethoven.* Oxford: Oxford University Press.

Cavell, Stanley. 1969. *Must We Mean What We Say? A Book of Essays.* New York: Scribner.

Chabanon, Michel-Paul-Guy de. 1785. *De la musique considérée en elle-même et dans ses rapports avec la parole, les langues, la poésie, et le théâtre.* Paris.

Chua, Daniel. 1999. *Absolute Music and the Construction of Meaning.* Cambridge: Cambridge University Press.

Churgin, Bathia. 1980. "The Symphony as Described by J. A. P. Schulz (1774): A Commentary and Translation." *Current Musicology* 29: 7–16.

Cole, Malcolm S. 1969. "The Vogue of the Instrumental Rondo." *Journal of the American Musicological Society* 22: 425–55.

Croce, Benedetto. 1992. *The Aesthetic as the Science of Expression and of the Linguistic in General.* Trans. Colin Lyas. Cambridge: Cambridge University Press. (Orig. pub. 1902.)

Cumming, Naomi. 2000. *The Sonic Self: Musical Subjectivity and Signification.* Bloomington: Indiana University Press.

Dahlhaus, Carl. 1989. *The Idea of Absolute Music.* Trans. Roger Lustig. Chicago: University of Chicago Press.

Danckwardt, Marianne. 1977. *Die langsame Einleitung: Ihre Herkunft und ihr Bau durch Haydn und Mozart.* Tutzing: Schneider.

Datson, Lorraine. 2001. "Enlightenment Fears, Fears of Enlightenment." In *What's Left of Enlightenment? A Postmodern Question,* ed. Keith Michael Baker and Peter Hanns Reill, 115–28. Stanford, Calif.: Stanford University Press.

Daube, Johann Friedrich. 1797–98. *Anleitung zur Erfindung der Melodie.* Vienna.

Davies, Stephen. 1994. *Musical Meaning and Expression.* Ithaca, N.Y.: Cornell University Press.

DeNora, Tia. 1997. "The Biology Lessons of Opera Buffa: Gender, Nature, and Bourgeois Society on Mozart's Buffa Stage." In *Opera Buffa in Mozart's Vienna,* ed. Mary Hunter and James Webster, 146–64. Cambridge: Cambridge University Press.

Derrida, Jacques. 1981. *Positions.* Trans. Alan Bass. Chicago: University of Chicago Press.

Deutsch, Otto Erich. 1932. *Mozart und die Wiener Logen.* Vienna: Verlag der Wiener Freimaurer-Zeitung.

Diderot, Denis. "Lettre sur le traité du mélodrame." In *Oeuvres complètes,* vol. 8, ed. J Assézat, 506–10. Paris: Garnier. (Orig. pub. 1771.)

———. 1922. *Jacques le fataliste et son maître.* Ed. Nobert Czarny. Paris: Seuil. (Orig. pub. 1778.)

———. 2000. *La religieuse.* Ed. Heather Lloyd. London: Bristol Classical Press.

Diderot, Denis, Jean le Rond d'Alembert, and Pierre Mouchon. 1751–56. *Encyclopédie, ou dictionnaire raisonné des sciences, des arts et des métiers.* Paris: Briasson.

Droysen, Johann Gustav. 1897. *Outlines of the Principles of History.* Trans. Elisha Benjamin Andrews. Boston: Ginn.

———. 1960. *Historik: Vorlesungen über Enzyklopädie und Methodologie der Geschichte.* Ed. Rudolf Hübner. Munich: Oldenbourg.

Du Bos, Jean-Baptiste. 1719. *Réflexions critiques sur la poësie et sur la peinture.* Paris.

Eagelton, Terry. 1990. *The Ideology of the Aesthetic.* Oxford: Basil Blackwell.

Eco, Umberto. 1989. *The Open Work.* Trans. Anna Cancogni. Cambridge, Mass.: Harvard University Press. (Orig. pub. 1965.)

———. 1994. *The Limits of Interpretation.* Bloomington: Indiana University Press.

Feldtenstein, C. J. von. 1767. *Die Kunst nach der Choreographie zu tanzen and Tänze zu schreiben*. Braunschweig: Schöderschen Buchhandlung.

Fielding, Henry. 1974. *The History of Tom Jones, a Foundling*. Ed. Fredson Bowers. Oxford: Clarendon Press. (Orig. pub. 1749.)

Film Culture 36. 1965. New York: Film Culture.

Fish, Stanley. 1980. *Is There a Text in This Class? The Authority of Interpretive Communities*. Cambridge, Mass.: Harvard University Press.

———. 1989. *Doing What Comes Naturally: Change, Rhetoric, and the Practice of Theory in Literary and Legal Studies*. Durham, N.C.: Duke University Press.

Fisher, Stephen. 1985. "Haydn's Overtures and Their Adaptations as Concert Orchestral Works." Ph.D. dissertation, University of Pennsylvania.

Fiske, John. 1987. *Television Culture*. New York: Methuen.

Foucault, Michel. 1978. *The History of Sexuality*. Vol. 1. Trans. Robert Hurley. New York: Pantheon.

Freud, Sigmund. 1989. "Formulations on the Two Principles of Mental Functioning." In *The Freud Reader,* ed. and trans. Peter Gay, 301–306. New York: W. W. Norton. (Orig. pub. 1911.)

Garcin, Laurent. 1772. *Traité du melodrama, ou réflexions sur la musique dramatique*. Paris: chez Vallat-la-Chapelle.

Gay, Peter. 1969. *The Enlightenment: The Science of Freedom*. New York: W. W. Norton.

Geiringer, Karl. 1968. *Haydn: A Creative Life in Music*. Berkeley: University of California Press.

———. 2002. *Joseph Haydn and the Eighteenth Century: Collected Essays of Karl Geiringer*. Ed. Robert N. Freeman. Warren, Mich.: Harmonie Press.

George, M. Dorothy. 1953. *England in Transition: Life and Work in the Eighteenth Century*. London: Penguin Books.

Gerard, Alexander. 1970. *An Essay on Taste, to which are annexed Three Dissertations on the Same Subject by Mr De Voltaire, Mr D'Alembert, Mr De Montesquieu*. New York: Garland. (Orig. pub. 1764.)

Gerber, Ernst. 1799. "Etwas über den sogenannten musikalischen Styl." In *Allgemeine musikalische Zeitung,* cols. 292–97, 305–12. Leipzig: Breitkopf und Härtel.

———. 1966–69. *Historisch-biographisches Lexikon der Tonkünstler (1790–1792) und Neues historisch-biographisches Lexikon der Tonkünstler (1812–1814)*. Graz: Akademische Druck- u. Verlagsanstalt.

Goehr, Lydia. 1992. *The Imaginary Museum of Musical Works: An Essay in the Philosophy of Music*. Oxford: Oxford University Press.

———. 1993. "'Music Has No Meaning to Speak of': On the Politics of Musical Interpretation." In *The Interpretation of Music: Philosophical Essays,* ed. Michael Krausz, 177–90. New York: Clarendon Press.

———. 1998. *The Quest for Voice: On Music, Politics, and the Limits of Philosophy*. Berkeley: University of California Press.

Goldmark, Daniel. 2005. *Tunes for Toons: Music and the Hollywood Cartoon*. Berkeley: University of California Press.

Goodman, Nelson. 1968. *Languages of Art: An Approach to a Theory of Symbols*. New York: Bobbs-Merrill.

———. 1970. "Some Notes on *Languages of Art*." *Journal of Philosophy* 67: 563–73.

Gorbman, Claudia. 1987. *Unheard Melodies: Narrative Film Music*. Bloomington: Indiana University Press.

Gotwals, Vernon. 1963. *Joseph Haydn: Eighteenth-Century Gentleman and Genius.* Madison: University of Wisconsin Press.

Greg, W. W. 1906. *Pastoral Poetry and Pastoral Drama: A Literary Inquiry, with Special Reference to the Pre-Restoration Stage in England.* London: A. H. Bullen.

Griesinger, G. A. 1963. *Biographische Notizen über Joseph Haydn.* Trans. Vernon Gotwals in *Joseph Haydn, Eighteenth-Century Gentleman and Genius.* Madison: University of Wisconsin Press. (Orig. pub. 1810.)

Habermas, Jürgen. 1989. *The Structural Transformation of the Public Sphere.* Trans. Thomas Berger and Frederick Lawrence. Cambridge, Mass.: MIT Press.

Hanslick, Eduard. 1990. *Eduard Hanslick: Vom Musikalisch-Schönen.* Ed. Dietmar Strauß. 2 vols. Mainz: Schott.

Harris, James. 1783. *Three Treatises Concerning Art.* 4th ed. London.

Hatten, Robert. 1980. "Nattiez's Semiology of Music: Flaws in the New Science." *Semiotica* 31: 1–2, 139–55.

———. 1985. "The Place of Intertextuality in Music Studies." *American Journal of Semiotics* 3, no. 4: 69–82.

———. 1994. *Musical Meaning in Beethoven: Markedness, Correlation, and Interpretation.* Bloomington: Indiana University Press.

———. 1996. "Grounding Interpretation: A Semiotic Framework for Musical Hermeneutics." *American Journal of Semiotics* 24, nos. 1–4: 25–42.

———. 2004. *Interpreting Musical Gestures, Topics, and Tropes: Mozart, Beethoven, Schubert.* Bloomington: Indiana University Press.

Hatting, Casten E. 1981. "The Enlightenment and Haydn." In *Haydn Studies,* ed. Jens Peter Larsen, Howard Serwer, and James Webster, 434–40. New York: W. W. Norton.

Haydn, Joseph. 1959. *The Collected Correspondence and London Notebooks of Joseph Haydn.* Ed. H. C. Robbins Landon. Fair Lawn, N.J.: Essential Books.

———. 1965. *Gesammelte Briefe und Aufzeichnungen: Unter Benützung der Quellensammlung von H. C. Robbins Landon herausgegeben und erläutert von Dénes Bartha.* Kassel: Bärenreiter.

Head, Matthew. 2000. *Orientalism, Masquerade and Mozart's Turkish Music.* London: Royal Musical Association.

Hiller, Johann Adam. 1970. "Abhandlung von der Nachahmung der Natur in der Musik." In *Historisch-kritische Beyträge zur Aufnahme der Musik,* ed. Friedrich Wilhelm Marpurg, vol. 1, 515–45. Berlin: Gottlieb August Lange. New York: Georg Olms. (Orig. pub. 1754.)

Hiller, Johann Adam, ed. 1970. *Wöchentliche Nachrichten und Anmerken die Musik betreffend.* 4 vols. Leipzig. New York: Georg Olms. (Orig. pub. 1766–70.)

Hilton, Wendy. 1981. *Dance of Court and Theater: The French Noble Style, 1690–1725.* Princeton: Princeton Book Company.

Hodgson, Antony. 1976. *The Music of Joseph Haydn: The Symphonies.* London: Tantivy Press.

Hoeckner, Berthold. 2002. *Programming the Absolute: Nineteenth-Century German Music and the Hermeneutics of the Moment.* Princeton: Princeton University Press.

Horowitz, Joseph. 2005. *Classical Music in America: A History of Its Rise and Fall.* New York: W. W. Norton.

Howard, Vernon A. 1972. "On Representational Music." *Noûs* 6: 41–54.

Hughes, Leo. 1971. *The Drama's Patrons: A Study of the Eighteenth-Century London Audience.* Austin: University of Texas Press.

Hume, David. 1965. "Of Refinement in the Arts." In *Of the Standard of Taste, and Other Essays,* ed. John W. Lenz, 48–59. Indianapolis: Bobbs-Merrill. (Orig. pub. 1752.)

———. 1965. "Of the Standard of Taste." In *Of the Standard of Taste, and Other Essays,* ed. John W. Lenz, 3–24. Indianapolis: Bobbs-Merrill. (Orig. pub. 1757.)

Hunter, Mary. 1997. "Rousseau, the Countess, and the Female Domain." In *Mozart Studies* 2, ed. Cliff Eisen, 1–26. New York: Oxford University Press.

———. 1999. *The Culture of Opera Buffa in Mozart's Vienna: A Poetics of Entertainment.* Princeton, N.J.: Princeton University Press.

Jauss, Hans Robert. 1989. *Question and Answer: Forms of Dialogic Understanding.* Trans. Michael Hays. Minneapolis: University of Minnesota Press.

Johnson, H. Earle. 1953. "The Germania Musical Society." *Musical Quarterly* 39: 75–93.

Johnson, James H. 1995. *Listening in Paris.* Berkeley: University of California Press.

Johnson, Samuel. 1755. *A dictionary of the English language: in which the words are deduced from their originals, and illustrated in their different significations by examples from the best writers. To which are prefixed, a history of the language, and an English grammar.* London: W. Strahan for J. and P. Knapton.

Kant, Immanuel. 1952. *Kritik der Urteilskraft.* Trans. James Creed Meredith. Chicago: Encyclopaedia Britannica. (Orig. pub. 1790.)

Katz, Ruth, and Carl Dahlhaus. 1989. *Contemplating Music: Source Readings in the Aesthetics of Music.* Stuyvesant, N.Y.: Pendragon Press.

Keefe, Simon P. 2001. *Mozart's Piano Concertos: Dramatic Dialogue in the Age of Enlightenment.* Rochester, N.Y.: Boydell Press.

Kirkendale, Warren. 1979. *Fugue and Fugato in Rococo and Classical Chamber Music.* Trans. Margaret Bent and Warren Kirkendale. 2nd ed. Durham, N.C.: Duke University Press.

Kirnberger, Johann. 1757. *Der allezeit fertige Polonoisen- und Menuettenkomponist.* Berlin.

Kivy, Peter. 1984. *Sound and Semblance: Reflections on Musical Representation.* Princeton: Princeton University Press.

Klein, Michael L. 2005. *Intertextuality in Western Music.* Bloomington: Indiana University Press.

Knepler, Georg. 1989. *Mozart und die Ästhetik der Aufklärung: dem Wirken Georg Kneplers gewidmet.* Berlin: Akademie.

———. 1994. *Wolfgang Amadè Mozart.* Trans. James Bradford Robinson. Cambridge: Cambridge University Press.

Koch, Heinrich Christoph. 1983. *Versuch einer Anleitung zur Composition.* Vol. 2. Leipzig: A. F. Böhme. Trans. Nancy Kovaleff Baker as *Introductory Essay on Composition,* vol. 2. New Haven, Conn.: Yale University Press. (Orig. pub. 1793.)

———. 1964. *Musikalisches Lexikon.* Frankfurt am Main: Bey A. Hermann. Reprint, Hildescheim: G. Olms. (Orig. pub. 1802.)

Koffka, Kurt. 1935. *Principles of Gestalt Psychology.* New York: Harcourt Brace.

Kollmann, August Friedrich Christoph. 1799. *An Essay on Practical Musical Composition.* London.

Korsyn, Kevin. 1999. "Beyond Privileged Contexts: Intertextuality, Influence, and Dialogue." In *Rethinking Music,* ed. Nicholas Cook and Mark Everist, 55–72. Oxford: Oxford University Press.

———. 2003. *Decentering Music.* Oxford: Oxford University Press.

Kramer, Lawrence. 1995. *Classical Music and Postmodern Knowledge.* Berkeley: University of California Press.

Krause, Christian Gottfried. 1973. *Von der musikalischen Poesie.* Berlin. Facsimile reprint, Leipzig: Zentralantiquariat. (Orig. pub. 1752.)

Lack, Russell. 1997. *Twenty-four Frames Under: A Buried History of Film Music.* London: Quartet.

Landon, H. C. Robbins. 1976. *Haydn: Chronicle and Works. Vol. 3: Haydn in England, 1791–1795.* Bloomington: Indiana University Press.

———. 1982. *Mozart and the Masons: New Light on the Lodge "Crowned Hope."* New York: Thames and Hudson.

———. 1991. *Mozart and Vienna.* New York: Schirmer Books.

Langer, Susanne K. 1942. *Philosophy in a New Key: A Study in the Symbolism of Reason, Rite and Art.* Cambridge, Mass.: Harvard University Press.

———. 1953. *Feeling and Form.* New York: Scribner's.

Lansky, Paul. 1990. "A View from the Bus: When Machines Make Music." *Perspectives of New Music* 28, no. 2: 102–10.

Le Huray, Peter, and James Day, eds. 1981. *Music and Aesthetics in the Eighteenth and Early-Nineteenth Centuries.* Cambridge, Mass.: Cambridge University Press.

Lerdahl, Fred, and Ray Jackendoff. 1983. *A Generative Theory of Tonal Music.* Cambridge, Mass.: MIT Press.

Levine, Lawrence W. 1988. *Highbrow/Lowbrow: The Emergence of Cultural Hierarchy in America.* Cambridge, Mass.: Harvard University Press.

Levinson, Jerrold. 1996. *The Pleasures of Aesthetics: Philosophical Essays.* Ithaca, N.Y.: Cornell University Press.

Levy, Janet. 1982. "Texture as a Sign in Classic and Early Romantic Music." *Journal of the American Musicological Society* 35, no. 3: 482–97.

Lillywhite, Bryant. 1963. *London Coffee Houses: A Reference Book of Coffee Houses of the Seventeenth, Eighteenth, and Nineteenth Centuries.* London: George Allen and Unwin.

Lippman, Edward A. 1992. *A History of Western Musical Aesthetics.* Lincoln: University of Nebraska Press.

Locke, John. 1961. *An Essay Concerning Human Understanding.* Ed. John W. Yolton. London: J. M. Dent & Sons. (Orig. pub. 1706.)

Loughrey, Bryan, ed. 1984. *The Pastoral Mode: A Casebook.* London: Macmillan.

Lowe, Melanie. 1998. "Expressive Paradigms in the Symphonies of Joseph Haydn." Ph.D. dissertation, Princeton University.

———. 2002a. "Claiming Amadeus: Classical Feedback in American Media." *American Music* 20, no. 1: 102–19.

———. 2002b. "Falling from Grace: Irony and Expressive Enrichment in Haydn's Symphonic Minuets." *Journal of Musicology* 19, no. 1: 171–221.

Lutteken, Laurenz. 1999. "Musik in der Aufklarung: Musikalische Aufklarung?" *Musiktheorie* 14, no. 3: 213–29.

Lyons, John O. 1978. *The Invention of the Self.* Carbondale: Southern Illinois University Press.

Lyons, Martyn. 1975. *France under the Directory.* Cambridge: Cambridge University Press.

Magazin der Musik. 1997. Ed. Carl Friedrich Cramer. Hamburg: Musikalische Niederlage. Facsimile edition, 4 vols., Hildescheim: Georg Olms. (Orig. pub. 1783–87.)

Manvell, Roger, and John Hartley. 1975. *The Technique of Film Music.* London: Focal Press.

Markley, Robert. 1987. "Sentimentality as Performance: Shaftesbury, Sterne, and the Theatrics of Virtue." In *The New Eighteenth Century: Theory, Politics, English*

Literature, ed. Felicity Nussbaum and Laura Brown, 210–30. New York: Metheun.

Marpurg, Friedrich Wilhelm. 1754–62. *Historisch-kritichse Beyträge zur Aufnahme der Musik.* 5 vols. Berlin.

Marx, Karl. 1976–80. "Über thematische Beziehungen in Haydns Londener Symphonien." *Haydn-Studien* 4: 1–19.

Mather, Betty Bang. 1987. *Dance Rhythms of the French Baroque.* Bloomington: Indiana University Press.

Mattheson, Johann. 1981. *Der vollkommene Capellmeister.* Hamburg: Herold. *Documenta Musicologica,* Kassel: Bärenreiter, 1954. Trans. Ernest C. Harriss, Ann Arbor, Mich.: UMI Research Press. (Orig. pub. 1739.)

McClary, Susan. 1986. "A Musical Dialectic from the Enlightenment: Mozart's Piano Concerto in G Major, K. 453, Movement 2." *Cultural Critique* 4: 129–69.

———. 1994. "Narratives of Bourgeois Subjectivity in Mozart's *Prague* Symphony." In *Understanding Narrative,* ed. James Phelan and Peter J. Rabinowitz, 65–98. Columbus: Ohio State University Press.

McVeigh, Simon. 1993. *Concert Life in London from Mozart to Haydn.* Cambridge: Cambridge University Press.

Melton, James Van Horn. 2001. *The Rise of the Public in Enlightenment Europe.* Cambridge: Cambridge University Press.

Mercier, Louis-Sébastien. 1974. *L'an deux mille quatre cent quarante rève s'il en sût jamalt.* London. Trans. as *Memories of the Year Two Thousand Five Hundred.* London, 1772. New York: Garland. (Orig. pub. 1771.)

Meyer, Leonard B. 1956. *Emotion and Meaning in Music.* Chicago: University of Chicago Press.

———. 1973. *Explaining Music: Essays and Explorations.* Berkeley: University of California Press.

Milligan, Thomas B. 1983. *The Concerto and London's Musical Culture in the Late Eighteenth Century.* Ann Arbor, Mich.: UMI Research Press.

Monelle, Raymond. 2000. *The Sense of Music: Semiotic Essays.* Princeton: Princeton University Press.

Moreno, Jairo. 2004. *Musical Representations, Subjects, and Objects: The Construction of Musical Thought in Zarlino, Descartes, Rameau, and Weber.* Bloomington: Indiana University Press.

Morrow, Mary Sue. 1989. *Concert Life in Haydn's Vienna: Aspects of a Developing Musical and Social Institution.* Stuyvesant, N.Y.: Pendragon Press.

———. 1997. *German Music Criticism in the Late Eighteenth Century.* Cambridge: Cambridge University Press.

Mulvey, Laura. 1975. "Visual Pleasure and Narrative Cinema." *Screen* 16, no. 3: 6–18.

Munck, Thomas. 2000. *The Enlightenment: A Comparative Social History, 1721–1794.* London: Arnold.

Narmour, Eugene. 1977. *Beyond Schenkerism: The Need for Alternatives in Music Analysis.* Chicago: University of Chicago Press.

Nattiez, Jean-Jacques. 1990. *Music and Discourse: Toward a Semiology of Music.* Trans. Carolyn Abbate. Princeton: Princeton University Press.

Nettl, Paul. 1957. *Mozart and Masonry.* Trans. Mrs. Robert Gold. New York: Philosophical Library.

Neubauer, John. 1986. *The Emancipation of Music from Language: Departure from Mimesis in Eighteenth-Century Aesthetics.* New Haven, Conn.: Yale University Press.

Norton Anthology of Western Music. Vol. 2: Classic to Twentieth Century. 2006. Ed. J. Peter Burkholder and Claude V. Palisca. 5th ed. New York: W. W. Norton.

Orwell, George. 1953. *A Collection of Essays.* New York: Harcourt Brace Jovanovich.

Papendiek, Charlotte. 1887. *Court and Private Life in the Time of Queen Charlotte: Being the Journal of Mrs Papendiek.* Ed. Mrs. Vernon Delves Broughton. London.

Peirce, Charles Sanders. 1958. *Collected Papers of Charles Sanders Peirce.* Vols. 7 and 8. Ed. Arthur W. Burks. Cambridge, Mass.: Belknap Press of Harvard University Press.

———. 1984. *Writings of Charles S. Peirce: A Chronological Edition.* Vol. 2. Bloomington: Indiana University Press.

Perl, Benjamin. 2000. "Mozart in Turkey." *Cambridge Opera Journal* 12, no. 3: 219–35.

Pezzl, Johann. 1991. *Skizze von Wien: Ein Kultur- und Sittenbild aus der josefinischen Zeit.* Ed. Gustav Gugitz and Anton Schlossar. Graz: Leykam, 1923. Partially trans. in *Mozart and Vienna*, H. C. Robbins Landon, 54–191. London: Thames and Hudson. (Orig. pub. 1786–90.)

Pisani, Michael. 1998. "'I'm an Indian Too': Creating Native American Identities in Nineteenth- and Early Twentieth-Century Music." In *The Exotic in Western Music*, ed. Jonathan Bellman, 218–57. Boston: Northeastern University Press.

Pole, David. 1957. "When Is a Situation Aesthetic?" *Proceedings of the Aristotelian Society Supplement* 31: 93–106.

Pope, Alexander. 1737. *First Epistle of the Second Book of Horace.* In *The works of Alexander Pope, Esq; Vol. II, part i, containing his Epistles, &c.* London: Printed for R. Dodsley and sold by T. Cooper, 1743.

Pople, Anthony, ed. 1994. *Theory, Analysis, and Meaning in Music.* Cambridge: Cambridge University Press.

Powers, Harold S. 1995. "Reading Mozart's Music: Text and Topic, Syntax and Sense." *Current Musicology* 57: 5–44.

Rabin, Ronald J. 1997. "Figaro as Misogynist: On Aria Types and Aria Rhetoric." In *Opera buffa in Mozart's Vienna*, ed. Mary Hunter and James Webster, 232–60. Cambridge: Cambridge University Press.

Ratner, Leonard. 1970. "*Ars Combinatoria:* Chance and Choice in 18th-Century Music." In *Studies in 18th-Century Music, A Tribute to Karl Geiringer*, ed. H. C. Robbins Landon and Roger Chapman, 343–63. London: George Allen & Unwin.

———. 1980. *Classic Music: Expression, Form, and Style.* New York: Schirmer Books.

Reichardt, Johann Friedrich, ed. 1792. *Musikalisches Wochenblatt* (Berlin) 2: 12.

Réti, Rudolph. 1951. *The Thematic Process in Music.* New York: Macmillan.

———. 1967. *Thematic Patterns in Sonatas of Beethoven.* New York: Macmillan.

Robertson, Ritchie, and Edward Timms. 1991. *The Austrian Enlightenment and Its Aftermath.* Edinburgh: Edinburgh University Press.

Rosen, Charles. 1988. *Sonata Forms.* Rev. ed. New York: W. W. Norton.

———. 1997. *The Classical Style: Haydn, Mozart, Beethoven.* New York: W. W. Norton.

Rousseau, Jean Jacques. 1969. *Dictionnaire de musique.* Paris. Reprint, New York: Johnson Reprint Corp. (Orig. pub. 1768.)

Rudé, George. 1971. *Paris and London in the Eighteenth Century: Studies in Popular Protest.* New York: Viking.

Scheibe, Johann Adolf. 1745. *Critischer Musikus: Neue, vermehrte und verbesserte Auflage.* Leipzig.

Schenker, Heinrich. 1979. *Free Composition.* Trans. Ernst Oster. 2 vols. New York: Longmans.

Schlegel, Johann Adolph. 1751. *Einschränkung der schönen Künste auf einen einzigen Grundsatz von Batteux.* Leipzig.

Schopenhauer, Arthur. 1958. *The World as Will and Representation.* Trans. E. F. J. Payne. 2 vols. Indian Hills, Colo.: Falcon's Wing Press. (Orig. pub. 1818.)

Schroeder, David P. 1990. *Haydn and the Enlightenment.* Oxford: Clarendon Press.

Schuler, Heinz. 1987. "Freimaurer und Illuminaten aus Alt-Bayern und Salzburg und ihre Beziehungen zu den Mozarts." *Mitteilungen der Inernationalen Stiftung Mozarteum, Austria* 35: 1–4, 11–39.

Scruton, Roger. 1979. *The Aesthetics of Architecture.* Princeton: Princeton University Press.

———. 1980. "Absolute Music." In *The New Grove Dictionary of Music and Musicians,* ed. Stanley Sadie, vol. 1, 26–27. London: Macmillan.

———. 1997. *The Aesthetics of Music.* Oxford: Oxford University Press.

Sisman, Elaine. 1982. "Small and Expanded Forms: Koch's Model and Haydn's Music." *Musical Quarterly* 62: 444–78.

———. 1990. "Haydn's Theater Symphonies." *Journal of the American Musicological Society* 48: 292–352.

———. 1993a. *Haydn and the Classical Variation.* Cambridge, Mass.: Harvard University Press.

———. 1993b. *Mozart: The 'Jupiter' Symphony.* Cambridge: Cambridge University Press.

———. 1997. "Genre, Gesture, and Meaning in Mozart's 'Prague' Symphony." In *Mozart Studies* 2, ed. Cliff Eisen, 27–84. Oxford: Clarendon Press.

———. 2005. "Haydn's Career and the Idea of the Multiple Audience." In *The Cambridge Companion to Haydn,* ed. Caryl Clark, 3–16. Cambridge: Cambridge University Press.

Small, Christopher. 2001. "Why Doesn't the Whole World Love Chamber Music?" *American Music* 19, no. 3: 340–59.

Solomon, Maynard. 1995. *Mozart: A Life.* New York: HarperCollins.

Somfai, László. 1973–74. "The London Revision of Haydn's Instrumental Style." *Proceedings of the Royal Musical Association* 100: 159–74.

Sparshott, F. E. 1980. "Aesthetics of Music." In *The New Grove Dictionary of Music and Musicians,* ed. Stanley Sadie, vol. 1, 120–34. London: Macmillan.

Splitt, Gerhard. 1998. *Mozarts Musiktheater als Ort der Aufklärung: die Auseinandersetzung des Komponisten mit der Oper im josephinischen Wien.* Freiburg im Breisgau: Rombach.

Sterne, Laurence. 1980. *Tristram Shandy.* Ed. Howard Anderson. New York: W. W. Norton. (Orig. pub. 1759–67.)

Stillwell, Robynn. 1997. "'I just put a drone under him . . .': Collage and Subversion in the Score of 'Die Hard.'" *Music and Letters* 78, no. 4: 551–74.

Stolnitz, Jerome. 1960. *Aesthetics and Philosophy of Art Criticism.* New York: Houghton Mifflin.

Stravinsky, Igor. 1924. "Some Ideas about My Octour." *The Arts* (January): 4–6. Reprinted in Eric Walter White, *Stravinsky: The Composer and His Works,* 528–31. Berkeley: University of California Press.

Subotnik, Rose Rosengard. 1991. "Evidence of a Critical Worldview in Mozart's Last Three Symphonies." In *Developing Variations: Style and Ideology in Western Music.* Minneapolis: University of Minnesota Press.

Sulzer, Johann Georg. 1967–70. *Allgemeine Theorie der schönen Künste.* 2 vols. Leipzig.

Rev. ed., 4 vols., 1792–97. Reprint of the rev. ed., Hildescheim: Georg Olms. (Orig. pub. 1771–74.)

Till, Nicholas. 1993. *Mozart and the Enlightenment: Truth, Virtue, and Beauty in Mozart's Operas.* New York: W. W. Norton.

Tolley, Thomas. 2001. *Painting the Cannon's Roar: Music, the Visual Arts, and the Rise of an Attentive Public in the Age of Haydn, c. 1750 to c. 1810.* Aldershot: Ashgate.

Trachtenberg, Alan. 1982. *The Incorporation of America: Culture and Society in the Gilded Age.* New York: Hill and Wang.

Treitler, Leo. 1989. "Mozart and the Idea of Absolute Music." In *Music and the Historical Imagination,* 176–214. Cambridge, Mass.: Harvard University Press.

Triest, Johann Karl Friedrich. 1801. "Bemerkung über die Ausbildung der Tonkunst in Deutschland im achtzehnten Jahrhundert." *Allgemeine musikalische Zeitung* 3: 24.

Türk, Daniel Gottlob. 1962. *Klavierschule.* Leipzig. Reprinted in *Documenta Musicologica.* Kassel: Bärenreiter. (Orig. pub. 1789.)

Twining, Thomas. 1789. *Aristotle's Treatise on Poetry, translated; with Notes on the Translation, and on the Original; and Two Dissertations, on Poetical, and Musical, Imitation.* London.

van den Toorn, Pieter C. 1995. *Music, Politics, and the Academy.* Berkeley: University of California Press.

Voltaire. 1959. *Essai sur le goût.* In Alexander Gerard, *An Essay on Taste, with Three Dissertations on the Same Subject. By Mr de Voltaire, Mrs d'Alembert, Mr de Montesquieu.* London: Millar. (Orig. pub. 1732.)

Waldoff, Jessica. 1998. "Sentiment and Sensibility in *La vera costanza.*" In *Haydn Studies,* ed. W. Dean Sutcliffe, 70–119. Cambridge: Cambridge University Press.

Wallace, Robin. 1999. "Myth, Gender, and Musical Meaning: *The Magic Flute,* Beethoven, and 19th-Century Sonata Form Revisited." *Journal of Musicological Research* 19, no. 1: 1–26.

Wangermann, Ernst. 1973. *The Austrian Achievement 1700–1800.* London: Thames and Hudson.

Waterman, George Gow. 1980. "French Overture." In *The New Grove Dictionary of Music and Musicians,* ed. Stanley Sadie, vol. 6, 820–23. London: Macmillan.

Webb, Daniel. 1769. *Observations on the Correspondence between Poetry and Music.* London.

Weber, Daniel. 1800. "Über komische Characteristik und Karikature in praktischen Musikwerken. *Allgemeine musikalische Zeitung* (Leipzig) 3: 9.

Weber, Gottfried. 1830. *Versuch einer geordneten Theorie der Tonsetzkunst.* Mainz.

Weber, William. 1997. "Did People Listen in the 18th Century?" *Early Music* 25: 678–91.

Webster, James. 1991a. *Haydn's "Farewell" Symphony and the Idea of Classical Style.* Cambridge: Cambridge University Press.

———. 1991b. "The Analysis of Mozart's Arias." In *Mozart Studies,* ed. Cliff Eisen, 101–99. Oxford: Clarendon Press.

———. 1997. "The Creation, Haydn's Late Vocal Music, and the Musical Sublime." In *Haydn and His World,* ed. Elaine Sisman, 57–102. Princeton: Princeton University Press.

———. 1998. "Haydn's Symphonies between *Sturm und Drang* and 'Classical Style': Art and Entertainment." In *Haydn Studies,* ed. W. Dean Sutcliffe, 218–45. Cambridge: Cambridge University Press.

Weiss, Piero, and Richard Taruskin. 1984. *Music in the Western World: A History in Documents.* New York: Schirmer Books.

Wheelock, Gretchen. 1992. *Haydn's Ingenious Jesting with Art*. New York: Schirmer Books.

White, Eric Walter. 1966. *Stravinsky: The Composer and His Works*. Berkeley: University of California Press. (Orig. pub. 1924.)

Wimsatt, William K., and Monroe C. Beardsley. 1954. "The Intentional Fallacy." In *The Verbal Icon: Studies in the Meaning of Poetry*, ed. William K. Wimsatt, 3–18. Lexington: University of Kentucky Press.

Winkler, Max. 1951. *A Penny from Heaven*. New York: Appleton-Century-Crofts.

Wolf, Eugene K. 1980. "On the Origins of the Mannheim Symphonic Style." In *Studies in Musicology in Honor of Otto E. Albrecht*, ed. James Walter Hill, 197–239. Kassel: Bärenreiter.

Zaslaw, Neal. 1989. *Mozart's Symphonies: Context, Performance Practice, Reception*. Oxford: Clarendon Press.

Zechmeister, Gustav. 1971. *Die Wiener Theater nächst der Burg und nächst dem Kärntnerthor von 1747 bis 1776*. Vienna: Hermann Böhlaus Nachf.

Zeman, Herbert. 1982. "Literarische Perspektiven um Joseph Haydn." In *Joseph Haydn in seiner Zeit*, ed. Gerda Mraz, Gottfried Mraz, and Gerald Schlag, 198–210. Eisenstadt: Amt der Burgenländischen Landesregierung.

Index

Page numbers in italics indicate musical examples and/or analytical discussion.

cultural capital, 6, 104, 105, 166, 171, 175.
    See also Bourdieu
cultural studies, 103
culture: commodification of, 3, 7; contemporary
    American, 164–79; contemporary American
    consumer, 7, 177; democratization of, 3;
    eighteenth-century commodity (or con-
    sumer), 3, 100; high, 166, 167, 170, 175; late-
    eighteenth-century entertainment, 5, 24, 99;
    polite (or proper), 103–105; sacralization
    of, 167, 181n6 (*see also* Horowitz; Levine;
    Trachtenberg); television, 6, 102
Cumming, Naomi, 19
cyclic organization, 5, 54–66

D'Alembert, Jean le Rond, 189n5
Da Ponte, Lorenzo, 196n39
Dahlhaus, Carl: on absolute music, 10, 108,
    182n7
dance: ballroom/dance hall, 58, 107, 138, 142
    (*see also* contredanse; minuet); popular and
    comic dances, 57–60, 64, 66, 124–32; rustic or
    peasant, 64, 69, 124–32; as topic, 13, 27
Danckwardt, Marianne, 187n20
Daube, Johann Friedrich, 27, 195n28
Davies, Stephen, 14
Dempster, Douglas, 178
DeNora, Tia, 189n2
Derrida, Jacques, 76
Descartes, René, 71, 189n3
Deutsch, Otto Erich, 196n40
Deutscher Tanz: in the ballroom, 84, 109, 156; as
    topic, 66, 125–31, 155–56
developing variation, 10
Diary; or Woodfall's Register, 198n2
Diderot, Denis, 73, 74, 75, 79, 103, 190n12
Die Hard, 200nn11,16
difficulty: topic of, 124, 185n3. *See also* Mozart
dignity: degree of, 62, 66–69, 108, 115. *See also*
    style: high; middle; low
displeasure, 124
Droysen, Johann Gustav, 78
drum call, 38–43
Du Bos, Jean-Baptiste, 71, 75, 103, 190n8

Eady, Martin-Patrick, 200n10
Eagleton, Terry, 75, 77, 78, 79, 191n18
Eco, Umberto, 76–77, 78, 190nn12,15, 191n17
Elvira Madigan, 200n15
ending, 29; 48–49, 54, 57–60; *See also* closing
the Enlightenment, 70–71, 77, 78, 87, 107, 111,
    161, 190n12; values and ideals of, 103–104,
    119, 133, 150
entertainment, 164–79; aesthetics of, 99–103;

late-eighteenth-century culture of, 24, 99;
    mere entertainment, 6, 99, 106, 112, 165,
    175; politics of, 2, 103–106; relationship
    with pleasure, 6, 99–100, 102–106, 112, 175
entrée, 30
Enya, 201n18
Esterházy, 30, 119
exalted march, 63, 195n23
the exalted, 115
expectancy, 34, 36–38
expression: abstract, 13; exactness of, 92; musi-
    cal expressivity, 24, 76, 97; relationship with
    formal process, 28–69; relationship with imi-
    tation, 71, 75, 183n14, 190n6; relationship
    with representation, 14; subjective nature of,
    182n7
expressive descent, 5, 66–69, 144, 159, 189n39
expressive dissonance, 122, 123, 142
expressive echo, 69, 134, 136, 159, 161–62, 179
expressive genre. *See under* Hatten
expressive kinship, 54–66, 142
expressive meaning. *See* meaning
expressive paradigm, 68
expressive syntax, 66
the extra-musical, 11–13

fanfare, 13, 34, 36–38, 39, 75–76, 131, 144, 145,
    155, 159, 163, 187n20
Fantasia, 167
fantasia: as topic, 13
feedback loop, 169, 170; reverse feedback, 177,
    178, 202n25
Feldtenstein, C. J. von, 107
Ferris Bueller's Day Off, 171
the fictive, 6, 70, 78–80
Fielding, Henry, 79
final interpretant. *See* interpretant
Fish, Stanley: on anti-professionalism, 22; on
    interpretive communities, 20
Fisher, Stephen, 56, 188n34
Fiske, John, 6, 102, 106, 112, 168
The Flying Dutchman (Wagner), 199n3
Ford Foundation, 176
formalism, 4, 8, 9, 11
Forman, Milos, 122
Foucault, Michel, 102, 106, 189n3
Franklin, Milt, 167
Frasier, 171–73, 175, 201n19
Freed, Arthur, 200n11
freedom: individual, 70; science of, 69
Freemasonry: Mozart and, 123, 196n40
French overture, 30, 32; as topic, 30–32, 183n12,
    187n21
French Revolution, 92–93, 192n33

Horowitz, Joseph, 177, 178, 181n6
Howard, Vernon, 14
Hughes, John, 171
Hughes, Leo, 197n48
humanism: secular, 69
Hume, David, 193n7
Hunter, Mary: on gender in late-eighteenth-century music, 189n2; on opera buffa and poetics of entertainment, 99; on sentimental heroine, 84, 86–87; on sentimental mode, 136
hunting call, 63, 81; as topic, 13, 26

iconicity, 15
idealism, 9–10, 183n6
imitation, 4, 91–92; Batteux's use of, 190n6; critiques of, 6, 8, 13, 70–75; relationship with expression, 71, 75, 183n14, 190n6; *See also* mimesis
instability: expressive, 29, 49–54, 138, 158; strategic, 29, 49–54, 158;
intelligibility: structural, 23–69, 76, 106, 136, 159
intention, 20–21, 27, 69, 73, 122–23, 144, 152, 159, 167, 184n24, 202n23
intentional fallacy, 21, 28, 185n24
interpretant, 17, 184n21; final interpretant, 77, 190n16
interpretation, 20–21; freedom of, 75; hermeneutic, 10; intersubjective, 77–78; metaphysical, 4
interpretive community, 20, 22, 76–77
intertextuality, 24, 70, 75–79, 168, 170; in aesthetics of the Enlightenment, 6, 12, 74–75; in music, 183n10; radical, 75–77

Jackendoff, Ray, 10
Jarhead, 199n4
Jauss, Hans Robert, 78–79, 191nn19,20
Johnson, James H., 191n31, 192n33
Johnson, Samuel, 191n21
Jomelli, Niccolò, 110, 188n29
Joseph II, 80, 103, 105, 124, 187n18
jouissance, 101–102

Kant, Immanuel, 6, 73–74, 100, 101, 112, 183n14, 190nn9,10, 192n3
Katz, Ruth, 108
Keefe, Simon P., 189n1
Kelly, Michael, 196n39
Kenner (or connoisseur), 30, 110, 133–34
Kerman, Joseph, 184n23
Khachaturian, Aram, 166
Kirkendale, Warren, 196n35
Kirnberger, Johann, 24, 193n10

Kivy, Peter, 14, 185n24
Klein, Michael, 183n10, 191nn19,20
Knepler, Georg, 58, 189n1
Koch, Heinrich Christoph: *Musikalisches Lexikon,* 27; on melodic expansion, 193n10; on sonata and symphony style, 182n7
Koffka, Kurt, 111
Kollmann, Augustus Friedrich, 182n7
Korsyn, Kevin, 76–77, 190n13, 191n18
Kramer, Lawrence, 19, 184n23; on internal and external meanings, 11, 181n8; on musical representation, 18
Krause, Christian Gottfried, 189n5
Ku Klux Klan, 166, 199n3
Kubrick, Stanley, 166, 200n11

Lack, Russell, 199n9
Ladies Concert, 94
Landis, John, 173, 174
Ländler, 66, 155
Landon, H. C. Robbins, 135, 146, 152, 157, 196n40, 198n4, 198n12
Langer, Susanne, 15
Lansky, Paul, 202n24
Larpent, Anna, 104–105, 167, 175, 193n8
Leo, Leonardo, 188n29
Lerdahl, Fred, 10
Levine, Lawrence, 167, 170, 181n6
Levinson, Jerrold, 101
Levy, Janet, 15, 28, 32, 43, 186nn9,15, 187n23
Liebhaber, 30, 110, 124, 134
Ligeti, György, 166
Lilliwhite, Edward A., 192n38
Link, Dorothea, 191n25
Link, Stan, 200n14
listener: American, 166; attentive, 27, 29, 43, 54, 119, 144, 150, 154, 159, 162; bourgeois, 30; contemporary, 2, 6, 21; enlightened, 164, 175; entertained, 103, 105–106; fictional, 6, 71, 80–98; harmonically astute, 54; historical, 21; lay, 2, 4, 29, 30, 32, 33, 99, 107, 108, 109, 110, 124, 125, 133; late-eighteenth-century, 2, 3, 4, 6, 24, 27, 28, 75–76, 80–98, 99, 107, 108, 109, 110, 115, 118, 119, 122, 124, 136, 144, 149, 153, 155, 156, 158; listener subjectivity, 21, 74, 76, 79, 97, 106, 115, 131, 136, 179; noble, 30; perception of, 27, 71, 75; perspective of, 30; postmodern, 164, 175; subordination, 165
listening modality, 24, 29, 33, 53, 141, 159
listening pleasure, 7, 146, 179; lack of, 176
listening subject, 12, 20, 21, 22, 24, 70–89
Locke, John, 71
Loony Tunes, 167

Symphony in C Major, "Jupiter," K. 551, 16, 19, 32, *67–68,* 119, 187n21, 196n37; *Thamos, König in Ägypten, 49–50; Die Zauberflöte,* 57, 123
Mozart Effect, 170, 174, 201n17
Mulvey, Laura, 101–102, 106, 112, 178
Munck, Thomas, 134
Murphy, Eddie, 173
the musical, 11–13
musical meaning, 2–3, 5, 8–22, 17, 29, 69, 72, 74–79, 97, 165–68; accessibility of, 4–5; control of, 124, 131–32, 134, 168–69; extra-musical, 5, 8, 17, 186n7; intersubjective approach to, 77–78; intra-musical, 12; meanings of, 17, 19–22; opposition of musical and extra-musical, 11–13, 17; purely musical, 4–5, 8, 12, 17, 18, 19, 186n7; syntactical, 29
Musikalisches Lexikon (Koch), 27

Narmour, Eugene, 10
Nattiez, Jean-Jacques, 17, 184n22; on subjectivity of meaning, 18
nature, 70, 71
Nettl, Paul, 196n40
Neubauer, John, 73
Neue Leipziger gelehrte Zeitungen, 186n13
New Musicology, 19
noble simplicité, 87, 95, 107–108, 128
nontragic, 68, 115
North, Alex, 166
Norton Anthology of Western Music, 187n25

obbligato recitative, 49
objectivity, 4, 11–12, 78, 79
ombra, 16, 45, 52, 53
opening, 5, 29, 30–48, 54–57, 68–69
opera buffa, 58, 60, 99
Oracle, 1, 181nn2,3
Orchestra e Corodi Roma Della RAI, 200n10
Orff, Carl, 176
Orwell, George, 4
overture, 54–57, 61, 187n28, 188n29

Pachelbel, Johann, 169; Canon and Gigue for 3 Violins and Continuo in D Major, 202n22
Papendiek, Charlotte, 133
parody, 115, 118, 123, 151–52, 189n41, 195n32
Passion, 123, 197n44
pastoral, 63, 153; pastoral mode, 61; 150–51, 152; as topic, 146, 149
Peer Gynt Suite No. 1 (Grieg), 177
Peirce, Charles Sanders, 77, 184n21, 190n16
Pergolesi, Giovanni Battista, 188n29
periodicity, 33

Perl, Benjamin, 189n2
Pezzl, Johann, 191nn23,29,30
philosophes, 198n6
Pierce, David Hyde, 172, 201n19
Pisani, Michael, 200n13
plaisir, 101–102
Plato, 71
pleasure, 2, 73, 99–132, 164–79; aesthetic, 102, 192nn2,3; aesthetics of, 100–103; cognitive (or intellectual), 100, 104; disinterested, 100, 192n3; relationship with entertainment, 6, 99–100, 102–106, 112, 175; filmic (or cinematic), 101–102; and Haydn's Symphony in D Major, No. 93, 133–63; of the listener, 75, 81, 98, 138, 176; pleasures of the body (or physical), 100, 101, 102; pleasures of the imagination, 100, 103, 104; of power, 106, 112; principle, 6, 101–102, 192n4 (*see also* Freud); psychoanalytic, 102; relationship with power, 102–106; of resistance, 172; social, 102; of subversion, 106; of television, 102
Pleyel, Ignace Joseph, 116
Pole, David, 101, 112
politeness, 193n5
Pope, Alexander, 99
Pople, Anthony, 19, 22
positivism, 11
postmodernism, 190n12
Powers, Harold, 183n8
presentational material (or quality), 27, 36, 159, 186n9
The Prince of Tides, 175
Prince of Wales, 3
private music, 3, 181n7. *See also* public music
probability, 79
progress, 70
public music, 3–4, 99, 119, 181n7; public instrumental music (late-eighteenth-century), 164–179. *See also* private music
public sphere, 3–4
the purely musical, 11–13

Rabin, Ronald J., 189n2
racism, 70
Rameau, Jean-Philippe, 189n3
Ranke, Leopold von, 79
rationalism (and rationality), 19, 69, 150
Ratner, Leonard, 27, 189n40; on fanfare, 187n20; on fantasia style, 183n13; on topics, 13, 183n12
Raucher, Francis, 201n17
realism: historical, 78
reason, 70
Redoutensaal (Vienna), 87, 191n30

Verdi, Guiseppe, 165, 199n2
Vertigo, 169, 170, 200n14
Vinci, Leonardo, 188n29
Vivaldi, Antonio: *The Four Seasons,* 202n22
Voltaire, 103, 193n6

Wackenroder, Wilhelm Heinrich, 4, 8–9
Wagner, Richard, 165, 167, 199nn2,3,4; on abso-
   lute music, 9; *Gesamtkunstwerk,* 9
Waldoff, Jessica, 189n1
Wallace, Robin, 189n2
Walt Disney, 167
Wangermann, Ernst, 191n23
Warner Bros., 166, 167
Waterman, George Gow, 187n20
Webb, Daniel, 189n5
Weber, Daniel, 189n41
Weber, Gottfried, 189n3
Webster, James: on an aesthetic of entertain-
   ment in Haydn's symphonies, 99, 192n1; on
   conventions of Austro-Bohemian symphony,
   195n25; on cyclic integration in Haydn, 144,
   188n36, 198n5; on extra-musical associations

in Haydn, 10; on Haydn's music and the En-
   lightenment, 189n1; on Haydn's Symphony
   No. 68, 39; on Haydn's Symphony No. 93,
   157, 198nn11,12; on Mozart's "Porgi amor,"
   191n28
What's Opera Doc?, 166, 167
Wheelock, Gretchen: on canonic minuets, 113,
   115–16; 195n29
Widerberg, Bo, 200n15
"widow's concert," 81
Wier, Peter, 170
Williams, John, 202n25
Wimsatt, William K., 21
Win Ben Stein's Money, 164, 165, 167
Winkler, Max, 165, 199n2
Wiora, Walter, 182n4
wit, 189n41
Wöchentliche Nachrichten (Hiller), 27, 109
work-concept, 12. *See also* Goehr

Zaslaw, Neal, 64, 185n2, 187n18, 196nn37,38
Zeman, Herbert, 189n1
Zinzindorf, Count Karl von, 81, 191nn24,25

MELANIE LOWE is Assistant Professor of Musicology in the Blair School of Music at Vanderbilt University.